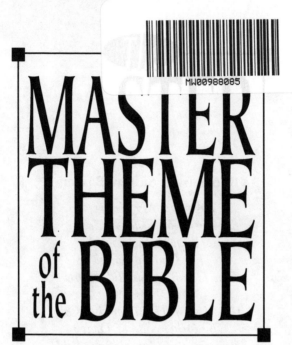

Books by J. Sidlow Baxter

Awake, My Heart
Does God Still Guide?
Explore the Book
For God So Loved
The God You Should Know
Mark These Men
The Master Theme of the Bible
The Other Side of Death
The Strategic Grasp of the Bible

The Christian Sanctification Series

His Deeper Work in Us
Our High Calling
A New Call to Holiness

The MASTER THEME of the BIBLE

A Comprehensive Study of the Lamb of God

J. Sidlow Baxter

kregel
PUBLICATIONS

Grand Rapids, MI 49501

The Master Theme of the Bible: A Comprehensive Study of the Lamb of God

Copyright © 1973, 1997 by J. Sidlow Baxter
Second Edition

Published by Kregel Publications, a division of Kregel, Inc., P.O. Box 2607, Grand Rapids, MI 49501. Kregel Publications provides trusted, biblical publications for Christian growth and service. Your comments and suggestions are valued.

For more information about Kregel Publications, visit our web site at http://www.kregel.com.

Cover design: Alan G. Hartman
Book design: Nicholas G. Richardson

Library of Congress Cataloging-in-Publication Data
Baxter, J. Sidlow (James Sidlow)
   The master theme of the Bible: a comprehensive study on the lamb of God / J. Sidlow Baxter.
      p.   cm.
   Originally published: Wheaton, Ill.: Tyndale House, 1973.
   1. Jesus Christ—Person and offices. 2. Jesus Christ—Crucifixion. 3. Atonement. I. Title.
BT202.B35   1997   232—dc21   96-46397
                                                         CIP

ISBN 0-8254-2147-0

Printed in the United States of America

1 2 3 / 03 02 01 00 99 98 97

Contents

Foreword

READERS OF THIS BOOK should realize right from the beginning that the chapters, although they may without presumption be called Bible studies, are not so in an academic or professionally theological sense. They are meant for the general public and the average reader. I believe, however, that such studies do not necessarily lose thereby any basic worth that they may have. Neither our Lord himself nor any of his apostles (except Paul) was an academician or a specialist theologian. The public always needs the general practitioner as well as the specialist. Often the general practitioner is far better understood.

Further, these chapters now reproduce in print spoken studies used at Bible conferences, and they largely retain their original form. Here and there they become conversational rather than merely declarative, but that suits my own disposition better and, I think, brings them closer to most readers. In both the preaching and the writing of these reflections, the subject has set my own heart singing with new love and gratitude to our inexpressibly glorious Savior-King, and my longing is that at least some other hearts may be moved to love and prize him more earnestly through the reading of this book.

J. SIDLOW BAXTER

PART ONE

The Doctrine of the Lamb

1

The Revelation of the Lamb

None other Lamb,
None other Name,
None other hope in heav'n or earth or sea;
None other hiding place from guilt and shame:
None beside Thee.

Harriet Beecher Stowe

Do not forget that the Atonement was made by God, and not simply to God. The initiative is with God. Then why should we preach God's reconciliation almost entirely from man's side, without realizing the Divine initiative as an act of God's self-reconciliation, timeless, eternal, in the "Lamb slain from the foundation of the world"?

Henry C. Mabie

OUR BIBLE IS A collection of humanly written documents. That does not mean, however, that it is merely a literary miscellany. There is a basic unity about the documents of the Bible that forms them into one, homogeneous whole, thus making the Bible a book.

In many ways the Bible is the most human book ever written. But it claims to be much more than that. In its various parts it claims to be nothing less than the written Word of God, given by direct and inerrant divine inspiration through chosen human writers.

If that claim is true, then the Bible is different from all other literature. It is not merely human and natural; it is superhuman and supernatural. Its inspiration is a miracle. Its revealing how the universe began and how the pre-Adamite earth was refashioned to become the abode of humanity is a miracle. Its foretelling of events and details accurately, centuries in advance, even to the end of time and even beyond time, is a miracle.

Moreover, the Bible records miracles—scores of them—such as the dividing of the sea to let the hundreds of thousands of Israelites cross over, the falling of fire from heaven on Mount Carmel at the prayer of Elijah, the bodily resurrection of the Lord Jesus Christ.

There is a certain kind of biblical scholarship today that thinks it must be all the time apologizing to modern science for the supernatural in the Bible. It has tried in one way or another to explain away all the biblical miracles, but if we are honestly to accept the clear wording of the Scripture records, then as plainly as can be, the Bible means us to understand that they were miracles.

We evangelicals take the position that if the evidences are demonstrably sound for the inspiration of the Bible and the veracity of its records, then we accept them. The Bible openly offers its credentials to human reason and logic. New Testament Christianity invites investigation and makes appeal to evidence. We believe that the truly scientific attitude is to weigh the evidence and thereby reach a verdict.

Our intuitive sense of logical fairness is strangely jarred, therefore, when a seminary professor or some Christian minister says to us, "Your evidences mean nothing to me. If they were a hundred times stronger they would still be valueless. As a modern thinker in an age of science and in a universe of inviolable natural law, I reject all talk of 'miracle' as absolutely inadmissible."

We have to agree with such people that our appeal to evidences is lost upon them, but we cannot help adding that in the name of science they are being utterly unscientific. To reject summarily all evidence for miracle on the a priori assumption that miracle is impossible is to forget that the a priori assumption itself was first reached by weighing evidence. It is an even worse fault to let that a priori assumption shut out all further and more recent evidence.

Actually, the one who absolutely disallows the possibility of miracle is no longer "modern." The same attitude was manifesting itself 150 years ago among Germany's radical theologians. Nobody has ever voiced it more strongly than David Strauss in his brilliant Leben Jesu (1835).

What is more, if I correctly interpret what I read, modern science itself is now much more inclined to accept the credibility of miracle. Some of the world's leading scientists are people of Christian faith who accept the Bible from cover to cover. They accept it as the Word of God on grounds of valid evidence. Is it not strange that when science is now much more open to evidence for miracle, a certain brand of Christian theologian still adamantly refuses it? Does it not show again that liberalism is not so much a matter of scholarship as an attitude of mind, a spirit, a temper, a set refusal to admit the supernatural in Christianity? Professing themselves to be modernly broad, the antisupernaturalists have become too narrow to admit even the soundest evidence if it is against them. Well, we must leave them and feel sorry for them. The kind of study that we are here opening up can have little meaning for such as they. On the other hand, if we have eyes to see and ears to hear, I believe that our present line of exposition will carry its own weight of edifying evidence to our minds, that the Bible is indeed the inspired Word of God. I entitle my theme: The Doctrine of the Lamb.

To my own mind, the most satisfying proofs that the Bible is divinely inspired are not those that one reads in volumes of religious evidences or Christian apologetics but those that we discover for ourselves in our own study of the Book.

To the prayerful explorer, the Bible has its own way of revealing its internal credentials. One fascinating study trail that continually repays exploration and always confirms faith in the divine origin of the Bible is that which we call "the progress of doctrine." Let me clearly explain what we mean by that term.

When we evangelicals speak about progress of doctrine in the Bible we do not mean, as certain others do, a groping progress from error to truth. To us, the whole Bible is the product of the Holy Spirit, but the revelation that it brings to us is progressive. By progress of doctrine we mean, so to speak, progress from the dimness of the dawn to the brightness of the noon. It is the same divine light that shines through all the pages, but the degree of the light increases as the revelation unfolds.

More particularly, by this progress of doctrine we mean that truths or teachings that first appear in Genesis or other early parts of the Scriptures are found to have a recurring mention and developing buildup right through the Bible, book after book, stage after stage, century after century, each successive mention contributing some further aspect in the progressive unfolding, until usually some New Testament passage is reached in which there is either a classic summary or a completive culmination. Indeed, in some instances, subjects that are first mentioned away back in early Genesis keep reappearing in succeeding books of Scripture until, in the closing pages of the New Testament, the Apocalypse unmistakably finalizes them.

In this progress of doctrine, seldom does the first mention of a subject seem likely to be the first link in a concatenated series, nor do the human agents who figure in the series suspect that in what they say or do they are contributing to a developing divine revelation. That, however, only makes such progress of doctrine the more obviously supernatural and fascinating.

One outstanding instance of this progressive unfolding is the Bible doctrine of the Lamb; it is that which we are to inspect somewhat in these studies. It is the kind of theme that, if we approach it with reverent and prayerful eagerness, will stir our hearts to love and prize and adore our Lord Jesus more than ever. I dare not claim originality for some of the germinative data, but the formulation and expansion of them are entirely my own. Let us then briefly examine the progressive doctrine of the Lamb. As an introduction, let me quote 1 Peter 1:18-21.

> *Ye were redeemed, not with corruptible things, with silver or gold, from your vain manner of life handed down from your fathers; but with the precious blood of Christ, as of a lamb without blemish and without spot: who verily was foreordained before the foundation of the world, but was manifested in these last times for your sake, who through Him believe in God, who raised Him up from the dead, and gave Him glory, so that your faith and hope might be in God.*

In the Bible there are ten notable passages in which the Lamb is conspicuously mentioned. They are as follows.

1. Genesis 4:3-7—Abel and his lamb
2. Genesis 22—Abraham offers the lamb in place of Isaac
3. Exodus 12—the Passover lamb, slain on the night before the exodus of the Israelites from Egypt
4. Leviticus—the sin-offering lamb that the Israelites offered on the altar of sacrifice outside the tabernacle
5. Isaiah 53—the suffering Lamb on whom "Jehovah laid the iniquity of us all"
6. John 1—the Lamb announced by John the Baptist: "Behold, the Lamb of God which beareth away the sin of the world"
7. Acts 8—the Ethiopian official, traveling in his chariot on the Gaza road from Jerusalem and reading about the Lamb in Isaiah 53, to whom Philip explains that the Lamb is Jesus the Messiah
8. 1 Peter 1:18-21—the paragraph that we quoted by way of introduction, which tells us that we were redeemed with the precious blood of Christ, as of a Lamb "without blemish and without spot"
9. Revelation 5—the vision that dramatizes the enthronement of the Lamb in heaven
10. Revelation 21-22—the final vision of the Apocalypse, in which the Lamb is seen reigning in the New Jerusalem, amid the "new heaven and new earth"

Successive Emphases

Those, then, are the ten special Lamb passages. Let us now look through them and observe the distinctive emphases developing successively through them. First, in Genesis 4:3-7 there is the account of Abel and his lamb.

Genesis 4:3-7

> *And in process of time it came to pass that Cain brought of the fruit of the ground an offering unto Jehovah. And Abel, he also brought of the firstlings of his flock and of the fat thereof. And Jehovah had respect unto Abel and to his offering; but unto Cain and to his offering He had not*

respect. And Cain was very wroth, and his countenance fell. But Jehovah said unto Cain, Why art thou wroth? and why is thy countenance fallen? If thou doest well, shalt thou not be accepted? and if thou doest not well, sin [or perhaps more correctly, a sin offering] croucheth at the [tent] door.

We notice at once that in this Abel incident the emphasis is upon the necessity of the Lamb. We are not told that the lamb was slain, though presumably it was both killed and burned. Cain's outwardly beautiful but bloodless offering was evidently in disobedience to divine instruction. We know this from the comment in Hebrews 11:5, that Abel offered his lamb "by faith," that is, faith in what God had spoken about it. Cain's offering had in it nothing of confessed sin or of need for propitiation. But God gave him another chance: "If thou doest well [that is, according to what is required of thee], shalt thou not be accepted? And if thou doest not well, [a sin offering] croucheth at the door." It is noteworthy that in the Hebrew language the same word means both "sin" and "sin-offering," remarkably indicating the identification of the sinner with the sin offering.

Cain still disobeyed and was rejected. Thus, both through Abel and through Cain, we see the indispensable necessity of the Lamb.

Genesis 22

The second passage where the Lamb significantly figures is the twenty-second chapter of Genesis, in the story of Abraham and the lamb that he offered in place of Isaac. It will be enough if we quote verses 6–8.

And Abraham took the wood of the burnt offering, and laid it upon Isaac his son; and he took in his hand the fire and the knife; and they went both of them together. And Isaac spake unto Abraham his father, and said: . . . Behold the fire and the wood: but where is the lamb for a burnt offering? And Abraham said: My son, God will provide himself a lamb for a burnt offering.

In this incident the emphasis is not upon the necessity of the lamb but upon God's provision of it: "God will provide himself the lamb." This is doubly emphasized by the way the incident ends. Just as the agonized patriarch lifts the knife, the voice from heaven arrests him with these words: "*Lay not thine hand upon the lad.*" And in that moment Abraham sees a ram caught in a thicket, which he at once understands is to be offered instead of Isaac. God had indeed provided the lamb. So impressed was Abraham that he named the place *Jehovah-jireh,* which means "Jehovah will provide." Yes, that is the aspect which is underscored—the provision of the Lamb.

Exodus 12

Here in this third passage we have the Passover lamb on the night before the exodus of the Israelites from Egypt. And now the emphasis is upon the slaying of the Lamb.

> *Speak ye unto all the congregation of Israel, saying, In the tenth day of this month they shall take to them every man a lamb, according to their fathers' houses, a lamb for a household. . . . And ye shall keep it up until the fourteenth day of the same month, and the whole assembly of the congregation shall kill it in the evening. And they shall take of the blood, and strike it on the two side posts and on the lintel of the houses wherein they shall eat it. . . . Ye shall take a bunch of hyssop, and dip it in the blood that is in the basin, and strike the lintel and the two side posts with the blood that is in the basin; and none of you shall go out of the door of his house until the morning. For Jehovah will pass through to smite the Egyptians: and when he seeth the blood upon the lintel and on the two side posts, Jehovah will pass over the door, and will not suffer the destroyer to come in unto your houses to smite you (vv. 3–7, 22–23).*

So there had to be one lamb for each family, and it had to be a male of the first year, without blemish (v. 5). It was to provide a covering from the stroke of the destroying angel. Most emphatically of all, it must be slain and its blood sprinkled protectively on the Hebrew dwellings. However blemishless, however qualified in itself the little lamb might be, it was of no covering efficacy while still alive. Jehovah's word was, "When I see the blood, I will pass over you" (v. 13). Let it be duly weighed in Exodus 12, in the case of the paschal lamb, the emphasis is on the slaying of the lamb.

Leviticus

And now, in the fourth place, we have the Lamb as set forth in the book of Leviticus. That third book of the Pentateuch is a manual for Israel's priests, giving them instructions about the sacrifices that were to be offered and informing them of regulations covering various other matters. All the way through Leviticus the emphasis is upon the character of the lamb. Some twenty times we are told that the Lord's offering must be "without blemish." Or, in the words of 22:21, "It shall be perfect to be accepted." Yes, the emphasis here is on the character of the Lamb.

Isaiah 53

Now turn to Isaiah 53 for the fifth of these Lamb passages. Here we have what is perhaps the most famous and treasured of all the Isaiah prophecies. The whole chapter is so well known that we need quote only verses 6–8:

All we like sheep have gone astray; we have turned every one to his own way: and Jehovah hath laid on him the iniquity of us all. He was oppressed, and he was afflicted, yet he opened not his mouth. He is brought as a lamb to the slaughter, and as a sheep before its shearers is dumb, so he openeth not his mouth. By oppression and judgment he was taken away; and who considers his generation? For he was cut off out of the land of the living: for the transgression of my people [saith Jehovah] he was stricken.

Here we take a big step forward in the developing revelation of the Lamb. Up to this point the lamb has been an animal, but now for the first time we learn that the Lamb God provides is a person. "He was wounded for our transgressions." "Jehovah hath laid on him the iniquity of us all." "He is brought as a lamb to the slaughter." Yes, the Lamb is a person.

John 1

In the sixth place we come to the first chapter of John's Gospel. From verse 19 onward we are at Bethabara (more correctly, Bethany) on the eastern side of the river Jordan and away up in the direction of Galilee. We are among the crowds who attended John the Baptist's startling ministry, to hear his preaching that the long-awaited "kingdom of heaven" was at hand.

On one of those days a deputation from the Pharisees in Jerusalem came to interview John. Since the ascetic prophet was teaching that the leaders and people of Israel needed some peculiar cleansing and baptismal admission into a fellowship holier than that which came by membership in the elect nation, the Jewish leaders wanted to know what it was all about. John plainly told them, "I am not the Christ." But he added, "There standeth One among you whom ye know not: he it is [i.e., the Christ] who cometh after me." So John already knew Jesus and who he really was. He had learned it when Jesus came for baptism in Jordan some days earlier. The "next day" after answering the deputation from Jerusalem, John sees Jesus coming to him and cries: "Behold, the Lamb of God, that taketh away the sin of the world!" (v. 29).

So here the Lamb is not only a person, he is identified as that person, even Jesus. By way of emphasizing this, verse 35 adds, "Again on the morrow John was standing, and two of his disciples; and looking upon Jesus as he walked John saith, Behold the Lamb of God!" So now we know who is the typified Lamb.

Acts 8

And now we move on to the eighth chapter of the Acts, where we have the seventh link in this tenfold chain of special reference to the Lamb. See the episode beginning at verse 26.

The angel of the Lord directs Philip the evangelist to the road from Jerusalem to Gaza. On that road, traveling southward in his chariot, is an important Ethiopian dignitary, chancellor of the exchequer to Candace, queen of the Ethiopians. As he sits in his chariot he is reading Isaiah 53. Philip calls, "Understandest thou what thou readest?" and the surprised official replies, "How can I, except someone shall guide me?" Then Philip joins him and finds him reading, "He was led as a sheep to the slaughter, and as a lamb before his shearer is dumb, so he openeth not his mouth."

The narrative goes on to tell us that Philip "began at the same Scripture and preached unto him Jesus." The result was that the Ethiopian requested baptism, and Philip said, "If thou believest with all thine heart, thou mayest." The Ethiopian replied, "I believe that Jesus Christ is the Son of God."[1]

The point here is that the Lamb of God is not only identified personally as Jesus, but that Jesus the Lamb is further identified as the promised Christ, the Son of God.

1 Peter 1:18–21

From that, we pass now to the eighth of these ten passages on the Lamb. It is the passage we quoted at the outset.

> *Ye were redeemed, not with corruptible things, with silver or gold, from your vain manner of life handed down from your fathers; but with precious blood, as of a lamb without blemish and without spot, even the blood of Christ: who verily was foreordained before the foundation of the world, but was manifested at the end of the times for your sake, who through him believe in God, who raised him up from the dead, and gave him glory; so that your faith and hope might be in God.*

This passage is of pivotal importance in the developing doctrine of the Lamb. It looks both backward and forward. That is, it gathers up all that has preceded it and then adds a startling new truth that points us on to wonderful consummations in the future.

Observe first how Peter's paragraph sums up all the different aspects of the Lamb that we have encountered thus far. We started with Abel and saw the *necessity* of the Lamb. Here it is in 1 Peter: "Not with corruptible things, with silver or gold"; the indispensable necessity is the Lamb.

Then, in the Abraham-and-Isaac incident, we saw the *provision* of the Lamb. And here it is again in this paragraph from 1 Peter; for the Lamb, Peter tells us, was "foreordained before the foundation of the world."

Next we saw the emphasis on the *slaying* of the Lamb in the Passover drama, and here it appears again in this summary by Peter. We are redeemed not by the immaculate life or sublime teaching of our Lord Jesus apart from his death but by the "precious blood of Christ."

Next, in Leviticus we saw the repeated emphasis on the *character* of the Lamb. It must be blemishless. So here in 1 Peter our Lord is said to be a Lamb "without blemish and without spot." It is that character of the Lamb which gives the blood its atoning virtue.

In Isaiah 53 we found that Jehovah's Lamb is a *person*. And in John 1 we saw that person identified as *Jesus*. In Acts 8 we saw Jesus the Lamb identified as *the promised Christ*. It is all here in this paragraph from Peter's pen, for he tells us that this foreprovided Lamb is the personal Lord Jesus Christ of the Gospel.

Is there any special reason for this interim summary? There is. Having looked back over all those aspects of the Lamb that were already revealed, Peter's paragraph now includes the *resurrection* of the slain Lamb. "God . . . raised him up from the dead, and gave him glory."

This resurrection of the slain Lamb was something never foredisclosed in Old Testament times. That the Lamb should die is foretold again and again, but nowhere is his resurrection predicted. With the light of the New Testament shining on the Old Testament, we who live in this Gospel dispensation can now discern in certain parts of the Old Testament latent or typical anticipations of our Lord's resurrection, but nowhere was it clearly revealed as were the other aspects of his saviorhood.

Observe also that as soon as Peter mentions the resurrection of the Lamb, he introduces the correlative feature of hope: "God raised him up . . . that your faith and hope might be in God." All the other aspects of the Lamb and his saving work call for faith, but as soon as we see the resurrection of the slain Lamb, faith becomes crowned with wonderful new hope. So, what is this new hope? What of the Lamb and the future? We begin to see the answer to that question in the next great Lamb chapter, Revelation 5.

Revelation 5

In this further chapter we see the enthronement of the Lamb in heaven. It takes the whole chapter to describe it, but for the moment we need not quote more than verses 6 and 8.

> *And I saw in the midst of the throne and of the four living beings, and in the midst of the elders, a Lamb standing, as though it had been slain. . . . And the four living beings and the four and twenty elders fell down before the Lamb, having each one a harp, and golden bowls full of incense, which are the prayers of the saints.*

So the Lamb is now in the throne of heaven, the very throne of the universe! What does that mean for the future? We find the answer in the tenth and last of these Lamb passages, namely, Revelation 21-22.

Revelation 21–22

What a climax of never-ending glory is portrayed in these last two chapters of the New Testament! In a passage that seems to grow more wonderful every time we read it reflectively, we see the ultimate goal reached in the endless bliss of a sinless society here on this earth, with the curse and pain and tears and death all gone forever. The untarnishable New Jerusalem forever supersedes the old. The earth itself is renewed and adapted to the new society. God himself dwells in the midst, and an ineffable, eternal day banishes darkness forever. It is indeed a sublime ending—an ending that merges into a prospect of never-ending felicity. The account runs from 21:1–22:5 and reaches its climax in these words:

> *And there shall be no curse any more; but the throne of God and of the Lamb shall be therein: and his servants shall serve him; and they shall see his face, and his name shall be on their foreheads. There shall be night no more. They need no light of a lamp, neither light of the sun; for the Lord God shall give them light; and they shall reign unto the ages of the ages.*

Thus, the final picture of the Lamb is that of his everlasting kingship. He sits in the very throne of God—the "throne of God and of the Lamb"—and reigns supreme in the glorious queen city of God's new order upon this earth, away beyond the Millennium in those ages, outlasting all time measurement, yet to unfold. His reign never ends. He is King of Kings forever!

Progressive Doctrine

But now travel through those ten Lamb passages again, and see the remarkable progress of doctrine that they exhibit. In the case of Abel, we are simply told that the lamb was an "offering." The New Testament comment is that it was a "sacrifice" offered by "faith"; that is, it was a propitiation to a gracious but holy God who cannot tolerate sin. We need not read more into it than that, but neither can we read less. The lamb was a *propitiation.*

In the Abraham incident the emphasis is not upon propitiation but upon *substitution,* for the lamb is offered as a substitute instead of Isaac.

Next, in the Passover story of Exodus 12, the emphasis is neither on propitiation nor on substitution but on *protection.* The sprinkled blood on the door frames is a protective covering from the angel of judgment and death.

In Leviticus, particularly in chapter 16 where we have the annual Day of Atonement, the emphasis is upon complete *absolution*—absolution from guilt, in both its Godward and manward aspects.

That annual Day of Atonement wonderfully typified our Lord's atoning work on Calvary, and in order to show this the lamb had to be represented by two goats[2]—one "for Jehovah," as a sin offering for the nation's guilt, and the other for *azazel* (or "removal," as the Hebrew word means). Our King James Version translates that Hebrew word *azazel* as "scapegoat," but perhaps we are wiser to keep to the Hebrew word itself—*azazel*, that is, "removal." After the one goat had been slain as a sin offering on behalf of the nation, Aaron the high priest was to lay both his hands on the head of the *azazel*, or "scapegoat," confessing over it all the iniquities of the nation, by which high priestly act all those sins were symbolically transferred to the *azazel* goat. Then the *azazel*, or goat of "removal," was driven away out to the wilderness, bearing upon itself (and thus removing) all those sins, to be lost forever in the trackless wilderness, never to be remembered against Israel any more. See verses 7-10 with 21-22.

Thus, the goat offered as a sacrifice typified the Godward aspect of our Lord's atoning work for us, while the *azazel* goat typified the manward aspect, that is, the removing of our guilt far from us forever. The two goats together therefore represent a complete and final absolution.

In Isaiah 53 all the foregoing aspects are included, but now the emphasis is on *expiation*. The suffering Lamb who is "wounded for our transgressions" expiates in his own soul and body the penalty of our sin.

In John 1 in the words, "Behold, the Lamb of God which beareth away the sin of the world," the emphasis is upon the complete *removal of our sin*, with all its ugly guilt and penalty. The Greek word means not only to bear, but to bear away. The immense, black barrier between God and our sinful race is removed in that one gigantic sin-bearing.

In Acts 8, where Philip preaches Jesus as the Lamb-Messiah-Savior to the high-ranking Ethiopian official, the emphasis is upon *individual human salvation* through the Lamb. On having the Lamb in Isaiah 53 explained to him, the Ethiopian exclaims, "I believe!" The end of the episode is: "And he went on his way rejoicing." What he had failed to find in Jerusalem, in the Law, in the temple, in the ceremonials, he had found in Jesus Christ the Lamb—personal salvation.

In 1 Peter 1:18-21, the emphasis is upon *redemption* through the Lamb. "Ye were redeemed . . . with precious blood, as of a lamb without blemish and without spot, even the blood of Christ." This is redemption not just as an objective concept but as a received and possessed reality.

In Revelation 5 the emphasis is upon *government* by the Lamb. He is not only risen and ascended; he now sits in sovereign control over history and destiny, as "the Lamb in the midst of the throne"!

Finally, in Revelation 21-22 we see the transfigured saints reigning in *eternal glory* through the Lamb. "The throne of God and of the Lamb shall be therein . . . The Lord God shall illumine them, and they shall reign unto the ages of the ages." Yes, that is the final emphasis—eternal glory through the Lamb!

How wonderful is this developing biblical theology of the Lamb! See the ten focus points in kaleidoscopic movement: (1) in Genesis 4, propitiation through the Lamb; (2) in Genesis 22, substitution by the Lamb; (3) in Exodus 12, protection through the Lamb; (4) in Leviticus, absolution through the Lamb; (5) in Isaiah 53, expiation by the Lamb; (6) in John 1, sin removal by the Lamb; (7) in Acts 8, personal salvation through the Lamb; (8) in 1 Peter 1, redemption through the Lamb; (9) in Revelation 5, government by the Lamb; (10) in Revelation 21-22, eternal glory through the Lamb!

Progressive Expansiveness

And now travel once more through those ten passages exhibiting the Lamb, and observe their progressive expansion.

In the case of Abel, we are told simply that the lamb was offered. It was offered as a propitiation *for sin.*

In the Abraham-and-Isaac incident the lamb was *offered in the place of one person,* namely, Isaac.

In the case of the Passover, each family must have its own lamb. It was the lamb *for one family.*

In the book of Leviticus, in the typical ritual on the annual Day of Atonement, we see the lamb *for one nation.*

Next, in Isaiah's great picture of the suffering Lamb-Messiah we find: "He shall sprinkle many nations"[3]—which looks beyond Israel; also, in verse 8, "He shall make many righteous, for he shall bear their iniquities." Here we have the Lamb *for all the elect.*

In John 1: "Behold the Lamb of God which beareth away the sin of the world," we have the Lamb *for the whole world.*

In Acts 8 it is the Lamb *for each individual*—not for the Jew only, but also for that Gentile Ethiopian. It is the Lamb for "*whosoever.*"

In 1 Peter 1 it is the Lamb "foreordained from before the foundation of the world"—that is, the Lamb *for all history.*

In Revelation 5, where the Lamb is enthroned in heaven, we see the Lamb *for the universe.*

In Revelation 21-22, where he reigns in endless glory amid the new heaven and new earth, we see the Lamb *for all eternity.*

Think of it: (1) the Lamb for sin; (2) the Lamb for one person; (3) the Lamb for one family; (4) the Lamb for one nation; (5) the Lamb for all the elect; (6) the Lamb for the world; (7) the Lamb for "whosoever"; (8) the Lamb for all history; (9) the Lamb for the whole universe; (10) the Lamb for all eternity!

Supernatural Inspiration

Is all this progressive presentation of the Lamb a product of blind chance or fortuitous coincidence? According to some moderns, I may be old-fashioned and naive, but to me this Bible doctrine of the Lamb is another internal evidence of supernatural inspiration. It confirms to me that the whole Bible is a developing unfolding of divine revelation and that the whole of it is the written Word of God. If that is being old-fashioned, then let me stay old-fashioned, for I believe that this good old fashion will still be new and true when the new fashion of the present hour has become dead and buried, with few mourners at the funeral. I recommend to one and all: Let such biblical phenomena as this progressive doctrine of the Lamb be a reassurance that these sixty-six documents which comprise our Bible are the "living oracles" of the Almighty.

Divine Testimony

To that I would add: Let this Bible doctrine of the Lamb show us what God thinks about the Lamb. In one way or another, right through the Bible, it is Jesus as the Lamb who has the preeminence. All other disclosures, whether through Pentateuchal law or Israelite history, whether psalmodic or philosophic, whether prophetic or doctrinal, whether visional or didactic, all are subservient to this onward-moving unveiling of truth concerning the Lamb. Supremely, our Bible is God's testimony to the Lamb. Should not our own testimony be in line with God's? Should not the Lamb be the outshining center and dominating accent of all our Christian preaching and witness bearing?

Tenfold Message

Think back again over the tenfold progress: the necessity of the Lamb, the divine provision of the Lamb, the slaying of the Lamb—right on to the heavenly enthronement and eternal sovereignty of the Lamb. Are not all these needing new enunciation in the pulpit ministry and public evangelism of today? Glance back over some of those ten doctrinal emphases of the Lamb: propitiation, substitution, absolution, expiation, redemption. All these, and indeed all ten, are being denied or glossed away or disdained today by ecclesiastical scholars at the one extreme, and in the hazy sophisms of crude "hedonists" at the other extreme. One of our easiest dangers just now is to give way either to the pressures of humanistic theologians or to the loud rebellions of misguided young collegians.

Already we are seeing everywhere around us today the sorry repercussions of the new and popular false gospels. You have only to turn on your television or scan your newspaper to see that the part of American society that gets most publicity at present is wallowing in muck and mire. Instead of accommodating our message to changing theological predilections or to carnalized social standards, we should preach with more consecrated resolve than ever our central, glorious Gospel of the Lamb—the Lamb of Calvary, of resurrection victory, of all-transcendent enthronement—the one and only true Savior and the predestined Administrator of a soon-coming new age!

See that stately oak tree proudly reigning on yonder hillside. How did it become the noble, mighty giant that it now is? Was it by bowing and cringing to hostile winds or sudden tempests? No, it was by holding on and standing firm. The more the storms tore in among the branches and ripped off the leaves, the deeper went the roots and the stronger grew the trunk and the sturdier became the branches. Even so, this is no time for us to be apologizing for our evangelical message. Like Goliath's sword, there is "none like it"! I believe that if we hold our ground and refuse to pander to the whims of a sick society and preach more prayerfully than ever redemption through the Lamb, we shall yet win new triumphs.

As we remember again how we ourselves have become saved through the Lamb, let us exult yet more gratefully that the precious blood shed on Calvary still cleanses from all sin and brings us eternal salvation. Let William Cowper's lines become afresh the language of our hearts:

> E'er since by faith I saw the stream
> Thy flowing wounds supply,
> Redeeming love has been my theme,
> And shall be till I die.
>
> Then, in a nobler, sweeter song
> I'll sing Thy power to save,
> With sinless heart and raptured tongue,
> In triumph o'er the grave.

2

The Centrality of the Lamb

Jesus is King!
True King of Israel, David's great Son,
Hope of the fathers, Heir to the throne;
Lion of Judah, Lamb that was slain,
True King of Israel yet shall He reign.

Jesus is King!
King of the angels, reigning in light,
King of His people, glorious in might,
Victor o'er Hades, Judge of all men,
King of all nations yet shall He reign.

Jesus is King!
King of all regions and ages of time,
King of the heaven of heavens sublime,
King of all creatures in every domain,
King of the universe yet shall He reign.

Jesus is King!
Sovereign of sovereigns, King evermore,
Godhead Incarnate, all must adore,
Soon now returning to end war and pain,
Boundless in empire yet shall He reign.
Jesus is King!

OUR LORD JESUS IS both the center and the circumference of divine revelation. As the sun is the center of our solar system and also the power that holds it together, so Christ is the magnetic center of Scripture and the unifying theme that makes all the three-score-and-six books of the Bible one self-consistent whole.

As Christ is the central figure of biblical revelation, so the Cross is the central factor. Whatever else our Bible may or may not be, it is distinctively and preeminently the book of salvation from sin, and its many-sided doctrine of salvation both centers in and radiates from the Christ of the Cross. The precious blood of Calvary, so to speak, sprinkles every page. The doctrine of redemption by the Lamb runs through Holy Writ like a crimson cord holding all the various parts of the sacred canon together in one. Amid the present-day whirl of new ideas, let this shine all the more clearly in our thinking: Jesus, as the Lamb of God, is the center-point of that message which we are to preach.

In the preceding study, we reviewed the progressive unfolding of biblical disclosure concerning the Lamb in ten notable passages. From those ten we now pick out three, and we may truly call them three classic passages exhibiting the centrality of the Lamb. The three passages are (1) Isaiah 53, (2) Revelation 5, and (3) Revelation 21–22. These three sections display the centrality of the Lamb in the following ways:

1. the Lamb amid the throes of his agony—Isaiah 53
2. the Lamb amid the throne of his glory—Revelation 5
3. the Lamb amid the throng of his people—Revelation 21–22

In Isaiah 53 we see the Lamb transfixed to the Cross here on earth. In Revelation 5 we see the Lamb triumphant on the throne in heaven. In Revelation 21–22 we see the Lamb transcendent forever in the new Jerusalem.

In the first of these three passages we look back to a humiliation that is now past. In the second we look up to an exaltation that is now present. In the third we look on to a consummation that is yet future.

The Centrality of the Lamb in Bearing Our Sin

We turn first to Isaiah 53, where we see the centrality of the Lamb in the bearing of our sin. That chapter is the most famous of all Isaiah's prophecies. It is quoted or alluded to again and again in the New Testament, and invariably it is applied to our Lord Jesus. Indeed, Angus's Bible Handbook says, "This chapter is almost reproduced in the New Testament and is applied at every point to Christ."

If we were to insist on strict chapter divisions, I suppose the fifty-third chapter should begin three verses earlier than it does, that is, at verse 13 of the preceding chapter. However, although those three verses introduce the new section, the "report" itself on our Lord's agonizing humiliation and ultimate exaltation does not begin until the first verse of the fifty-third chapter, in the words, "Who hath believed our report?"

In both a literary and a prophetic sense it is a wonderful chapter. It gathers into vivid concentration all the various scattered references of the Hebrew prophets to our Lord's redemptive work. In its photographic description of our Lord's unattractiveness and rejectedness, his unretaliating submissiveness and vicarious sufferings, his fearful travail and final triumph, it is all together of a sublime character unexcelled anywhere, either inside or outside the Bible.

Unfortunately, in our Authorized Version, in the English Revised, and in the *American Standard Version,* Isaiah 53 reads as prose, whereas in the original it is superb poetry, as more recent English versions, such as NIV and NASB, show. It is not poetry in the mold of rhyme or rhythm but the flexible Hebrew poetry of thought parallelism. In Hebrew poetry there are three kinds of parallels: (1) completive, (2) contrastive, (3) constructive. Isaiah 53 consists of twenty-four completive parallels. Completive parallels are those in which the second member of a pair extends or completes the thought in the first member. For instance, the first completive parallel is

> *Who has believed our report?*
> *And to whom is Jehovah's arm revealed?*

In line one the report is not received. In line two the Lord's arm is not revealed. Line one gives a human aspect. Line two gives a divine aspect. Line two grows out of line one: it expresses something on the Godward side that grows out of unbelief on the manward side in line one. In all such completive parallels that is the feature: the second member carries forward or intensifies or amplifies or completes the content of the first member. Take just the next two parallels in this fifty-third chapter:

> *For he grows up as a sapling before him,*
> *And like a root out of arid ground.*
> *He has no form or regality that we should regard him*
> *Or appearance that we should desire him.*

We will not linger over these couplets or the others throughout the chapter, though there is a peculiar fascination about them. The one thing to which we here call attention as being noteworthy is that the exact center of these twenty-four parallels is

> *He is led as a lamb to the slaughter;*
> *As a sheep, dumb before its shearers.*

If we are to be truly modern, then of course our immediate reaction is to regard this as purely accidental: we are too enlightened to allow that divine inspiration would descend to mere grammatical contrivances—(even though it does use alphabetic mnemonics in Lamentations and certain of the Psalms!) But if that reference to the Lamb at exact center-point is mere coincidence, is it not even more remarkable that in the verses preceding it there are just seven expressions of vicarious atonement viewed from the human side, while in the verses following it there are another seven expressions of vicarious atonement viewed from the divine side? Let me point them out. First, in the earlier half of the chapter:

1. "He hath borne our griefs" (v. 4)
2. "And carried our sorrows"
3. "He was wounded for our transgressions" (v. 5)
4. "He was bruised for our iniquities"
5. "The chastisement of our peace is on him"
6. "And with his stripes we are healed"
7. "Jehovah hath laid on him the iniquity of us all" (v. 6)

Notice, it is "our griefs" and "our sorrows"; "our transgressions" and "our iniquities." All seven are from our side, the human side of the Cross.

Each of these seven statements expresses one distinct aspect of our Lord's representative and substitutionary identification with us, until the final, comprehensive statement is reached: "Jehovah hath laid on him the iniquity of us all"—which makes our Lord's death on our behalf an act of God, not just a human deed; that is, an atonement, not just a crucifixion.

And now glance through the second half of the chapter. Here we find seven expressions of vicarious atonement viewed from the divine side. Some of them are so worded that we hear God speaking through the pronoun "my"; or else, instead of "our," we now have "their," as though God is viewing the Cross objectively.

1. "For the transgression of my people he was stricken" (v. 8)
2. "Thou shalt make his soul an offering for sin" (v. 10)
3. "By his knowledge shall my righteous Servant justify many" (v. 11)
4. "For he shall bear their iniquities"
5. "He was numbered with the transgressors" (v. 12)
6. "And he bore the sin of many"
7. "And made intercession for the transgressors"

Well, there it is: seven aspects of vicarious atonement from our point of view, then seven aspects of it from God's side, and between the two sevens,

He is led as a lamb to the slaughter;
As a sheep, dumb before its shearers.

Are we still quite sure that its center position happened accidentally? That is where it belongs. That is where the prophet-poet put it, speaking in the Holy Spirit. That is where God has put the Lamb—absolutely central in our redemption and salvation.

In this fifty-third chapter of Isaiah, this prophetic passion-poem describing our Savior's vicarious sufferings, every strophe, every couplet should be examined and pondered separately. We are dealing with supernatural literature in which every word is carefully placed and full of meaning. Let me here touch on just two of the poetic parallels. The first of those that actually declare the vicarious nature of our Lord's sufferings says:

> *Surely it was our griefs he bore;*
> *It was our sorrows he carried.*

Note the two verbs here: He "bore" and he "carried." Neither of them means to bear away. Thank God, our Lord did bear our guilt away from us forever, but that is not the emphasis here. Both the Hebrew verbs used here stress the idea of his bearing our sins and sorrows as a consciously endured pressure of weight.

We need only reflect on what the fearful pressure of our whole race's sin, guilt, and sorrow must have been on the mind of our Lord to find ourselves soon lost in wondering thought too deep for words.

Even during the three years of his public ministry that burden must have pressed heavily upon him. In some mysterious way even then he became inwardly identified with the very sicknesses that his miracles healed, for Matthew 8:17 tells us that in those healings he fulfilled "that which was spoken by Isaiah the prophet: himself took our infirmities, and bare our sicknesses." He suffered even as he healed.

But it was as he drew near to Gethsemane, with its agony and sweat of blood, that the pressure intensified into a monstrous, crushing horror. Mark 14:33 tells us that he "began to be sore amazed and very heavy." The Greek verb translated as "sore amazed" is an awesome word to be used of our divine Savior. It means to be astounded, staggered, bewildered, utterly dumbfounded. The root meaning of the second verb is "not at home"—as though our Lord was driven beyond himself in an "anguish of the soul struggling to free itself from the body under such pressure of mental distress."

That we are not overstating the force of those two verbs may be seen in the way recent Greek scholars translate them. To mention only two: Weymouth renders the phrase "full of terror and distress," and Moffatt gives it as "appalled and agitated."

> Oh, never, never can we know
> That crushing weight of sin and woe,
> When He, our great Sinbearer bled,
> The Lamb of Calvary, in our stead.

But take just one more couplet from Isaiah 53. It is in that fifth verse and is unspeakably precious to all those of us who have fixed our hope of eternal salvation on that Lamb of Calvary.

> *He is wounded for our transgressions,*
> *And is bruised for our iniquities.*

That word "wounded" represents a Hebrew verb that more strictly means "pierced." After looking up its use in other parts of the Old Testament I think there is reason to translate it as "pierced" here. It points to the spear that was driven into our Lord's side, to the iron spikes that transfixed him to the rough beam and transom, and to the crown of piercing thorns that tore his brow.

That other verb in the couplet—"bruised"—is a fearful word to be used in such a connection. It means to crush or beat to pieces! It does not refer so much to our Lord's outward, physical sufferings as to the inconceivable extreme of his inward excruciation.

The prophet sees it all in the present tense—"He is pierced . . . he is bruised," and that is how we should see it again in times of prayerful contemplation. It is true that we should always see the cross in the light of our Lord's resurrection. It is true that he is no longer on that cross. Yet equally truly there is a sense in which our Lord and that cross are united forever. As we see him rising from the dead and ascending to heaven, our exulting gratitude ascends to God with him; nevertheless, if we want the deepest love of our hearts to well up and overflow toward him, we must keep seeing, in vivid memory and adoring contemplation, those pierced hands and feet, that spear-torn side, that thorn-crowned brow, that cross of sin-atoning anguish.

Most of us, in these days of rush and speed, spend far too little time in rapt contemplation of that cross. We are needing to relearn the need and enrichment of lingering there. We preachers need to spend hours of aloneness before that cross with our Bibles open at Isaiah 53, slowly going over it line by line. If we are really to preach the Cross of Christ with compelling influence, we need inwardly to see it, as Isaiah did, with a vividness that breaks and melts and disturbs and inspires us. Every sermon on the Cross should come to our hearers wet with the preacher's tears.

Years ago I knew a fine Christian in Canada. He was born and bred among the poor. At an early age he had to leave school and go to work. While still young he came to know the Lord Jesus as his Savior. He started a small business and covenanted to give one-tenth of all his earnings to God. His business grew and grew until it was one of the largest of its kind in Canada. Faithfully he gave his tithe to the Lord. Then he made it a fifth, then a quarter, then a half, then three-quarters, then nine-tenths, until eventually he was running the whole business practically to make money for supporting the Lord's work in various ways. Thousands received financial help from him without ever knowing where it came from.

One day I asked him what brought about his conversion to Christ. He replied, "It was the example of my godly father." Then he told me he was one of four boys who grew up in the little old home. From their youngest days their father used to gather them round his knee while he read to them from the Bible and then prayed with them. On Sunday evenings he always read Isaiah 53. With a glow on his face he would start to read it. Then, on reaching verse 4, "Surely he hath borne our griefs," or verse 5, "He was wounded for our transgressions, he was bruised for our iniquities," his voice would falter, his throat would become husky, the tears would begin to drip down his cheeks, and he would have to say in broken syllables, "I'm sorry, boys, I canna' go on; it's too upsettin'—that such a dear, divine Savior should suffer for us sinners . . . like *that!*"

My friend added, "Sometimes my dad would struggle on a bit, but I never once knew him to get right through Isaiah 53. Even if he managed to get beyond verses 5 and 6, he never got beyond verse 7—'He is led as a lamb to the slaughter.' It broke him down to think that the Son of God should suffer for us 'like that.'"

In the deepest sense of the words, can we ever get beyond that seventh verse? He, the Creator of stars and systems and aeons, the Firstborn of all creation, in whom all things cohere, the delight of the Father's bosom, "He is led as a lamb to the slaughter"! Can any Christian heart ever get over that as long as eternity lasts? Those nail-torn hands and feet are more marvelous to us than twice ten billion stars. Those Calvary scars shine with lovelier luster than all the flashing gems of the New Jerusalem.

As we bring the eye of a telescope or the lens of a camera into clear focus upon an object, so the fifty-third chapter of Isaiah sets the Lamb in clear focus as the center point. There it is, between those two sevens that express vicarious atonement first from the human side and then from the divine—which is only another way of saying that the Holy Spirit has put the Lamb there. There is no soul-saving message for sinners apart from the Lamb. No one is truly preaching the Gospel who leaves out the Lamb or makes him anything other than the vital center.

In these days, much so-called Christian scholarship and preaching sneers with fancied intellectual superiority at the idea of salvation through the blood. Much that goes under the name of Christianity among our Prot-estant denominations is a new version of the Cain religion that wants to worship God with bouquets of flowers and fruits but refuses the sacrifi-cial Lamb of propitiation and atonement. There is a humanistic elegance about it, but it has no confession that the members of Adam's fallen race are hell-deserving sinners needing redemption and regeneration. God re-jects it. What is more, it leaves sinful people fundamentally unchanged. Cain would not lower himself to shed the blood of a poor little lamb—it was so "cruel"—yet he would in anger shed the blood of his own brother! If you want to know what religion without the Lamb does, look around at the pitiful wreck of morals and decency in Christendom today!

Let there be no apology in our preaching of the Lamb. Instead of secretly wondering whether we are preaching something outmoded or no longer relevant, let the desperate breakdown today be a new call to uplift the Lamb more than ever as the vital center of the only Gospel that truly saves people!

The Centrality of the Lamb in Wearing the Crown

We turn now to the book of Revelation, to the other two passages where the centrality of the Lamb is especially displayed. The first of the two is chapter 5, where we see the Lamb enthroned as universal Administrator.

The setting of this chapter is one of surpassing magnificence. In all of Holy Writ there is nothing to eclipse the grandeur and majesty of the scene that is here unveiled to us. The vision is of the rainbow-circled, glory-flashing throne of the Deity in the heaven of heavens, with the heavenly worshipers prostrating themselves around the throne in pro-found adoration and exulting praise. The vision quickly moves on to the climactic act in which the slain but now risen Lamb is constituted Joint Occupant with the eternal Father in the seat of supreme authority. There-upon the chapter reaches its spectacular and moving finale with the "one hundred millions" and "millions" more of angels and all other beings throughout the universe unitedly expressing themselves in a thunder of adoring praise to the Lamb-Lion-King amid the throne! Look at verses 1-5.

> *And I saw in the right hand of him that sat on the throne a book written within and on the back, sealed with seven seals. And I saw a strong angel proclaiming with a loud voice: Who is worthy to open the book, and to loose the seals thereof? And no one in heaven or on the earth or under the earth was able to open the book or to look thereon. And I wept much because no one was found worthy to open the book or to look thereon. And one of the elders saith unto me: Weep not; behold, the Lion of the tribe of*

Judah, the Root of David, hath overcome to open the book and the seven seals thereof.

That seven-sealed book, or scroll, obviously is not the book of the past, for that is already unrolled and open. Nor is it the record of the unfolding present, for the hand of time itself is unrolling that. It is the book of the yet-to-be, revealing the finalities of human history, the winding up of present mysteries, the future climaxes of the divine purpose, and the ultimate issues of human destiny. We know that such is the meaning of the seven-sealed book because of what we see and hear and learn as the Lamb afterward successively opens the seven seals.

It is not surprising that John "wept much" because no one was found equal to breaking the seven seals, for is there anything of more concern to us human beings than to learn the ultimate outcome of the mysterious conflict of good and evil through the ages—and to know what our destiny will be in that endless future on the other side of the grave? We recall the consternation of Egypt's magicians when none of them could unseal the meaning of Pharaoh's dream—and how Joseph overcame to unloose the meaning of it, for doing which he was exalted by Pharaoh to be over all the land of Egypt. We remember, too, the furious threat of Nebuchadnezzar to destroy all the wise men of Babylon because they could not interpret his forgotten dream—and how Daniel unlocked the mystery and meaning of it, for which he was exalted to be ruler over the whole province of Babylon. There was the same kind of scene when the awesome handwriting appeared on the palace wall at Belshazzar's feast, and only Daniel could unseal its fateful message.

On an immeasurably grander scale, such is the vision in Revelation 5. Those seven seals symbolize not only the sacred inviolability of the scroll, but also the sevenfold completeness of the revelation contained in it. Only one hand in the universe can unfasten those seals, for there is only the One who is worthy to do so.

But why must he be "worthy"? It is because the unsealing of that book carries with it the administrative authority to dispense its contents—just as, in a much lesser sense, the unsealing of the royal dreams lifted Joseph and Daniel to the highest administrative authority. In other words, the One who can unloose those seals belongs in that rainbow-circled throne as the Executive of the Godhead. That is why, coinciding with our Lord's taking the book, John suddenly sees the Lamb "in the midst of the throne."

The first big wonder that we should clearly appreciate is that this chapter describes not something that is yet to happen but something that has occurred already. Admittedly, there are prospects in it that will reach their final fulfillment in the future, but the main event, that is, the enthronement of the Lamb, has happened already. Our Lord is even now in that throne of thrones. We know this from a verb that occurs in verse 5: "The Lion of the tribe of Judah hath overcome to open the book." In the Greek the verb tense is the aorist, which is more exactly rendered here as "overcame." It links back at once to Revelation 3:21, where our risen Lord says, "To him that overcometh will I grant to sit with me in my throne [i.e., his messianic throne], even as I also overcame and sat down [note the past tense again] with my Father in his throne." So our ascended Lord himself tells us that when he sent those letters to the seven churches his investiture as supreme Administrator in the midst of the throne had already taken place.

What a comfort it is in these days of widespread moral breakdown, of defiant lawlessness and social violence and unblushing sexualism and organized anti-Godism and overhanging threat of nuclear war—what a comfort to know that despite all appearances to the contrary, the sovereign control of history and destiny is still in the hands that bear the nail prints and that these divinely permitted latter-day excesses are the very things that (as foretold) will precipitate his return in flaming power to trample out all such evil and bring in his global Christocracy!

But now glance at a few of the arresting features of this fifth chapter. The elder says to John, "Weep not; the Lion of the tribe of Judah, the Root of David, overcame to open the book." John therefore looks to see the Lion, but instead, to his utter surprise, he sees a Lamb right in the midst of all that glory—a Lamb with all the marks of having just been killed and yet standing there alive, as the center, along with God himself, of all that celestial splendor!

So the Lamb is the Lion! Here is the supreme vindication of the truth that right is might, that humility is majesty, that the final inheritance is with the meek, that light has the final victory over darkness, and that virtue shall at last trample evil underfoot. The Lamb who once was slain is the Lion who now must reign. The Victim is the Victor! The Crucified is the Crowned! The Servant and Savior of all is the Sovereign and Ruler of all. As Lamb he is Redeemer. As Lion he is King. He is the Lamb-Lion Redeemer-King.

Observe in verses 5–6 the seven great facts about the Lamb (like other symbolic sevens in Scripture, comprised of four and three)—four things that he is and three attributes that he has; four features belonging to his human nature and three pertaining to his divine being. Note first the four aspects of his humanity:

1. the "Lion of Judah," that is, the promised Deliverer of his people
2. the "Root of David," that is, the promised Shepherd-King
3. the "Lamb slain," that is, the promised Sin-Bearer and Redeemer
4. the "Worthy One," that is, the promised "glory of Israel," in whom

is fulfilled all that seers ever saw and prophets ever promised and psalmists ever sang

See now the three infinite attributes predicated of him. The Lamb has "seven horns, and seven eyes which are the seven Spirits of God sent forth into all the earth." The horn is the symbol of strength. Seven is, among other significations, the number of completeness, of perfection. Thus we have here three infinite attributes:

1. "seven horns," that is, perfect power—omnipotence
2. "seven eyes," that is, perfect wisdom—omniscience
3. "seven spirits into all the earth"—omnipresence

Those are the attributes of God. The Lamb, besides being promised Deliverer, Governor, Redeemer, and Glory of Israel, is God Incarnate! He to whom these divine attributes are ascribed must not only be exalted, he must be worshiped. Therefore we are immediately told that "the four living beings, and four-and-twenty elders fell down before the Lamb, having, every one of them, harps, and golden vials full of odors which are the prayers of saints." The harps represent worship in the form of praise. The incense vials represent worship in the form of prayer. The same kind of praise and prayer that are offered to God are now offered to the Lamb, that is, to the risen and exalted Lord Jesus as God the Son incarnate in manhood. There is no unitarianism in heaven! Our Lord Jesus is no mere ideal human with a God-given laurel on his head; neither is he some exalted demiurge or demigod of the Jehovah's Witnesses brand. In that pure worship up yonder, where the Lamb is in the midst of the throne, he is worshiped not only as a son of God, but as God the Son.

See now the tremendous climax of the whole scene. The countless myriads of angel hosts unite in the following sublime outburst of sevenfold praise to the Lamb: "Worthy is the Lamb that was slain, to receive: [1] the power, [2] the riches, [3] the wisdom, [4] the might, [5] the honor, [6] the glory, [7] the blessing"!

Then, augmenting and consummating the praise of the angelic hosts, the whole vast universe joins in the superglorious anthem of acclamation described in the closing verses of the chapter. "And every creature which is in heaven, and on the earth, and under the earth, and on the sea, and all that are in them, I heard saying, 'Blessing, and honor, and glory, and dominion, unto him that sitteth on the throne, and to the Lamb, unto the ages of the ages.'"

How plain is the meaning of all this! God has put the Lamb in the place of absolute supremacy and centrality. Let us keep him where God has put him! He is central in prophecy and history, central in the worship of heaven, central in the adoration of saints and angels, central in the government and ultimate homage of the whole universe, central in his atonement as the one true Savior of human beings; central in his exaltation as the one true King of all creation.

The Centrality of the Lamb in Sharing His Glory

Finally, look at the third passage where the centrality of the Lamb is outstandingly exhibited, Revelation 21-22. These last two chapters of the Apocalypse are the matchlessly sublime consummation of divine revelation as given to us in the Holy Scriptures. See again the opening words of chapter 21.

> *And I saw a new heaven and a new earth: for the first heaven and the first earth are passed away; and the sea is no more. And I saw the holy city, new Jerusalem, coming down out of heaven from God, made ready as a bride adorned for her husband.*

So the passage that ensues is not a description of heaven but of a "city" that "comes down out of heaven" and is set up here on this earth. In verse 24 we are told that "the nations shall walk by the light of it; and the kings of the earth bring their glory into it." Verse 26 adds that the "glory and honor of the nations" shall be brought to it, and 22:2 tells us that the tree of life, made accessible again through it, shall yield its fruit monthly for the "healing [i.e., continually renewed health] of the nations." See the glory of that apocalyptic city:

> *And he carried me away in the Spirit to a great and high mountain, and showed me the holy city, New Jerusalem, coming down out of heaven from God, having the glory of God. Her light was like unto a stone most precious, as it were a jasper stone, clear as crystal. . . . And the building of the wall thereof was jasper; and the city was pure gold, like unto pure glass . . . And the twelve gates were twelve pearls . . . (21:10–11, 18, 21).*

Yet we miss the sublimest meaning unless we see that it is the Lamb who is the center of it all. In the description of this queen city amid the new heaven and new earth, running from 21:1 to 22:5, there are just seven references to the Lamb. Well may we gratefully wonder at what they tell us.

1. "Come hither; I will show thee the bride, the wife of the Lamb" (21:9). So the Lamb is the Bridegroom.
2. "The city had twelve foundations, and in them the names of the twelve apostles of the Lamb" (21:14). So the Lamb is the foundation.

3. "I saw no temple . . . the Lord God Almighty and the Lamb are the temple" (21:22). So the Lamb is the temple.
4. "The glory of God did lighten it, and the Lamb is the light thereof" (21:23). So the Lamb is the luminary or radiance.
5. "Only they [enter] that are written in the book of life of the Lamb" (21:27). So the Lamb is the portal.
6. "A pure river of water of life, clear as crystal, [flowed] from the throne of God and the Lamb" (22:1). So the Lamb is the life.
7. "The throne of God and of the Lamb shall be in it" (22:3). So the Lamb is the King.

Think of it—this sevenfold relationship of the Lamb to that ineffable city and society of the new world that is yet to be. The Lamb is the Bridegroom. The Lamb is the foundation. The Lamb is the temple. The Lamb is the radiance. The Lamb is the portal. The Lamb is the life. The Lamb is the King—the center of everything!

How sublimely wonderful is this sevenfold relationship between the heavenly Bridegroom and that queen city of the new earth! How rapturously it lights up the indissoluble bond that binds the people of Christ to their Lord and Savior! The Lamb is the Bridegroom and his people are the bride, so it is a loving union. The Lamb is the foundation and his people are the building, so it is a lasting union. The Lamb is both the temple and the object of his people's worship, so it is an adoring union. The Lamb is the luminary or irradiating glory-light, so it is a transfiguring union. The Lamb is the portal and "nothing that defileth" can ever gain access, so it is a holy union. The Lamb is the life and we live in his life for ever, so it is a life-renewing union. The Lamb is the King and his people reign with him forever, so it is a royal union.

Thus the Lamb is the ever-living, ever-loving, everlasting center and supreme glory of the celestial city and its sinless society. The light of the city is the face of Jesus. The music of the city is the name of Jesus. The harmony of the city is the praise of Jesus. The theme of the city is the love of Jesus. The joy of the city is the presence of Jesus. The employment of the city is the service of Jesus. The strength of the city is the omnipotence of Jesus. The magnetic center and superglory of the city is Jesus himself. The duration of the city is the eternity of Jesus.

> Jerusalem the golden,
> With fadeless treasures blest,
> Oh, heavenly Zion glorious,
> By raptured saints possessed!
> I know not, oh, I know not
> What joys await me there,

> What radiancy of glory,
> What bliss beyond compare.

As we think of what awaits us there, perhaps we can sympathetically enter into the wistful sentiment of the old Puritan who said, "When I get yonder, I'll spend the first thousand years gazing on Jesus; then I'll have a look around"!

> The Bride eyes not her raiment.
> But her beloved's face;
> I will not gaze on glories,
> But on my King of grace:
> Not on the crown He giveth,
> But on His pierced hand:
> The Lamb is all the glory
> In Emmanuel's land.

Yes, the Lamb is all the glory in that fair realm where, with sin and the curse utterly done away, Christ and his own are one forevermore. And how wonderfully it climaxes the Bible doctrine of the centrality of the Lamb! We have seen the centrality of the Lamb as set forth in Isaiah 53 and in Revelation 5 and in Revelation 21-22: the Lamb amid the throes of his agony, the Lamb amid the throne of his glory, the Lamb amid the throng of the glorified. We have seen him bearing our sin on earth, wearing the crown in heaven, sharing his glory with us forever.

Behold, then, the triune centrality of the Lamb—the Cross, the Crown, the City, Crucifixion, Coronation, Consummation. He is central not only in prophecy and history, not only in the adoration of the heavenly hosts and in the government of the universe, but throughout the future even to "the ages of the ages." He is the one true Savior, the King of Kings and Lord of Lords; the Consummator of the ages, and the everlasting glory of his people. Glory to the Lamb!

Let changing theological fashions come and go. Let twentieth-century cynicisms be what they may. Let people deride and demons fume. Let oppositions multiply. The only message that saves people is the Gospel of the Lamb. More than ever, the Lamb must be the center of our preaching and planning and serving, of our faith and hope and love. More concentratedly than ever let us proclaim him, uplift him, glory in him, love him, live for him, and, if need be, die for him. And let us beware of becoming so professionally theological or so religiously busy or so pragmatically antisentimental that we do not thrill at the prospect of seeing him at last—the "King in His beauty, in the land of far distances." Think of it:

Not merely one glimpse, but forever,
At home with Him, ever to be;
With Him in that glory celestial,
Where shimmers the crystal sea:
Yet there, even there, in such glory,
Will anything ever efface
That rapturous moment of moments,
My first, first sight of His face!

3

The Sovereignty of the Lamb:
(1) Preincarnate

Certainly we need to guard against any morbid or merely sentimental dwelling on the harrowing details of our Lord's crucifixion. Yet perhaps there is renewed reason in these days of unmeditating hurry why we should deliberately pause sometimes to think what that Calvary horror must have meant to that gentle mind and even to that pinioned flesh of our Saviour. The nailing of the crucified victim to the Cross was the first in a series of agonies. The second factor causing keen suffering was the abnormal position of the body, the slightest movement occasioning acutest torture. A third factor was the traumatic fever induced by hanging for so long. Within six to twelve minutes blood pressure would drop to 50 with pulse racing at double rate. Under such agonizing excruciation the heart is deprived of blood and eventually collapses.

Anonymous

> Oh, never, never can we know
> That midnight of mysterious woe
> When, God-forsaken, there He cried,
> And thus forlorn and pain-racked died.

THE FURTHER WE INQUIRE into this Bible doctrine of the Lamb, the more impressive it becomes. In our first study we followed the unfolding manifestation of the Lamb through successive books of Holy Writ. Then, in our second survey, we saw how movingly the Bible exhibits the centrality of the Lamb. We now examine a further feature of the subject, namely, the Bible testimony as to the sovereignty of the Lamb. The Bible reveals the sovereignty of the Lamb in three main aspects. First, there is his preincarnate sovereignty as the Lamb designate: the Lamb "slain from the foundation of the world" (1 Peter 1:20; Rev. 13:8). Second, there is his postresurrection sovereignty as the Lamb now crowned in heaven: the Lamb "in the midst of the throne" (Rev. 5). Third, there is his never-ending sovereignty as the Lamb destined to rule over all worlds and beings in the ages to come: the Lamb supreme amid the new heaven and new earth (Rev. 21–22).

His Preincarnate Sovereignty

First we think of his sovereignty prior to his incarnation in our humanity, that is, his sovereignty as the Lamb "foreordained before the foundation of the world." In this connection we turn again to the prophet Isaiah.

In many quarters today it is fashionable to hold that our book of Isaiah comes from a plurality of authors rather than from the one well-known Isaiah who was the ablest writer in King Hezekiah's guild of literary experts. Some of the earlier German higher critics supposedly discovered seventy or more different hands in the work, and one of them, who evidently wanted to excel all his brother-dissectors in this latter-day quasi-science of literary vivisection, "discovered" no fewer than one hundred twenty-two authors instead of just the one Isaiah, the "son of Amoz"!

The comical peculiarity about these higher critical discoveries is that all those other writers who had a part in the supposedly composite product that we call the book of Isaiah are unidentifiable anonymities about whose existence there is not a wisp of evidence save in the fertile imaginations of the critics!

A more conservative theory now is that there were at least two Isaiahs—one of them the pre-Exile Isaiah of Hezekiah's day, who wrote chapters 1–39, the other a supposedly post-Exile, so-called Deutero-Isaiah, who compiled chapters 40–66—though once again the so-called Deutero is a Mr. Nobody so far as historical identification is concerned.

The rasher extravagances of the earlier higher critical detecting and dividing that reduced the book of Isaiah to a literary patchwork quilt have been disproved by their own obvious inanity, but still today the supposition is that modern scholarship has established a greater or lesser plurality of authorship in the book, so that instead of its being strictly a "book," it is a congeries from various contributors and redactors.[1] At the very least, so it is generally supposed, there were two main Isaiahs, but both sections have supposedly been abundantly tinkered with by a literary class known as the Hebrew sopherim, or scribes, or Scripturists.

This duality (or plurality) of authorship, especially between part one (chaps. 1–39) and part two (chaps. 40–66) has been argued on three grounds: (1) differences of vocabulary, (2) differences of ideas and forms of expression, (3) differences in historical references and geographical background. All these have been examined and answered again and again. We need not go into them here. (For a particular examination of them I recommend volume 3 of my *Explore the Book*).

But there is one aspect of the matter that I do want to mention again here, because it has been strangely neglected: the overall structure of the book, which binds all its parts into one progressive whole. I make bold to submit that if only more attention had been paid to the literary structure and architectural design that are evident in this book of the prophet Isaiah, its unity of authorship would have become convincingly clear, and the inventive genius of the higher critics might have been spared the need of discovering so many supposed joint authors who never existed. Let me quickly explain what I mean. With all other Bible students, I accept that the book of Isaiah falls into those two main parts: that is, chapters 1-39 and then chapters 40-66, though even that needs one incidental correction. To be strictly accurate, the book is in three parts: (1) chapters 1-35, which are a complete catena of poetic prophecies in themselves; (2) chapters 36-39, which are not prophetical at all in the predictive sense: they are a historical interlude, and they are written in prose, not poetry; (3) chapters 40-66, which are one continuous messianic poem-prophecy.

If we now look carefully through the first main chain of prophecies (chaps. 1-35) and then through the second (40-66) we shall find plan and pattern developing through each of them, indicating composition by one author. Also, we shall find a key chapter in each of those two series, and those two key chapters tell us something stupendous about the sovereignty of the Lamb.

Isaiah 1-35

An observant reader will notice that chapters 1-6 are all confined to Judah and Jerusalem. But that sixth chapter marks a crisis. Isaiah experiences his transforming vision of Jehovah as the King—King of all nations and of all history, transcendent above all the convulsions of time, and reigning in sovereign, purposive control over all developments. From that point onward Isaiah's prophecies reach out, ever widening and further seeing into the future.

The first six chapters, as noted, are limited to Judah. The next six chapters (7-12) reach out to the northern kingdom, Israel. The next eleven chapters (13-23) spread out to include ten great nations of Isaiah's own era: Babylon (13-14), Philistia (14:28-32), Moab (15-16), Syria (17-18), Egypt (19-20), and so on.

Next, in chapters 24-27, we have the "Day of Jehovah" in relation to the whole world. From special denunciations of woe on particular nations, Isaiah passes to tremendous predictions involving the whole human race. Expositors uniformly agree that the language of these mighty predictions does indeed embrace the entire earth. We only need quote a few verses.

> *Behold, Jehovah maketh the earth empty . . . and scattereth abroad the inhabitants thereof. . . . the world languisheth and fadeth away. . . . And it shall come to pass in that day, that Jehovah will punish the host of the high ones on high, and the kings of the earth upon the earth. . . . Jehovah*

of hosts will make unto all peoples a feast of fat things. . . . And he will destroy in this mountain the face of the covering that covereth all peoples, and the veil that is spread over all nations (24:1, 4, 21; 25:6-7).

The dominant subject in all the chapters, so far, is the Day of Jehovah—a day that certainly came upon all those powers of Isaiah's pre-Christian era but that, in coming on them, forepictured a final Day of Jehovah yet to be.

See, then, how Isaiah's outreach is broadening: first the message to Judah, then outward to Israel, then to all the surrounding Gentile nations, then to the whole world!

In chapters 28-33 we find a sharply distinguished group of six chapters pronouncing six "woes" on Jerusalem, which is ever the center of all God's earth-dealings. The city of highest privilege is the city of heaviest responsibility:

1. on drunkards of Ephraim and Judah (28)
2. hypocrites of Ariel (29:1-14, especially note v. 13)
3. evil schemers of Jerusalem (29:15-24)
4. the revolters against Jehovah (30)
5. the unholy alliance-makers (31-32)
6. the spoiler of Jerusalem (33)

Finally, in chapters 34-35, this first series of prophecies reaches its climax. The two chapters are an inseparable but sharply contrasting pair. Not only do they girdle the globe, they wing right on to the end of our present age and into the coming Millennium. They depict Jehovah's world-wide vengeance (34) and Zion's final restoration (35) or, in other words, the wrath to come at the end of this present age and the kingdom to come—our Lord's global empire that crowns the history of our Adamic race. See how chapter 34 begins:

Come near, ye nations, to hear; and hearken, ye peoples. Let the earth hear, and the fulness thereof; the world and all things that come forth from it. For Jehovah hath indignation against all the nations, and wrath against all their host. He hath utterly destroyed them; he hath delivered them to the slaughter. . . . And all the host of heaven shall be dissolved, and the heavens shall be rolled together as a scroll. . . . For Jehovah hath a day of vengeance, a year of recompense for the cause of Zion (vv. 1-2, 4, 8).

Thus does Isaiah carry us on, right to the fearful storm of the divine wrath that shakes all nations and all the powers of evil and culminates the present age. But in chapter 35 we are right through it and on into the glorious new day of the Millennium:

The wilderness and the dry land shall be glad; and the desert shall rejoice and blossom as the rose. . . . The eyes of the blind shall be opened, and the ears of the deaf shall be unstopped. Then shall the lame man leap as a hart, and the tongue of the dumb shall sing. . . . And the ransomed of Jehovah shall return and come with singing unto Zion; and everlasting joy shall be upon their heads: they shall obtain gladness and joy, and sorrow and sighing shall flee away! (vv. 1, 5–6, 10).

Yes, that is the millennial climax. How remarkable, then, is the expanding development in this first part of Isaiah! Glance back again. In the first six chapters we are limited to Judah, but after that transforming vision in chapter 6, the prophecies reach out more and more until they have comprehended all nations and all history!

See it in vivid summary: the first six chapters, Judah only. The next six chapters, the ten-tribed Israel. The next group of chapters, all the main kingdoms of Isaiah's era. Then, in the next group the whole world is revolving before the eye of prophecy. Next, in chapters 28–33, Jerusalem becomes the focus point as being the center of all Jehovah's controversy and ultimate purpose with the nations of our earth. Finally, in chapters 34–35, we are plunged into the age-end Great Tribulation and then brought through to the golden climax of the Millennium! Is not that indeed wonderful expansion, development, progress, design? And does it not argue one human author behind the whole of it?—even as it also indicates the one divine Author behind the human?

How much more meaningful becomes that sixth chapter with its overwhelming vision of Jehovah as King of all nations and ages—the vision that turned a parochial scribe into a worldwide prophet of God, with a clarion voice reverberating through centuries right on to the end of time!

Isaiah 40–66

But now we turn to that other weighty scroll of the prophet's oracles: Isaiah 40–66. Here, as presented in our English versions, we have twenty-seven chapters, and in them there is evident plan and pattern as much as in the earlier set of prophecies.

These twenty-seven chapters taken collectively shape themselves into one developing messianic poem-prophecy, and there is a significant grouping of the twenty-seven into three groups of nine chapters each, the end of each group being marked off by the same solemn refrain. At the end of the first nine (48:22) we read: "There is no peace, saith Jehovah, to the wicked." At the end of the second nine (57:21) we read: "There is no peace, saith my God, to the wicked." Finally, at the end of the third nine (66:24) we have the same in an amplified form: "Their worm shall not die, neither shall their fire be quenched."

In the first nine, the accent is on the supremacy of Jehovah; in the second nine, the servant of Jehovah; in the third nine, the challenge of Jehovah. The middle nine consists of chapters 49–57. So the middle chapter of that middle nine is chapter 53, which by common consent is the greatest of all Old Testament passages on the expiatory and atoning sufferings of our Lord Jesus (see Appendix). And in the exact center of that fifty-third chapter we find:

> *He is led as a Lamb to the slaughter (v. 7).*

Is that arresting singularity merely another coincidence? To some no doubt, nothing more. But think of it: one long, messianic poem-prophecy consisting of twenty-seven chapters, self-punctuated into three groups of nine chapters each—and the middle chapter of the middle nine the great Sin-Bearer chapter—and the middle couplet of that center most chapter:

> *He is led as a Lamb to the slaughter, and as a sheep before its shearers . . .*

Shall we insist on calling it sheer accident that in this orderly, progressive poem-prophecy the Lamb is thus put at dead center in the middle chapter of the middle nine? Are we not meant to see one more peculiarly captivating indication that the Lamb is the crux, the vital focus, the very heart and center of God's message to humanity? That fifty-third chapter is the hub around which the whole wheel of Isaiah's message of coming redemption revolves.

How can we ever read that fifty-third chapter of Isaiah without tears of grief and shouts of wondering praise? Oh, the mystery of that profound and agonizing substitution! Oh, the wonder of that glorious love which endured for us that immeasurable woe! Amid the shifting sands of human speculation and despite the popular new philosophies of our time, we must keep the Lamb at the very center of our message. We are not preaching mere religion or philosophy or some novelty that panders to modern thought. We are preaching the one and only authentic revelation of God and the one and only true redemption of humanity. At the very center of that revelation and redemption is the Lamb. There is no other Savior, and there is no other salvation. We must keep the Lamb where God has put him—utterly central—in our faith and hope and love, in our preaching and testifying, in all our planning and Christian enterprise.

Even that, however, is not the final significance of Isaiah's focus on the Lamb. All that we have seen so far, in his two series of prophecies, rises to its supreme meaning when we compare the two key chapters in those two series. As we saw, the key or pivot in the first series (1–35) is chapter 6 with its electrifying vision of the heavenly throne, from which point prophecies so spectacularly expand. The key chapter in the second series (40–66) is that central fifty-third chapter, the Lamb chapter.

First Key Chapter: Isaiah's Vision of the Great King

The opening words of chapter 6 are very familiar to most of us, but it is good to pause anew and try to visualize realistically what Isaiah describes.

> *In the year that king Uzziah died I saw the Lord, sitting upon a throne, high and lifted up; and his train filled the temple. Above him stood the seraphim: each one had six wings; with twain he covered his face, and with twain he covered his feet, and with twain he did fly. And one cried unto another, and said, Holy, holy, holy is Jehovah of hosts: the whole earth is full of his glory. And the foundations of the thresholds shook at the voice of him that cried, and the house was filled with smoke. Then said I: Woe is me! for I am undone; because I am a man of unclean lips, and I dwell in the midst of a people of unclean lips: for mine eyes have seen the King, Jehovah of hosts! (vv. 1–5).*

The vision soars to its high point in that awed exclamation, "Mine eyes have seen the King, Jehovah of Hosts!" There was the glory-flashing throne "high and lifted up," and the royal "train" filling the heavenly temple (or palace), and "the King"—even Jehovah of Hosts, the Creator and Controller of the universe. There were the firelike "seraphs," or "burning ones," crying, "Holy, holy, holy is Jehovah of hosts"—at which cry the very "foundations" moved, as though the whole building was awed into trembling, and the house became "filled with smoke," as though even the heavenly temple or palace sought to veil itself, as the six-winged seraphs did.

But the two predominant impressions that prostrated Isaiah were those of sin-exposing holiness and all-transcendent sovereignty. It was a sight of sheer glory and absolute supercontrol. Supreme over the histories and destinies of all nations and peoples Isaiah saw that flaming super-throne and the all-controlling purpose of a sovereign omnipotence. That was the strongest impact of the vision. All the globe-circling, history-spanning prophecies that later flowed from Isaiah's pen were implicit in that one terrific sight of the universe's King.

That overpowering apocalypse, however, assumes an even more eloquent splendor from the New Testament comment upon it. In John 12:41 we read: "These things said Isaiah because he saw his [i.e., Christ's] glory, and spake of him." When young Isaiah saw "the Lord" (Hebrew, *Adonay*) he was beholding the preincarnate Son of Man!

Second Key Chapter: The Lamb

And now turn to that other key chapter, Isaiah 53, the Lamb chapter. "Who hath believed our report? And to whom is the arm of Jehovah revealed?" Remarkably enough, that twelfth chapter of John, just quoted, which says that it was our Lord Jesus Christ who was on the heavenly throne in Isaiah 6, tells us equally clearly that it was our Lord Jesus whom Isaiah saw as the atoning Sufferer in chapter 53. See John 12:37–38: "But though he had done so many signs before them, yet they believed not on him: that the word of Isaiah might be fulfilled which he spake: Lord, who hath believed our report?"

The marvel that staggered Isaiah was that the despised, rejected, humiliated, bruised, wounded, pierced, broken, unresisting, meek and lowly, suffering Sin-Bearer whom he saw "led as a lamb to the slaughter" was the very One whom he had earlier seen surrounded by overwhelming heavenly splendor, sitting on the glory-flashing throne, reigning in supersovereignty over all nations and centuries! His omnipotent sovereignty that could crush a million alpha stars underfoot and never feel them, that sovereignty with its blaze of sin-consuming holiness that could burn up the whole race of human sinners in instantaneous extinction, that eternal sovereignty which governs all worlds and all beings—that sovereignty incarnates itself in the person of Jesus, descends from that ineffable throne of glory, and hangs on that gory, felon's cross as the Lamb that bears away the sin of the world!

That diademed Prince of glory, hanging in shame on that fearful cross is the most astonishing thing that ever happened in the history of the universe or in the life of the uncreated Creator himself! How can we ever be anything other than "lost in wonder, love, and praise"?

> Wonder of wonders! Vast surprise!
> Could bigger wonder be,
> That He who built the starry skies
> Once bled and died for me?
>
> Amazing, startling sacrifice,
> Confounding all our thought!
> Stupendous, staggering purchase-price
> Which our redemption bought!

The Sovereign of all becomes the Sin-Bearer of all! The regal Lion becomes the bleeding Lamb! The most baffling spectacle that angel hosts ever saw was that almighty divine sovereignty fastened by iron spikes to a criminal's cross on this earth. So, then, in Isaiah see the sovereignty of the Lamb: reigning as King over all, then hanging on a cross as Savior of all. What a Savior!

4

The Sovereignty of the Lamb:
(2) Postresurrection

It was one of the immeasurable evils which the Roman Church inflicted on Christendom, that it held constantly before the eyes of the Church the exhausted, suffering, agonized form of Christ on the Cross—fastened the thought and imagination of Christian men on the extremity of His mortal weakness, and so deprived them of the animation and the courage inspired by the knowledge that He is now on the throne of the Eternal. A similar loss may be inflicted on ourselves if our thoughts are imprisoned within the limits of the earthly life of Christ, and if we do not exult in His resurrection and in His constant presence in the Church. The historic Christ is the Object of memory: the present, the living Christ, is the Object of faith, the Source of power, the Inspiration of love, the Author of salvation.

R. W. Dale

IT IS TIME NOW to turn from the poetic oracles of Isaiah to the Patmos apocalypse of John, in the last book of our Bible. If in Isaiah we have a heart-moving preview of the suffering Lamb, in the book of Revelation we have the soul-stirring sequel.

We should be paying special attention to the book of Revelation just now. Unless many of us are strangely mistaken, history on this earth is now quickly moving into that age-end convulsion and transition to a new global order that the book of Revelation largely forepictures to us.

Many among us have the idea that the book of Revelation is mostly a mystifying riddle of cryptic signs and uninterpretable symbols. That is a pity, for it is the one book of Holy Writ that is actually named a "Revelation"! A revelation is meant to reveal and to be understood. Perhaps some of us are so busy imagining hidden meanings everywhere in it that we miss the big simplicities that are plainly written.

Admittedly, many of the apocalyptic visions do have symbols that are purposely enigmatic for the time being and that wait to be eventually unlocked by recognized fulfillment, but in its overall meaning and focal message the book of the Revelation is one of the plainest parts of Holy

Writ. No book of Scripture develops according to a clearer plan. It runs in three main movements, and those three movements issue in three successive enthronements—three enthronements of the Lamb. In fact, the book of Revelation might well be called the book of the three enthronements. Let me open up those three movements a little.

The First Enthronement

The first movement runs through chapters 1-5. Observe the progress in it. In chapter 1 we have the vision of the risen and glorified Son of Man amid the lampstands. What is the essential truth symbolized in it? Clearly, we are meant to see Christ in heaven operating through the church on earth. Then come chapters 2-3, with their brief, concentrated letters of appraisal, correction, and instruction to the seven churches. What is the predominant meaning? Surely it is that of the church on earth functioning for the Christ in heaven. Thus, the vision of the Son of Man amid the lampstands and the letters to the seven churches are the converse sides of the one great truth. In the one case it is the heavenward aspect: in the other, the earthward. In the first, it is Christ in heaven operating through the church on earth; in the other, the church on earth functioning for the Christ in heaven.

Our Lord, then, is risen. He operates through the church on earth. What is his last word to the church? It is this: "To him that overcometh will I grant to sit with me in my throne, even as I also overcame, and sat down with my Father in his throne" (3:21). This reference to our Lord's joint occupancy of the throne in heaven opens the door to the great vision of chapters 4-5. Chapter 4 spends itself in describing the throne of the Deity and the worship of heaven. In a word, we are shown the place of supreme authority—the "throne." Then comes chapter 5, the chapter of the Lamb and the seven-sealed book, in which we see the Lamb himself put amid the throne. The ruling purpose in this first movement of the Apocalypse is to put the Lamb there—in that throne of all-transcendent sovereignty. The book cannot continue until it has shown us the Lamb there. So this first movement reaches its climax with the Lamb in the place of supreme control.

What is the prime significance of the fifth chapter and its enthroning of our Lord Jesus in that seat of universal authority? It is a tremendous truth that all of us ought to see clearly but that we easily miss if we allow preoccupation with details to obscure the main meanings. Read the first few verses again:

> *And I saw in the right hand of him that sat on the throne a book written within and on the back, close-sealed with seven seals. And I saw a strong angel proclaiming with a great voice: Who is worthy to open the book, and*

to loose the seals thereof? And no one in the heaven, or on the earth, or under the earth, was able to open the book, or to look thereon. And I wept much because no one was found worthy to open the book, or to look thereon. But one of the elders saith unto me: Weep not; behold, the Lion that is of the tribe of Judah, the Root of David, hath overcome to open the book and the seven seals thereof.

As we noted in our former study, the seven-sealed scroll is obviously not the book of the now-open past nor of the now-opening present. It has to do with the future. We learn its contents soon afterward in pictorial form, as the Lamb successively opens the seven seals. It is the book of final issues, of God's ultimate purposes with the Adamic human race and with the nation Israel and with the redeemed people of Christ. It is the book that tells how the enigmatic mystery of humanity's sin-cursed history will eventually be cleared up. So we need not be surprised at John's weeping because no one was found "worthy" to open the book. His tears were those of godly anxiety.

The loud challenge resounds in earth and skies: "Who is worthy to open the book?" The question is really tantamount to "Who is worthy to sit in that throne of supreme authority as the executive administrator of the divine purposes?" or "Who is worthy of such all-controlling sovereignty?" Therefore, apart from our Lord Jesus, none was found worthy anywhere in the universe.

But are there not myriads of unfallen, sinless angels? Is there not one among all of them who is worthy? What of archangel Michael? What of the illustrious angel Gabriel? What of all the other high-ranking intelligences among the "morning stars of heaven"? Is there not one among all those princes of light who is worthy to open that book? What of the seraphim or cherubim, those exalted beings of flaming holiness who seem to be nearer the throne of the ineffable Deity than all other creatures? Are they not "worthy?" The answer is: No, not one among all those unsullied, resplendent heavenly hosts has the peculiar qualifications that would make him worthy to break the seals of that mystery scroll.

What, then, are the unique qualifications that give our Lord Jesus his absolutely solitary worthiness to reveal and execute the plan and purposes of the Almighty? They are principally three.

First there is the worthiness of his incomparable moral conquest. See verse 5 again: "Weep not; behold, the Lion that is of the tribe of Judah, the Root of David, overcame."[1] That past tense, "overcame," refers to our Lord's victory over sin and Satan here on earth. It was not in the omnipotent power of his Godhead that our Lord defeated the mighty Tempter (which would have been easy for the omnipotent One) but in the moral power of his humanity, as our new champion against the usurper.

From that first major temptation in the wilderness, when, although he was at the point of collapse through protracted hunger, he would not risk getting out of the Father's will by turning the stones into food, right on to the last agony of temptation in Gethsemane when he cried to the Father, "Nevertheless, not my will, but thine be done," he conquered. As our Champion David he laid Goliath Satan low. In our Lord's holy humanity Satan had at last met more than his match. In the "meek and lowly" Jesus he met the "stronger than the strong." The utter simplicity and transparent purity of that holy humanity proved stronger than all the dark-minded duplicity of the deceiver. The archfiend had reached his Waterloo. His power over humanity was broken. The future banishment of Beelzebub-Apollyon was assured. For the first time in human history the serpent's head was crushed. And it was the Man, Christ Jesus, who did it. None of the unfallen myriads of angels and principalities and powers of the heavenly regions has that worthiness! As the solitary conqueror of sin and Satan, Jesus alone is worthy!

But besides his being worthy by virtue of moral conquest, our Lord Jesus is worthy as the purchaser of costly redemption. See verse 9 again: "They sing a new song, saying: Thou art worthy to take the book and to open the seals thereof; for thou wast slain and didst purchase unto God with thy blood men of every tribe and tongue and people and nation." Not only is he Satan's Vanquisher; he is mankind's Redeemer, and he is so at the cost of his own voluntary sin-bearing and unspeakable humiliation. Among all the sinless, shining hosts of heaven, none but Jesus has that worthiness!

And in addition to that, our Lord Jesus is alone the worthy One by reason of his infinite governmental capacity. Consider verse 6 again: "I saw in the midst of the throne . . . a Lamb, having seven horns and seven eyes which are the seven spirits of God sent forth into all the earth." As we observed in our earlier study, the seven horns symbolize omnipotence and the seven eyes, omniscience, and the seven spirits encompassing the whole earth, omnipresence. Those are not only superhuman and superangelic qualities, they are exclusively divine attributes. The only one who can be worthy to open that fateful scroll of future history and destiny is one who, besides being uniquely supreme in moral conquest and in redemptive achievement, is commensurately worthy in constitutional capacity. Here on earth many a one who has been morally worthy of being a ruler has lacked the personal gifts and force that are necessary to true rulership. But our Lord Jesus is the absolutely worthy One because he conjoins with his incomparable moral conquest and redemptive self-sacrifice the possession of infinite capacity: omnipotence, omniscience, omnipresence. None can withstand his power. None can escape his all-seeing eye. None can elude his infallible knowledge. None can evade his ubiquitous presence.

Grasp it firmly: those are the three ways in which our dear Lord is the Lamb-Lion, the solitarily worthy One. (1) He is the vanquisher of Satan; (2) he is the redeemer of man; (3) he is the incarnation of God. As such he overcame to open the book and to loose the seals thereof. The mighty wonder is that when John looks to see a lion, he sees a lamb; and that Lamb—alive yet bearing evidence of having been slain—is on that throne of thrones! That is the all-eclipsing biblical picture of the divine sovereignty. You and I are meant to see on the throne of the universe, this very day, God in the form of that Man, the Lion ruling there as the Lamb, the Judge who is none other than the Redeemer, and the divine sovereignty sublimated in saviorhood. When I see the Lamb there, I am no longer afraid of the universe or of the unknown future or of what lies on the other side of the shadowy grave. With the Lamb there on that throne the universe is safe, the future is guaranteed, and beyond the grave there are assured fulfillments which will rectify the frustrations of this sin-spoiled present. The baffling mystery of permitted evil is answered by the absolute mastery of the Lamb in the throne. The Dragon's days are numbered! A new earth is on its way! The whole universe shall yet sing, "He has done all things well!"

Some years ago I was invited to become the minister of a large church in the U.S.A. The invitation was warmly worded, but it contained the following question: "Do you fully hold the doctrines of sovereign grace?" Not long afterward another church, wanting a series of special Bible-teaching gatherings, asked me the same question: "Do you go all the way with the doctrines of sovereign grace?"

It is a great phrase: "sovereign grace" (though I am not sure it is always used in just the way John Calvin meant). What is "sovereign grace"? If we would see it in its most vivid meaning we need to rivet our minds on those three chapters: Isaiah 6, Isaiah 53, and Revelation 5. We need to take a long, thoughtful look at the preincarnate Christ of Isaiah 6, high on that exquisite throne of universal empire amid the blaze of heaven's glory light. Then we need to turn our intent gaze upon that same Lord of glory descending from his peerless sovereignty in chapter 6 to that blood and shame and suffering and substitutionary sin-bearing in chapter 53. That is sovereignty becoming grace! Then we need to watch and wonder as that willingly slaughtered Lamb, the lowly Son of Man, conquers death and ascends to that all-transcendent throne again, carrying there his now glorified humanity as the representative of the countless millions he has redeemed. As we see him, the Lamb of Calvary, thus reoccupying that throne of universal dominion, we see grace becoming sovereign. Yes, that is "sovereign grace"; and that is why that throne is now called in Scripture, "the throne of grace" (Heb. 4:16).

We Christian believers, and especially those of us who are public voices of the faith, are needing a new vision of that sovereign grace today. No one whose inward eyes have really seen that overwhelmingly holy Christ in Isaiah 6 ever talks again about his or her own sanctity. No one who has ever really seen with the soul that bruised, broken, bleeding, disfigured Sufferer in Isaiah 53 ever talks of self again. No one who has ever really seen the revolutionary meaning of that Lamb amid the throne in Revelation 5 is ever a pessimist or defeatist again. With Jesus on that throne, final issues are certified.

In the early phase of the Second World War, it appeared that Hitler and his Nazis would win, but a point came later when it was plain he would lose. The war dragged on for weary and costly months after that, but the outcome was no longer in doubt. Similarly, the war of light against darkness, of evil against goodness, still drags on, but since the Lamb occupied that throne of sovereign control the result is settled. The archrebel in God's universe is a beaten foe. He and his accomplices still wreak vast havoc. They sweep around us today with a new and damaging offensive. They have largely captured the radio and television. They have surged in afresh under the battle flag of the "permissive society" or "new morality." They have broken in to de-Christianize society not by frontal attack on the church from outside it but through quislings who betray it from the inside by undermining faith in the Bible. They have launched a mighty offensive of anti-Godism through the global outreach of communism. But if Satan is flinging away disguise and ravaging as a beast of prey today, it is because the age is nearly over, and he "knoweth that he hath but a short time" (Rev. 12:12). The Lamb is on the throne. Soon, now, he will tread all rebels to the dust in everlasting obliteration.

I say again: we are needing a new vision of all this. I used to be suspicious of visions and the visionary type of person. Perhaps I still am. Many so-called visions are products of high-strung imagination or of emotional excitement, and some people are peculiarly prone to them. But there is a kind of vision that is healthily different from all that. It is not optical and transient but spiritual and lasting. It is no figment of autosuggestion but is powerfully luminous to the mind and sanctifying in one's character. The mind "sees" and grasps something in such a way that life is never quite the same again. I believe our Lord had some such revealing of himself in mind when he said, "He that hath my commandments and keepeth them, he it is that loveth me; and he that loveth me shall be loved of my Father; and I will love him, and will manifest myself unto him" (John 14:21).

Living as we are in times of unprecedented abnormality and chaotic mental confusion, if we are to be true prophets of our Lord to the present generation, we need such a vision. We need to see that throne of flaming holiness until we are prostrated in awed adoration. We need to see that dear Savior on Calvary until the wonder of his great love melts us into lifelong surrender. We need to see that Lamb in the midst of the throne until the absolute sovereignty of the Lamb dominates all our thinking about the world, about history, and about the future, and lives with us day after day.

The marvel of marvels is that the sovereignty of the universe's Creator is exercised through the Lamb. In terms of earthly time reckoning, God put him on the throne two thousand years ago. All other figures of history pale into insignificance. Despite all temporary appearances to the contrary in the present hour, the decisions of world government, the disposing of history, and the destinies of nations are all in the controlling hand of our sovereign Lord Jesus. That includes prodigal-son America, turning away from the godly convictions of its founding fathers and wasting its wealth in riotous fleshliness. It also includes Gog, alias the Prince of Resh, that is, Russia, with its mail-fisted tyranny and iron-curtain empire. It also includes the vast land of Sinim, the new China, with its seven hundred millions of brainwashed communists.

That is not mere rhetorical hyperbole: we are declaring the most stupendous reality of the centuries. All earth's billions are in those hands that were once spiked to that rough-hewn cross on Calvary! We need to see it all with new mental clearness and proclaim it with eager, undiscouraged insistence.

I sometimes wonder whether in our overseas missionary outreach and in our evangelism at home we have slipped away somewhat from the central emphasis of the New Testament. We keep telling people (and rightly so) that they need something, but the central emphasis of the New Testament is that God in sovereign grace has done something—something that all people have a right to know. He did it once for all, and for all people. He did it in the person of his eternal Son—born as a babe at Bethlehem, crucified as the world's Sin-Bearer on Calvary, and now exalted as our glorious brother and representative in that all-sovereign throne of heaven. We are to tell people now not so much that they are born into a lost world but into a lost world that has been saved, that all of us have a God-given inheritance in that effected salvation, and that

> None are excluded thence but they
> Who do themselves exclude.

One of our Savior's words after rising from the dead was: "All authority is given unto me in heaven and on earth," and it was on the basis of that all-comprehending sovereignty that he sent his disciples to "preach the glad news to every creature." That is sovereign grace. That is the church's central and continuous message. The Lamb who died on that cross now reigns on that throne.

The Second Enthronement

But now, with that in mind, follow on through the second main movement of the Apocalypse, the object of which is to crown our Lord Jesus on the throne as sole Emperor here on earth. In Revelation 6–11 our Lord successively unlooses the seven seals of the mysterious scroll. When he breaks open the seventh there appear seven angels having seven trumpets. The climax is reached when the seventh trumpet sounds, ending the intense three and a half years called the "wrath of the Lamb" (6:16) and the "wrath of God" (11:18 with 14:10, 19, etc.).

> *The seventh angel sounded; and there followed great voices in heaven, and they said: The world-kingdom of our Lord and of his Christ has come; and he shall reign for ever and ever (11:15).*

Chapters 12–19 then amplify various aspects of that three-and-a-half-year wrath period and then climax in a more detailed account showing how the world kingdom of the Lamb is brought in. This is how the whole movement heads up in the nineteenth chapter:

> *And I heard as it were the voice of a great multitude, and as the voice of many waters, and as the voice of mighty thunders, saying: Hallelujah, for the Lord our God, the Almighty reigneth. Let us rejoice and be exceeding glad, and let us give the glory unto him; for the marriage of the Lamb is come, and his wife hath made herself ready. . . . And I saw the heaven opened; and behold, a white horse, and he that sat thereon, called Faithful and True; and in righteousness he doth judge and make war. His eyes are as a flame of fire, and upon his head are many diadems . . . and his name is called the Word of God. And the armies which are in heaven followed him upon white horses, clothed in fine linen, white and pure. And out of his mouth proceedeth a sharp sword, that with it he should smite the nations: and he shall rule them with a rod of iron: and he treadeth the winepress of the fierceness of the wrath of Almighty God. And he hath on his garment and on his thigh a name written: KING OF KINGS, AND LORD OF LORDS. . . . And I saw thrones and they [the overcomers] sat upon them, and judgment was given unto them. And I saw the souls of them that had been beheaded for the testimony of Jesus and for the Word of God, and such as had not worshipped the beast, neither his image, and received not his mark upon their forehead and upon their hand; and they lived, and reigned with Christ a thousand years (19:6–7, 11–16; 20:4–6).*

That this reign is indeed to be on earth is certified by six locating particulars. First: our Lord's descent as King of Kings and Lord of Lords is to this earth, to "smite" and then "rule" the "nations" (19:15). Second: the armies of "kings" and "captains" and "mighty men" are overthrown on earth, for the "fowls" are filled with their "flesh" (19:15, 18, 21). Third: Satan is bound for a thousand years, that he should no more "deceive the nations" until the end of that millennium (20:3). Fourth: when Satan is briefly released about the end of the "thousand years" he goes out to the "four quarters of the earth" once again to "deceive the nations" (20:7-8). Fifth: those who "live" and "reign" with Christ during the "thousand years" include those who were "beheaded" for his sake on earth, and they now live again bodily, having been physically raised in "the first resurrection" (20:4-6). Sixth: when Satan emerges at the end of the "thousand years" he gathers his insurrectionists from "the breadth of the earth" against the "beloved city"; then fire comes "down from God out of heaven" and devours them (20:7-9).

Symbols or no symbols, could Scripture make it any plainer that the thousand-year reign is to be on earth? If, as some assert, the reign of Christ and the resurrected saints is purely spiritual, why such repeated attaching of it to the earth? And why does it need a resurrection of the body in order for the saints to participate in it? All the way through the book of Revelation, when the wording specifically states that something will happen on the earth it means this earth—otherwise the book would be a farce. One of its leading purposes is to tell how things will eventuate on this earth at the end of the present age and afterward.

All the way through both Old and New Testament prediction, the eventual earth rule of our Lord Jesus as the Seed of Abraham and the Son of David and the Christ of Jehovah is foretold. That earth rule has never yet happened. It certainly is not on earth today in this time of widespread apostasy in the organized Christian church, catastrophic moral landslide throughout Christendom, and internationally organized anti-Godism plainly spreading. But it yet will happen, unless Old and New Testament prophecy is deceptive in its most deliberate and specific assurances.

To say, as do the amillennialists, that the thousand years are the present Gospel age is indeed strange exegesis! This present age is distinctively the age of grace, whereas in the coming millennial age our Lord shall first "smite the nations" and then "rule them with a rod of iron" (19:15). To say th..t this present age of heaven's grace and permissive forbearance fulfills those predictions is surely a surprising kind of exposition!

During the thousand years of our Lord's messianic world-reign, Satan is to be completely removed from the earth scene so that he cannot then any longer "deceive the nations" (20:3). Could anything make that complete removal of Satan plainer than the fivefold enactment by the angel who comes "down out of heaven, having the key of the abyss [the deepest depth of hades] and a great chain in his hand"? The angel (1) laid hold on (*ekratesen,* "overpowered") him, (2) bound him with the great chain, (3) hurled him down into the abyss, (4) shut it, (5) and sealed it over him.

If that fivefold buildup does not describe an utter removal and confinement of Satan, then nothing could. To make the matter even surer, however, verse 7 adds, "And when the thousand years are finished [notice that here we have direct statement, not merely a vision] Satan shall be loosed out of his prison [so it has been a real incarceration] and shall come forth to deceive the nations"—a final exposure of his innate incorrigibility, whereupon his deserved doom is effected. We can hardly believe our eyes when we find amillennialist believers writing that the chaining and removing of Satan is now, during this age of gospel grace. I quote anonymously:

> One of the chief prohibitions laid upon him was that he should *deceive the nations no more* until the end of the period symbolized by the thousand years which represent the Gospel age (italics mine).
>
> This is his present place of abode [i.e., the abyss] from which he carries on his activities.
>
> He walks about as a roaring lion, but is a chained lion and can go only so far as the chain allows.

What kind of exegesis is that? What pitiful draining away of meaning from the clear wording of Scripture! As for the present age, Satan is not even chained, much less flung into the abyss. Nay, as John says, "The whole world lieth in the evil one" (1 John 5:19). And in the words of Paul, "If our gospel be veiled, it is veiled in them that are perishing, in whom the god of this age [this present, so-called Gospel age] hath blinded the minds of the unbelieving" (2 Cor. 4:3, 4). Nor is Satan operating from the abyss; he is the prince of the power of the air, "the spirit that now worketh in the sons of disobedience" (Eph. 2:2). All the way through the New Testament we are warned about a Satan who is terribly powerful, still free, and everywhere active, both as an angel of light to deceive and as a roaring lion to devour. Also, the written Word tells us that near the end of the present age Satan is flung out of the heavenly sphere (Rev. 12:7–10) from where he comes down to this earth (not up from the abyss), "having great wrath, knowing that he hath but a short time" (v. 12).

No, this present Gospel age certainly is not the thousand years of Satan's banishment to the dungeon of hades, nor is it the age of our Lord's plentifully predicted messianic empire on earth. But that coming millennial Christocracy is just as certainly on its way as our Lord is certainly enthroned already in heaven as the Lamb in the midst of the throne. And its duration will be for the specified thousand years. One feature that must impress any open-minded reader of Revelation 20 is the prominence given by reiteration to the time period of a "thousand years." No fewer than six times the expression occurs, and in four out of the six it has the definite article—"the thousand years"—as though by repeated definition to fix a specific period in our minds. Moreover, in verses 6–7 the wording passes from description of a vision to direct prediction: "They shall reign with him the thousand years."

As we said at the beginning of these studies, one of the most impressive phenomena of the Bible is its progress of doctrine. One outstanding instance of such progress is the Bible doctrine of the Lamb, which we are here examining. Other examples are the progress of revelation concerning the being of God, the progress of disclosure about life beyond the grave, and the progress of prophecy on the coming messianic kingdom. One feature after another contributes to the buildup of information about the global reign of the Messiah that will consummate the history of Adam's race on this earth, until here, in Revelation 20, we are given the final information as to its duration.

The history of Adamic humanity on this earth thus becomes a heptadic cycle, or week, of seven great thousand-year days: four thousand years B.C., then two thousand years A.D., and finally one thousand years R.D., that is, *regno Domini:* in the reign of the Lord. As the seventh day, this coming Millennium will be history's completive sabbath of worldwide, warless peace and rest. It will be so because our Lord Jesus will then be visibly back on earth and reigning as global Sovereign.

The Third Enthronement

From that millennial enthronement of our Lord on earth the apocalyptic panorama moves on through the final insurrection and abolition of evil to the general judgment of mankind at the Great White Throne. In that awesome, immeasurably vast and fateful assize, which both congregates and yet discriminates all human beings of all the centuries before the divine Judge, the deciding factor is: "And whosoever was not found written in the book of life." That book of life is "the book of life of the Lamb" (Rev. 13:8; 20:27). So the Lamb is sovereign not only in the throne of heaven, and in the wrath to come, and in the future global empire, but also in racial judgment.

That judgment of the whole human race at the Great White Throne not only decides the eternal destiny of human individuals, it terminates the present world forever. If we rightly understand the language of Scripture, there is going to be a fundamental refashioning of our earth to become the habitation of a new humanity in Christ, surrounded by heavenly spheres that have been forever freed from all evil powers. Gone forever all need for the "rod of iron"! Gone forever the curse, the blight of sin, the scourge of pain, the shadow of sorrow, the tyranny of the grave.

Gone forever all frustration, weeping, sighing, aging, dying. John says, "I saw a new heaven and a new earth; for the first heaven and the first earth are passed away."

Thus begins the third and final movement of the grand Apocalypse, in which we see the enthronement of the Lamb as eternal King of God's new order on and around the earth. In the words of Tennyson, that is

> The one far-off, divine event
> To which the whole creation moves.

Let it not be lost sight of for one moment that this event brings the further coronation of our Lord Jesus as the Lamb. Calvary is never to be forgotten. He is the beloved Redeemer, yesterday and today and unto the ages.

5

The Sovereignty of the Lamb:
(3) Never Ending

Then onward and yet onward! for dim revealings show
That systems unto systems in grand succession grow;
That what we deemed a volume, one golden verse may be,
One rhythmic, flowing cadence in God's great poetry.
Francis Ridley Havergal

Far o'er yon horizon gleam the city towers
Where our God abideth: that fair home is ours!
Flash the walls with jasper, shine the streets with gold,
Flows the gladdening river, shedding joys untold!
Henry Alford

YES, A NEW HEAVEN and a new earth! So our Bible not only begins with "Genesis," it ends with a "genesis": a new beginning, a re-creation. That coming new order is described in the last two chapters of the Apocalypse in terms that are at once august and exquisite. The inaugural motto, uttered by a voice from the throne and written across the new order, is: "Behold, I make all things new."

And I saw a new heaven and a new earth: for the first heaven and the first earth are passed away; and the sea is no more. And I saw the holy city, new Jerusalem, coming down out of heaven from God, made ready as a bride adorned for her husband. And I heard a great voice out of the throne saying, Behold the tabernacle of God is with men, and he shall dwell with them, and they shall be his people, and God himself shall be with them, and be their God: and he shall wipe away every tear from their eyes; and death shall be no more; neither shall there be mourning, nor crying, nor pain, anymore: the first things are passed away. And he that sitteth on the throne said, Behold, I make all things new (Rev. 21:1-5).

Such is the introductory paragraph. It is followed by a description of the New Jerusalem, with accompanying comments on the new earthly conditions, ending at chapter 22, verse 5. Seven great "new" features stand out and captivate the mind:

1. the new heaven—"And I saw a new heaven," that is, the terrestrial expanse and solar system
2. the new earth—"And [I saw] a new earth," that is, the present planet, but after a fundamental refashioning
3. the new center—"I saw the holy city, new Jerusalem, coming down out of heaven from God," that is, to this earth
4. the new society—"They shall be his people, and God himself shall be with them," that is, the "nations"
5. the new worship—"I saw no temple therein"—no need of one when there is open vision of the Shekinah and the Lamb
6. the new light—"The city has no need of sun . . . for the glory of God illumines it. . . . The nations walk in the light thereof"
7. the new paradise—"He showed me . . . the tree of life, . . . the leaves . . . were for the healing of the nations"

This is that ultimate splendor and complete felicity into which our Lord's millennial reign eventually merges. Notice that it is all on this earth. However common the idea may be, we must never think that when the history of our fallen human race is over, we Christian believers will then be millions of bodiless spirits living in a purely spiritual sphere. If that were our intended future, what purpose would there be in the coming resurrection of the body? Is it not to give us supernal bodies, after the pattern of our Lord's resurrection body, fitted for a higher quality of life and service in that new heaven and new earth—yes, and in those ages to come (Eph. 1:7) that lie beyond the reach of all the apocalyptic descriptions?

Nor must we mistakenly suppose that our Bible teaches any such eventuality as "the end of the world"—at least not in the sense of the obliteration or disappearance of the earth. Whether or not this tiny planet of ours will pass into nothingness at some future point is not revealed in Scripture. That phrase, "the end of the world," certainly does occur in our standard English translations of the New Testament (e.g., Matt. 28:20), but as every informed reader knows, the Greek word translated as "world" is *aion* (Anglicized into "aeon" or "eon"), and means, more exactly, "the end of the age." The Bible nowhere speaks of the end of the earth. It does say that the earth in its present condition will be "dissolved," or "burnt up," but that is preparatory to its becoming again refashioned into a new earth, with a new genesis of occupation and history.

Let me repeat for emphasis: it is erroneous to think that after the all-inclusive judgment at the Great White Throne (Rev. 20:11-15) brings to an end the drama of our fallen human race, the earth will then go spinning unoccupied through space for ages until it gradually disintegrates into nonexistence. Listen to Isaiah 45:18 again: "Thus saith Jehovah that created the heavens, God that formed the earth and made it; he established it; he created it not a waste; he formed it to be inhabited."

In the coming new order there will be on this earth the most wonderful cosmos, or world system, that it has ever yet known. It is to be that which is described in Revelation 21-22. If anyone should say that we are unduly literalizing something that is a vision and not actual prediction, we reply that the same dissolution and re-creation is taught in direct statement elsewhere in Scripture. The following passage is representative:

> *But the day of the Lord will come as a thief, in the which the heavens shall pass away with a great noise, and the elements shall be dissolved with fervent heat, and the earth and the works that are therein shall be burned up. . . . But, according to his promise, we look for new heavens and a new earth wherein dwelleth righteousness (2 Peter 3:10–13).*

Peter's statement is a plain prediction of that coming new heaven and new earth that are pictured to us in Revelation 21-22. Furthermore, in John's own Patmos vision of it he recurrently passes from the visional description of it to direct statement. For instance:

> He that overcometh shall inherit these things (21:7).
> The nations shall walk in the light of it (21:24).
> They shall bring the glory and honor of the nations into it (21:26).
> There shall be no curse any more: and the throne of God and of the Lamb shall be in it (22:3).

These are some of the plain foretellings that accompany John's vision and that settle how we are to understand the vision.

This advance unveiling of that new heaven and new earth which are yet to be may well fascinate us, though it need not surprise us. Away back in the opening verses of Genesis we are told that before the earth was adapted for human occupancy it was "without form and void." Yet Isaiah 45:18, already quoted, says: "God created it not without form" (or "waste," the same word as in Gen. 1:2). So the earth must have become waste and void at some point after its original creation.

How and when did it become so? Where the written Word does not give us definite statement let us tread warily, yet on the other hand let us not hesitate to follow clear pointers. We cannot digress here to discuss Lucifer's relationship to this planet. From a variety of Scripture references it would seem that in a long-ago, pre-Adamite age this earth was under the overlordship of Lucifer, who by his vain infidelity and duplicity not only forfeited his position as "prince of this world," but involved a world full of others in his downfall, occasioning the cataclysmic judgment by which the earth became "without form and void."

Until recently, modern science has rejected the idea of any such cataclysmic epoch in our planet's history and has held that it reached its present state by a gradual, unbroken evolution. However, that is now doubted or discarded by many. One of the most recent hypotheses is that there have been a succession of such cataclysms.

After the Luciferian revolt, the desolated earth was refashioned to become the abode of mankind, as described in the six days of Genesis 1. How long after, we do not know, but the earth was now put under the lordship of man (Ps. 8:6, etc.). Thereupon Lucifer-Satan by subtle deception contrived the human fall, with all the pitiful havoc that has ensued. The archfiend usurper at length met his defeat. Our Lord Jesus, by incarnation the Second Adam, overcame all the Tempter's wiles and powers. Then, as the sinless Sin-Bearer, he made complete atonement on Calvary for the sin of the whole Adamic race, after which he rose in irresistible triumph over the grave, with this announcement: "All authority is [now] given unto me, in heaven and on earth."

Our Lord Jesus, as Son of Man and as the Lamb slain from the foundation of the world, is the world's true prince and Savior (Acts 2:32–36; 5:31). The mystery of permitted evil will run its course to the end of the present age, when our glorified Lord Jesus, as the Head of the new humanity, will return to earth in absolute command and reign in millennial world rule. Then, after the final judgment of mankind at the Great White Throne, instead of another long, dark interval "without form and void," the ages-to-ages reign of God and the Lamb will go on from glory to glory, Satan and all evil having been banished for ever.

It is in that new heaven and new earth that our ultimate destiny lies as the redeemed people of Christ and as the members of his mystical body, the Church. What we are told about it therefore becomes of captivating interest. Some of its aspects are full of surprise. One is the far-reaching perpetuity of the nation Israel. The twelve gates of the new Jerusalem are inscribed, respectively, with the names of the twelve tribes of Israel (21:12–13). The twelve foundations of the city bear the names of the twelve apostles—one name on each (21:14). It would seem that the Abrahamic covenant and messianic prophecies reach right on to an ultimate sublimation in that flawless new heaven and new earth.

Another surprise is the presence of "nations" and "kingdoms" in that eternal regime (21:24), all revering the new Jerusalem and the throne of the Lamb as the divinely adorned center of the new cosmos.

It further appears that the new humanity—that fair society of the pure in heart—will use a form of time reckoning like that of the present solar system, if the word "months" in Revelation 22:2 has a literal meaning.

Again, since death shall be no more there is to be immortality, while the "tree of life," then available to all, bears fruit continuously for the healing, that is, the continual health, of all peoples.

Apparently, too, there is to be a blending of the natural and the supernatural, for at the center of that new global organization, the queen city is not dependent on either sun or moon for light. The divine presence gently floods it with Shekinah glory-light. That benign, soft radiance never tires the eyes of the immortals who live in it, so there is never any need for relief such as darkness now affords, and therefore "there shall be no night there" (21:25).

The sovereign, central magnet of it all is our Lord Jesus as the glorified Lamb. All who live in it know that they owe it all to him and his glorious love. It is all his, and his joy is to make it all theirs. It is the fulfillment of his prayer in John 17. In that prayer he speaks to the Father about "the glory which I had with thee before the world was" (v. 5), but later he speaks of "the glory which thou hast given me" (v. 24). The former was his preincarnate divine glory as God the Son, the Father's coequal. The latter is the glory given by the Father to our Lord as the guileless, stainless, sinless Son of Man, the utterly yielded Sin-Bearer of the human race. Up from hades and the grave God raised that spotless Victim-Victor and exalted that resurrected manhood to the very throne of the universe! That is the glory which the Father has given him as the New Man.

But now, as we think of the latter glory that the Father has given him, let us grasp with clearer understanding the meaning of verse 22: "And the glory which thou hast given me, I have given them"! It is in the new heaven and new earth that those words of our Lord will reach their rapture of fulfillment. The glory that the Father has given him, he will share to the full with us, through endless ages!

It is then, in those ages to come, and there, in that new heaven and new earth, that we shall drink in the full meaning of John 1:16: "Of his fullness have we all received, and grace upon grace" (i.e., successive accessions of grace). The New Testament speaks again and again about the divine grace. It also speaks about "abundance of grace," and the "glory of his grace," and the "riches of his grace." But there is only one place where we find the lavish expression, "The exceeding riches of his grace." It is in Ephesians 2:7, and it refers not to the present age nor even to the millennial age to come but to those ages upon ages beyond the Millennium, in that new heaven and new earth.

He [God] quickened us together with Christ (by grace have ye been saved)
and raised us up with him, and made us to sit with him in the heavenlies,

*in Christ Jesus; that in the ages to come he might show the exceeding
riches of his grace in his kindness toward us in Christ Jesus.*

Those ages to come are also called the "ages of the ages," meaning
"age upon age as far as the farthest-seeing eye can peer." Perhaps it is
then and there, when the New Jerusalem and its new peoples comprise
the sinless future society on earth—when there is open fellowship of heaven
with earth's occupants—that we shall at last understand Jehovah's word
to Israel long ago:

> . . . *visiting the iniquity of the fathers upon the children to the third and
> fourth generation of them that hate me; but showing lovingkindness unto
> a thousand generations in them that love me and keep my command-
> ments (Ex. 20:5–6).*

> *Know therefore that Jehovah thy God, he is God, the faithful God, who
> keepeth covenant and lovingkindness with them that love him and keep
> his commandments, to a thousand generations (Deut. 7:9).*

Think of those words and then turn again to Ephesians 3:21, where
the apostle, with his gaze on those ages to come, uses that word "generations" in a way that occurs nowhere else in the New Testament.

> *Now unto him that is able to do exceeding abundantly above all that we
> ask or think, according to the power that worketh in us; unto him be the
> glory in the Church and in Christ Jesus unto all the generations of the
> ages of the ages.*

Think of it: "all the generations of the ages of the ages"! One golden
age gives birth to another in a never-never-ending progress of blessedness
beyond all that we can now imagine—until the whole history of the human race now on earth becomes a mere dot in the past.

We must add no more. Our pen runs away with us! But see how the
apocalyptic vision of it ends, in Revelation 22:3–5.

> *And there shall be no curse any more: and the throne of God and of the
> Lamb shall be therein: and his servants shall serve him; and they shall see
> his face; and his name shall be on their foreheads. And there shall be night
> no more; and they need no light of lamp, neither light of sun; for the Lord
> God shall give them light: and they shall reign unto the ages of the ages.*

It is the most wonderful conceivable climax and prospect. The more
one's mind lingers over it, clause by clause, the more it shines with an

opalescent radiance that has no parallel on earth. Every facet flashes with a rapture that our present modes of thinking are incapable of comprehending. It pictures a future state in which every lovely aspiration will be realized and in which every high capacity of our beings will be fulfilled to the uttermost. Pick out the seven ultimate perfections that are indicated in that final paragraph:

1. perfect sinlessness—"There shall be no curse any more."
2. perfect government—"The throne of God and of the Lamb shall be therein."
3. perfect service—"And his servants shall [thus] serve him."
4. perfect communion—"And they shall see his face" (i.e., in open vision).
5. perfect holiness—"His Name shall be written on their foreheads" (Christlikeness).
6. perfect illumination—"No night . . . The Lord God giveth them light."
7. perfect blessedness—"And they shall reign unto the ages of the ages."

What a picture! What a prospect! What a consummation! A faultless, flawless, fadeless bliss of self-fulfillment to the praise of God and of the Lamb!

Note again that the center of it all is the sovereign throne in which reigns the Lamb. He reigns there in complete oneness with God the Father, for it is "the throne of God and of the Lamb." He reigns with God. He reigns for God. He reigns as God. Also, he does not cease to be the Lamb! Recently I read a book in which the author (expressing what seems to be a fairly common idea) says that when our Lord, as Messiah-Sovereign, hands over the kingdom to the Father at the end of the Millennium, with all foes subjugated (1 Cor. 15:28), he thereupon ceases to be the Lamb; his manhood then disappears by absorption into his "original Godhead." I quote: "At that abdication Christ leaves His human glory to retire into the Divine. He ceases to rule the universe as Man, that He may rule it for ever and ever as God."

Surely that idea is wrong. As Hebrews 13:8 says, our Lord, by his incarnation, is now "Jesus Christ, the same yesterday and today and unto the ages." His incarnation gave him not merely a human body, but a human nature. Forevermore now he is God-Man, the Lion-Lamb, the Creator-Redeemer, the Sovereign-Savior. That is why, in the Patmos Apocalypse, the throne is said to be that of "God and the Lamb unto the ages of the ages." It is the tremendous, glorious, unmistakable picture of *the Lamb in absolute sovereignty forever!*

Oh, the wonder of it: the divine sovereignty now and unendingly expressed through that utterly beautiful Humanhood and Saviorhood! Try to think what it will mean to each of us through those ages to come. The infinite love of the Father's boundless bosom comes to us through the incomparable tenderness of that meek and lowly human heart! His infinite mind will hold and surround all the millions of us who love and adore him, but (which is possible only to the infinite) he will affectionately discriminate in such a way as to love and cherish each one of us, individually. In that boundless ocean of immeasurable yet individualizing love there can be no food for even adoring jealousy among us! The song of each one of us will be, "The Son of God loved me, and gave himself for me!" (Gal. 2:20). We will sing, "My Beloved is mine, and I am his!" (Song of Sol. 2:16). Did not his redeeming love come to us individually? Did he not save us individually? Did he not keep us individually? Has he not a plan for us individually? Then will his love ever lose sight of us individually? Never! Each one of us is uniquely precious to him. Moreover, one of the sweetest constituents of our bliss in those coming ages will be our sharing in his love for others! Thus we shall evermore discover that his joy in all of us is simply the aggregate of His loving joy in each of us.

> O Savior mine,
> King all-divine,
> What can I say, to see Thee hanging there?—
> Bleeding, reviled mid vulgar jeer and glare;
> Lamb of Calvary!
>
> Oh, gladdest morn!
> Hope! hope new-born!
> Victor resplendent o'er the fearsome grave!
> Rising with endless, boundless power to save!
> Mighty Savior!
>
> Now Thou dost reign,
> Jesus once slain,
> High on the sapphire, rainbow-circled throne!
> Thine, now, the crown and scepter, Thine alone;
> King of glory!
>
> On that fair shore
> Myriads adore;
> Yet Thou dost deign my human heart to share!
> Foretaste of heav'n to have Thee reigning there:
> Mine forever!

6

The Finalities of the Lamb:
Lord and Savior

What hope we friends of Jesus share,
    To whom His name is dear!
What cheer in days of anxious care,
    As His return draws near!
Oh, with what longings do we burn,
    His coming reign to see,
And skyward leap at His return,
    With Him at last to be!

For every tear will then be dried,
    And every fear be quelled,
And every yearning satisfied,
    And every cloud dispelled:
And every heartache will be healed,
    And every problem solved,
And every myst'ry be revealed,
    And every doubt dissolved.

With deathless body, sinless mind,
    Around the Savior's throne,
Unending rapture we shall find
    With Jesus and His own:
Oh, with such raptures on before,
    Should we not patient be,
And love and serve Him yet the more
    Until "that day" we see?

THE MORE WE READ the book of Revelation with its graphic unveilings, the more communicative it becomes, if we have observant and teachable minds. Unmistakably, too, it authenticates itself as being rightly the last book in our Bible, for it is obviously full of divinely designed completions.[1] This and that and the other subject of biblical revelation all reach their completive culmination in the Patmos disclosures.

That is most of all true in the Bible doctrine of the Lamb. Earlier in this book we singled out and considered the main references to the Lamb in successive books of Scripture. In the book of Revelation they reach a multiple culmination. The Lamb is actually named no fewer than twenty-eight times. In fact, more than anything else, the last book of the Bible is the revelation of the Lamb. That may well arrest us. Its meaning is bigger than words can tell.

The last book in our Bible is mainly about the finality of the Lamb. All else is incidental to that. All the ruling lines of Scripture doctrine reach their finality in the Lamb. Human history is to find its finality in the Lamb. All the divine purposes ultimately converge into the finality of the Lamb. Our Lord's lambhood is no temporary role. It has become, and will forever remain, the supremely determining factor of the universe. That is the main thrust of the Apocalypse. If we miss seeing that, we miss everything that is really vital.

Finality in the Church

In the introductory vision our risen Lord is exhibited as the final Arbiter in the church. Clothed in a glory-light outshining the meridian sun, he appears amid the seven golden lampstands, holding the seven stars in his hand. Of all numbers used in Holy Writ with a mystical meaning, seven appears most frequently. That is markedly so in the book of Revelation. Usually it is to be taken representatively, which is the case in this first vision. The seven lampstands are the "seven churches" (1:20). Those seven seem meant to represent all the churches which in the aggregate comprise the one organized church on earth.

Note that the seven are all equal. None is superior or leader to the others. They are not arranged as six around one central metropolitan lamp! There is no maternal priority of Jerusalem or papal primacy of Rome. Those two are not even mentioned! As to organization, each of the seven is independent. Their sevenfold oneness is solely in the living Lord who moves among them and in the soul-saving light of truth that they are meant to diffuse: a oneness of privilege and responsibility in functioning here on earth for the Lord now in heaven.

Those seven churches are a sore problem to some expositors, because in the seven letters sent to them by our Lord they seem to sustain a legal rather than an evangelical relationship to him. For instance, E. W. Bullinger says, "The Bible student . . . finds himself suddenly removed from the ground of grace to the ground of works." It is said that, all through, there is a doubtful "if" on the human side that seems to make salvation dependent on human works rather than on divine grace.

That mistaken view of the seven letters comes from reading them as letters to individuals instead of to churches. We have to see those churches as plural units. First, they are a mixture of individuals, with the true believers among them saved by grace alone on God's part and by faith alone on their own part, through the atonement of Christ and regeneration by the Holy Spirit. But second, they are a membership collectively as a functioning unit, and although the salvation of each individual member is a matter of pure grace, the functioning of the whole assembly as a unit or "church" cannot be, for a corporate unit has no consciousness of its own. As individuals, the members are saved by grace, but the churches as collective bodies stand or fall according to their fidelity.

If a church, or "lampstand," is removed because of apostasy or other failure, its removal does not mean that it is eternally lost, for churches as corporate entities cannot be either saved or lost in that eternal sense. Only individuals are saved or lost in that sense. The removing of a church, or lampstand, is a purely historical rejection, and even then the "overcomers" in the dishonored church (i.e., those who remain true in doctrine and practice) still inherit the reward of faithful individuals. Moreover, in the case of those individual overcomers, although their reward is for faithful service, their eternal salvation as human souls is altogether of grace.

We do well to remember, then, that those seven churches were addressed as visible, organized units—which is why each letter begins with the singular: "I know thy works." There is no shift from grace to works so far as individuals are concerned.

Those seven churches represent all such visible, organized churches and, aggregately, the whole visible, organized church on earth, as distinct from that inner, spiritual church composed of spiritually reborn individuals.

In each of those seven churches of long ago (just as today) there were the truly born again, as also there were others who, although professors of Christ, were not really possessors of Christ. So the seven churches are each addressed not only as collective units, but as collectively mingled. It is that which accounts for the phraseology of the seven letters.

Those seven churches of Revelation were not Jewish assemblies, as some aver. They were all churches in Gentile cities, comprised of both Jews and Gentiles who were all one in Christ Jesus. In that, again, they well represent the whole, outward, organized church.

As it was in the beginning, so is it now, and shall be till this present age is over: our living Lord moves amid the lampstands, and he is the final Arbiter of each, of all.

Each of the seven letters begins with "I know," and ends with "I will." The "I know" indicates an all-seeing omniscience, as the penetrating diagnoses in the letters evince. The "I will" is the sign of royal sovereignty, of him who is "the First and the Last" (2:8), who has "the sharp two-edged sword" (2:13), and wields "authority" over "all nations" (2:27). Each church is addressed as being accountable directly to that all-seeing, sovereign Lord.

It is an awe-inspiring picture: those seven lampstands diffusing their light of saving truth in a world of spiritual darkness while hostile powers of evil strive to quench them, while at the same time, moving among those lampstands is that mysterious Figure clothed in dread splendor invisible to natural eye but awesomely vivid to evil spirit-powers. The symbolic two-edged sword that proceeds from his mouth means that he can slay his enemies with a word. His "eyes as a flame of fire" mean that his holiness can consume them with a look. His countenance, outflashing the blaze of noonday sun, bespeaks his overwhelming power to obliterate all opposition. To demon powers, that "sword," those "eyes," that "countenance," are torture. They belong to a Son of Man (1:13) who met Satan on his own ground and trod the venomous serpent's head to the dust.

In his hand he holds "the seven stars," the "angels" or leaders of the seven churches. None can pluck them thence, which means that if they are faithful none can harm them, and if they are unfaithful none can save them. They and the lampstands function solely for him. He is Son of Man and Son of God; Lamb of Calvary but Lion of Judah; boundless in grace but also absolute in wisdom, holiness, power, and sovereignty; Lord of the church and of the churches; absolutely final in all he directs and in all he permits, whether in rewarding the praiseworthy or removing the unworthy.

Finality in Administration

The first place where our Lord is actually named the Lamb in the book of Revelation is chapter 5, where in vision we see the Lamb occupy the throne of heaven. Standing out above all the incidental elements, there are three features that give that enthronement its all-eclipsing wonder.

First is the kind of lamb our Lord is said to be. The Greek word for a sheep is *probaton*. The word for a lamb or young sheep is *amnos*, and that is the word used of our Lord in the other New Testament passages outside the Apocalypse where he is called the Lamb (John 1:29, 36; Acts 8:32; 1 Peter 1:19). That is the word anyone would naturally expect. But throughout the book of Revelation the word is *arnion*, a diminutive that means the youngest and smallest even among the lambs. On being told that the "Lion of the tribe of Judah" had overcome to open the mysterious, seven-sealed scroll, John looked to see what would happen, but to his surprise—

I saw in the midst of [or between] the throne and the four living beings, and in the midst of the elders, a little lamb standing, as though it had been killed (i.e., as a sacrifice; Rev. 5:6).

John gazed and wondered at the seeming incongruity of it: a "little lamb"—the meekest, gentlest, most harmless and defenseless of all little animals, standing there! But the transfixing surprise is to see that "little lamb" approach the throne of the Deity, take the seven-sealed book, occupy the throne, and assume sole authority to release the fateful contents of the scroll into operation.

That diminutive, *arnion,* is used all through the book of Revelation with the same peculiar incongruity. For instance, at the opening of the sixth seal, just before the "wrath to come" breaks loose on the earth, we see kings, princes, rich, and poor calling on the rocks and mountains to fall on them, to hide them from "the face of him that sitteth on the throne, and from the wrath of the [little] lamb"! The vainglorious Lucifer once aspired to that throne of the Most High. What an exasperating backfire on the self-exalting traitor, to see the "little Lamb" seated there with seraphs and elders and angel hosts all worshiping him!

But second, that "little Lamb" was "as though it had been slain." If the expression "little lamb" tells of our Lord's self-humbling, his having been "slain" speaks of his humiliation. There is a wide difference between self-humbling and humiliation. The former is a movement from within one's own heart and mind and is altogether voluntary, whereas humiliation is something inflicted from without and usually against one's own will. Besides our Lord's vast and voluntary self-humbling was his humiliation, his being despised and rejected, scourged, mocked, spat upon at Satan's instigation, and then hung up in naked shame before the vulgar mob. From that fathomless humiliation on the ugly cross, the slain Lamb is lifted to the very throne of heaven, to be universally extolled as having "the Name which is above every name." Even Lucifer and his coinsurrectionists must yet cringe before that "little lamb."

Third, and as a crowning honor, the "little lamb" is exalted to expedite the seven-sealed divine program not as a deputy administrator for the Almighty, not even as the highest regent whom God could appoint, but as cooccupant of the throne! That is why the seraphs and elders immediately fall down before the little Lamb with their harps (praises) and incense vials (prayers) and render to him exactly the same worship as they do to the everlasting Father. This means that our Lord Jesus as the Lamb has absolute finality of administration throughout heaven and earth.

Finality of Saviorhood

Turn now to Revelation 7, where we see in our Lord Jesus as the Lamb a consummating finality of Saviorhood. Many of the visions in the Apocalypse refer exclusively to the future. Others may be called *vista* visions: they describe something going on now but that will reach consummation in a climax yet to be. One such vista vision is that of the innumerable multitude in chapter 7.

> *I saw, and behold, a great multitude which no man could number, out of every nation and of all tribes and peoples and tongues, standing before the throne and before the Lamb, arrayed in white robes, and having palms in their hands: and they cry with a great voice, saying: Salvation unto our God who sitteth on the throne, and unto the Lamb. And all the angels were standing round about the throne, and about the elders and the four living beings; and they fell before the throne on their faces, and worshiped God, saying: Amen; blessing and glory and wisdom and thanksgiving and honor and power be unto our God for ever and ever, Amen. And one of the elders answered, saying unto me: These that are arrayed in the white robes, who are they, and whence came they? And I say to him: My lord, thou knowest. And he said unto me: These are they that come out of the great tribulation, and they washed their robes and made them white in the blood of the Lamb. Therefore they are before the throne of God, and they serve him day and night in his temple. And he that sitteth on the throne shall spread his tabernacle over them. They shall hunger no more, neither thirst any more, nor shall the sun strike upon them, nor any heat. For the Lamb that is in the midst of the throne will shepherd them, and guide them to fountains of the waters of life: and God shall wipe away every tear from their eyes. (Rev. 7:9–17)*

There are those who teach that this vision refers exclusively to the end time of the present age, to a short period of seven years (some say three and a half) which they mark off as the Great Tribulation. Others maintain that the words "these that come out of the great tribulation" cover the whole of the Christian dispensation. Either way, the vision depicts the ultimate bliss of our salvation in Christ.

Note the Greek present tense in verse 14: "These are they who are coming out of." It seems perhaps to connote a continuity of coming rather than one total transference from earth to heaven. In any case, John is given to see the multitude in its eventual complete immensity.

The scene is in heaven. In their countless thousands upon thousands the vast multitude are "standing before the throne and before the Lamb." Here again, as in chapter 5, the classification is fourfold: "nations, tribes, peoples, tongues," the number four being, as usual, the symbolic number pertaining to the earth and the physical creation.

Those who compose that countless throng are "arrayed in white robes"— symbol of stainless purity. In their hands they hold "palm branches"— symbol of final victory. They unite in exulting acclamation: "Our salvation [be ascribed] to our God who sitteth on the throne, and unto the Lamb!"

Here, as in chapter 5, the angels blend in with their sevenfold praise: "The blessing and the glory and the wisdom and the thanksgiving and the honor and the power and the might be [ascribed] to our God unto the ages of the ages."

How came those countless humans to wear those robes of now spotless white? The answer is: "They washed their robes and made them white in the blood of the Lamb." That past tense refers to what they did while still on earth and apart from which they would never have been in heaven. They were now in heaven through the blood. That is why verse 15 says, "Therefore are they before the throne of God." Their absolute cleansing from the guilt and stain of sin they owe utterly to the Lamb. In the vision of chapter 5 the praise was for our having been "purchased" by the blood. Here, in chapter 7, it is for our having been "purified" by the blood. In 12:11, we see the overcomers "prevailing" through the blood. Oh, the wonder of that precious blood!

But now see the further felicity of that raptured multitude. Not only are they "before the throne of God," bathed in its ineffable glory-light, but they "serve him day and night" in his heavenly "sanctuary," which means that their blissful state is augmented by the serene joy of sinless ministry. Furthermore, "He that sitteth on the throne shall spread his tabernacle over them," pavilioning them in unending tranquillity and security and overspreading them as the Shekinah (symbol of the divine presence) covered the mercy seat with its gentle splendor long ago. And again: "They shall not [emphatic] hunger any more, nor thirst any more; the sun shall not strike on them; no, nor any heat"—phraseology that blends both the literal and the symbolic to indicate that every need—physical, mental, spiritual—and all worthy desire is forever satisfied, with nothing ever to cause weakness or fatigue.

Do we ask how all this is theirs? Verse 17 answers: "For [i.e., because] the Lamb in the midst of the throne shall shepherd them." So he is both Lamb and Shepherd! That is no mixing of metaphors: it is a union of precious realities in the one manifold Savior. That which opens heaven to us is the blood of the Calvary Lamb. That which makes heaven for us is the love of that divine-human Shepherd. And he leads us to "springs of living waters," which means unending renewal in a life of rapturous purity and buoyant energy.

The concluding word is: "And God shall wipe away every tear from their eyes," which implies that every cause of tears is forever obliterated: no more pain, fear, regret, persecution, privation, misunderstanding, temptation, failure, weakness, martyrdom, imprisonment, poverty, hunger, sickness, death, bereavement. Every pain and pang and imperfection will be gone, even the memory of them becoming lost in ages of unfolding compensations.

This, then, is the tenfold picture of final salvation in that uncountable host of saved sinners now transplanted to heaven as the glorified saints.

1. beatific vision—"before the throne"
2. unsullied holiness—"white robes"
3. finalized victory—"palm branches"
4. highest ministry—"they serve him"
5. unending security—"he covers them"
6. fulfillment for ever—"hunger no more"
7. felicity without flaw—"sun smites not"
8. serenity in his love—"he shepherds them"
9. ageless immortality—"living waters"
10. joy, perfect, fadeless—"every tear" dried

Amid our present limitations of mortal flesh and impaired mental faculties, even when we enjoy most vigorous health of body and keenest agility of mind, we simply cannot imagine realistically what it will be to experience that life of utter ecstasy yonder. With sinless hearts and with minds continuously penetrated by direct rays of holy radiance from that dearest face in the universe, with perfected powers and expanded capacities of thought and worship and love and service, surrounded by lofty opportunities and incentives and amplitudes such as we have never known before—all that, amid the unclouded, open vision of his smile—what must it be!

We are not being sentimentally impractical when we long for such a bliss as that! On the contrary, we are strangely calloused and spiritually phlegmatic if we do not! To let our minds linger gratefully on that coming glory rather than turning us into inactive visionaries animates us with one of the healthiest stimulants of the Christian faith.

> Artistic Spring awakes the flowers,
>   And paints the landscape fair,
> But Autumn wilts the gayest bowers,
>   And Winter strips them bare.
> Oh, for the land of light and love
>   Free from all blight and gloom!
> Oh, for that Paradise above,
>   Where flowers unfading bloom!
>
> The questing eye and supple limb
>   Of youth's romantic hour,
> How swiftly gone! Its vigors dim
>   In quickly jaded power:

Oh, for the life of ageless day,
  Mounting on eagle's wings!
Oh, for the youth beyond decay,
  To serve my King of Kings!

How oft on earth the spirit faints
  And mourns o'er inward sin!
But yonder the enraptured saints
  Know sinless bliss within!
Oh, for a deeper faith and prayer!
  Stir us, dear Lord divine;
Seal us and guard us till we share
  That bliss with Thee and Thine.

It is years since I wrote the above three verses to be used as a hymn in connection with a sermon of mine. I was still a young man. I can recall the feelings, the longings, that prompted my pen to write away back then, during a season of busy and very tiring activity in Christian work. Were those lines a product of dreamy listlessness? Did those longings cause my hands to drop into pious inactivity or luxurious uselessness? The very opposite! Always my thoughts of what awaits us yonder have nerved me afresh to persevere in earnest Christian endeavor amid the ugly sin and poignant need everywhere around us.

But take another look at that "multitude which no man could number" there in that "excellent glory." How came they there? Every one of that numberless throng came there "through the blood of the Lamb" (v. 14). Where do they gather and exult? "Before the throne and before the Lamb" (v. 9). What is their heaven of joy? It is this: "The Lamb in the midst of the throne shall shepherd them" (v. 17). It is a surpassingly wonderful photograph of final glorification, and it all centers in the finality of the Lamb as our Savior. He is the sweetness, the fullness, and the everlasting finality of it all. Well may we sing with C. E. Mudie,

To Thee, dear Calvary Lamb,
  I all things owe:
All that I have and am,
  And all I know.
All that I have is now no longer mine,
And I am not my own, Lord, I am Thine.

How can I, Lord, withhold
  Life's brightest hour

From Thee, or gathered gold,
   Or any power?
How can I keep one precious thing from Thee,
When Thou hast giv'n Thine own dear Self for me?

I pray Thee, Savior, keep
   Me in Thy love,
Until death's holy sleep
   Shall me remove
To that fair realm where, sin and sorrow o'er,
Thou and Thine own are one for evermore.

7

The Finalities of the Lamb:
Judge and King

Kingdoms and empires, age by age,
File quickly by on history's page;
Vaunting in conquest, one by one,
They waxed a season, and were gone:
Lord of the Church, whom we adore,
Thy crown alone lasts evermore.

Strangely and swiftly in our day
Historic thrones have passed away;
Earth-girdling new philosophies
Spread vast, collective tyrannies:
Lord of the Church, again appear,
Thy reign of truth establish here.

Despots, inflated, scorn Thy crown;
Thy iron rod shall smite them down;
Satan to Hades shall be hurled,
Thy worldwide banner be unfurled:
Lord of the Church, return, we pray;
Bring in Thy warless, global sway.

No weapon men may yet employ
Can ever Thy dear Church destroy;
No nuclear missile man invents
Can breach its lofty battlements:
Lord of the Church, no more refrain;
The time is ripe: return and reign!

LET US CONTINUE OUR reflections on the finalities of our Lord as the
Lamb. It is a subject flashing with brilliant and varied facets. Some of its

gladder implications we have reviewed, though all too inadequately, and our hearts have already blended in chorus with that raptured multitude on high as they sing, "Glory to the Lamb!"

Finality in Retribution

But there are aspects in the finalities of the Lamb which may well be frightening to the ungodly. He is the Executive of the divine wrath, particularly of the age-end "wrath to come"—that concentrated few years of catastrophe with which the present dispensation is to close. That cloud-burst of terminal wrath is plainly foretold in various Scriptures and startlingly depicted in some of the apocalyptic visions. Its breaking forth is seen when the Lamb unlooses the sixth seal of the seven-sealed scroll.

> *And I saw when he opened the sixth seal, and there was a great earth-quake; the sun became black as sackcloth of hair, and the whole moon became as blood: and the stars of heaven fell unto the earth, as a fig tree casteth her unripe figs when she is shaken of a great wind. And the heaven was removed as a scroll when it is rolled up; and every mountain and island were moved out of their places. And the kings of the earth, and the princes, and the chief captains, and the rich and the strong and every bondman and freeman, hid themselves in the caves and in the rocks of the mountains: and they say to the mountains and the rocks: Fall on us, and hide us from the face of him that sitteth on the throne, and from the wrath of the Lamb; for the great day of their wrath is come; and who is able to stand? (Rev. 6:12–17).*

I would not presume to speak with any dogmatism on this point, but it seems to me that Scripture makes a distinction that is usually disregarded. I mean a distinction between the "great tribulation" and the "wrath to come." Our Lord makes that distinction in his Olivet forecast in Matthew 24. In verses 21–28 he certainly speaks of the "great tribulation," telling us that it will be "such as hath not been from the beginning of the world." But at verse 29 he makes a sharp time distinction, saying, "Immediately after the 'tribulation' of those days, the sun shall be darkened, and the moon shall not give her light, and the stars shall fall from heaven, and the powers of the heavens shall be shaken: and then shall appear the sign of the Son of Man in heaven; and then shall all the tribes of the earth mourn."

That same distinction between the "great tribulation" and the "wrath of God" is marked by that sixth seal in Revelation 6. Up to that point there certainly has been "tribulation" (see vv. 3–11), but now "the great day of the wrath is reached" (vv. 16–17). Indeed, there is a parallel between our Lord's Olivet predelineation and those seven seals of the Apocalypse that is too pronounced and significant to be overlooked.

Matthew 24

Many shall come in my name, saying, I am the Christ, and shall lead many astray (v. 5).

You will hear of wars and rumors of wars . . . for these must needs come to pass. . . . Nation will rise against nation and kingdom against kingdom (vv. 6–7).

And there shall be famines . . . in various places (v. 7).

And earthquakes in various places. . . . All these are the beginning of travail (vv. 7–8).

They shall deliver you to tribulation, and kill you; and ye shall be hated of all nations for my Name's sake (v. 9; amplified in vv. 15–28).

Immediately after the tribulation of those days the sun shall be darkened, and the moon shall not give her light, and the stars shall fall from heaven and the powers of the heavens shall be shaken: and then shall appear the sign of the Son of Man in heaven: and then shall all the tribes of the earth mourn: and they shall see the Son of Man coming on the clouds of heaven

Revelation 6

First seal: "A white horse; and he that sat thereon had a bow . . . and he came forth conquering and to conquer" (v. 2).

Second seal: "A red horse; and to him that sat thereon it was given to take peace from the earth, that they should slay one another" (v. 4).

Third seal: "A black horse; and he that sat thereon had a balance . . . . A measure of wheat for a shilling . . . hurt not the oil and wine" (vv. 5–6).

Fourth seal: "A pale horse; and he that sat upon him, his name was Death; and Hades followed him" (v. 8).

Fifth seal: "I saw underneath the altar the souls of them that had been slain for the Word of God, and for the testimony which they held" (vv. 9–10).

Sixth seal: "There was a great earthquake; and the sun became black as sackcloth of hair, and the whole moon became as blood: the stars of the heaven fell unto the earth . . . and the heaven was removed as a scroll . . . And the kings of the earth, and the princes . . . bondman and freeman hid themselves . . . and say to the mountains and rocks: Fall on us and hide us from the face of him

with power and great glory (vv. 29–30).	that sitteth on the throne and from the wrath of the Lamb" (vv. 12–16).
And he shall send forth his angels with a great sound of a trumpet, and they shall gather together his elect from the four winds, from one end of heaven to the other (v. 31).	Seventh seal: First the 144,000 elect are sealed on earth (7:4–8) and multitudes in heaven (vv. 9–17), then the seventh seal: "seven angels" with the "seven trumpets" of the now-beginning "wrath" (8:1).

So, then, that sixth seal brings us to the point when (with the seventh seal) the "wrath to come" breaks forth. Up to that point it has been the "great tribulation," but that now runs into the "wrath of God." The "great tribulation" is something caused by humans—especially by "the man of sin," the culminating embodiment of Antichrist, the "beast" whose cryptic number is 666; whereas the "wrath to come" is something inflicted by God—even "the wrath of the Lamb." The seven unloosed seals bring us right to that epoch of "wrath." The seven "trumpets" and seven "bowls" that follow show us what will happen in it. My own reading of the Apocalypse along with other Scriptures convinces me that this "wrath to come" covers the last three and a half years of the present age.

We are often asked, "Will the church go through the great tribulation?" The question itself is out of focus. How can the church go through that future period here on earth when the vast majority of those who compose the church are already in heaven and will remain there until our Lord's visible return to this planet? The real question at issue is: Will there be Christian believers on earth at that time? Over dogmatism as to that has too often been unloving and damaging to our Lord's work through his people. To my own mind it seems wiser at present to be tentative rather than headstrong on that point. My own persuasion is that there will be Christian believers on earth then, though I am open for further guidance.

This, however, is certain, that whenever God allows his Shadrachs, Meshachs, and Abed-negos to go through the seven-times heated furnace there is always One "like the Son of God" who walks with them in it. If we had asked those three worthies about their ordeal afterward, they would have said, "We wouldn't have missed it for anything." In line with that, as I now look back, I can see in my own experience that my larger discoveries of the heavenly presence with me have come in times of trial or stress. Those, I agree, are comparatively minor considerations belonging to just one individual, but they are reassuring to me, and I am content to let the matter rest there. Whatever may or may not immediately precede the sudden "shout" of the descending heavenly Bridegroom, I want to be ready for that! I would not needlessly provoke either tribulation or martyrdom—but I fain would have the Shadrach, Meshach, and Abed-nego spirit!

What a picture of consternation that sixth seal releases! See who they are who call on the rocks and mountains to fall on them. They are "kings, nobles, military commanders, the rich, the strong, the bondman, the freeman." The first six categories are people of power, courage, daring—not easily terrified but used to scenes of conflict or challenge. At the other extreme, "bondmen" are usually least alarmed, for they have least to lose. But here is something that terrifies all kinds of people.

What is it? Well, for one thing, there is the greatest earthquake in history. Of all the freak phenomena of nature, none excites such frenzy, distraction, and stark terror as a major earthquake. Whatever other catastrophe may overtake us, so long as the ground beneath us remains firm—the "solid earth" as we call it—there is at least a sense of basic stability. But when the earth itself reels and rolls, rocks and cracks, there is absolutely no hiding place, nowhere to run. Our whole system of thinking and reasoning loses its equilibrium. Not only humans, but the lower animals also give way to strangest panic.

Until recently many orthodox expositors have held that the sun's becoming as black sackcloth and the moon becoming as blood and stars falling to the earth must be taken as purely visional symbols, not as actual disturbances of the elements. But present-day happenings, discoveries, unprecedented weapons of vast destruction, and predictable likelihoods in nature itself may well make us revise our thinking. If such an earthquake, with such hitherto unknown accompaniments, seems unthinkable because unprecedented, we should reflect that this coming upheaval is by sovereign intention to exceed all former earthquakes. It is to be the most fearful ever.

Furthermore, in the correspondence that we have noted between Matthew 24 and Revelation 6, our Lord's Olivet words that parallel this sixth seal certainly do foretell, not in symbol but with obviously intended literalness, unprecedented and frightening abnormalities in the heavenly bodies. "Immediately after the tribulation of those days the sun shall be darkened, and the moon shall not give her light, and the stars shall fall from heaven, and the powers of the heavens shall be shaken." The wording is neither rhetorical nor hyperbolic. It is the language of phenomenal appearance and as such is accurate and unexaggerated. The content of that sixth seal will thus be terrifyingly actual.

That, however, is not the only cause of the frantic alarm. Amid those bewildering cosmic terrors the godless and the wicked of the earth see

Someone right in the center—as if the moon were suddenly to swing so near to the earth as to fill the sky and seem about to smother us all. Instinctively they know who it is, and they cry out, "Hide us from the face of the Sitter on the throne and from the wrath of the Lamb; for the great day of their wrath is come, and who is able to stand?" What they now see is, as Paul expresses it, the overpowering "glory of God in the face of Jesus Christ" (2 Cor. 4:6).

That which makes their remorse and sickening dread the more torturing is that the inescapable retribution is "the wrath of the Lamb"—the unanswerable vengeance of the meek and lowly Jesus whom they have despised and rejected, the One whose redeeming love and atoning blood they have "trodden underfoot" like some "unholy thing" (Heb. 10:29). His wrath carries a condemnation from which there is no escape, for besides being condemned of God they are now uselessly self-condemned.

The "wrath of the Lamb"! Wrath is not mere temper; temper is always irrational, emotion gone berserk; therefore temper is never right. Nor is wrath some savage personal revenge. Wrath is righteous anger executing vengeance against wickedness. Righteous wrath is an awesome thing. The wrath of a noble father whose long-suffering forgiveness has been outraged is far more awesome than the temper of a tyrant. The eventual wrath of mocked love is far more terrible than hate. It is "the wrath of the Lamb" (the "little Lamb") which is so crushing. Whoever saw a lamb in a rage? A lion, a tiger, or any other tantalized beast, yes, but the "wrath of the Lamb"! The degree to which wrath is terrible is determined by three factors: (1) whose it is, (2) the reason for it, (3) the form it takes. Let those three together tell us why the wrath of the Lamb is so prostrating.

That sixth seal, then, marks the transition from the "great tribulation" to the "wrath of God"; for with the opening of the seventh seal the seven trumpets of that sevenfold wrath begin to sound, one after the other. During the "great tribulation" history's culminating Antichrist, namely, the "beast," the "man of sin" whose number is 666, has had things his way, raging against Israel and all who hold the testimony of Jesus. But now "wrath from heaven" is rained down on him, along with all his accomplices and followers. The seventh seal brings us to that last three and a half years, or forty-two months (Rev. 11:2; 12:5), or 1,260 days (11:3; 12:6), or "time and times and half a time" (12:14), or the second half of the seventieth week (Dan. 9:27) when "wrath shall be poured out upon the desolator" (see especially ERV or RSV).

It is at once arresting that between the sixth and seventh seals the 144,000 of Israel are sealed on earth for preservation through the coming wrath period (Rev. 7:1-8), and then the countless multitude of the saved from "every nation" is seen in heaven singing "salvation to our God." We are meant to see thereby God's preservation of his elect both through and from the "great tribulation" and the "wrath" that follows it. Then there is a solemn pause or suspenseful silence (8:1) before the seven trumpets of the wrath begin sounding (8:6).

Observant readers will have noticed that from the first trumpet (8:6) to the seventh (11:15) we are inside that final three and a half years of concentrated intensity (compare 9:11 with 11:7 and references to the forty-two months). Chapters 12–14 confirm that the "dragon" and the "beast" and the "false prophet" are all here together on earth at that time. Then, as if to give us decisive confirmation, we are shown the seven angels with the seven bowls containing the seven plagues in which is "finished the wrath of God" (15:1).

The parallel between those seven bowls and the preceding seven trumpets is too clear to be doubted, and it confirms (at least to my own mind) that the period is one and the same. Both the trumpets and the bowls are coterminous, that is, they end at Armageddon and the actual coming of the messianic kingdom. If the trumpets and bowls are not the same "wrath" period, then the bowls are surely the final intensification of it.

The Seven Trumpets	The Seven Bowls
First: On the earth (8:7)	On the earth (16:2)
Second: On the sea (8:8)	On the sea (16:3)
Third: On the rivers (8:10)	On the rivers (16:4)
Fourth: Sun, moon (8:12)	On the sun (16:8)
Fifth: Men smitten (9:1–11)	Men smitten (16:10)
Sixth: Euphrates (9:13–21)	Euphrates (16:12–16)
Seventh: Divine wrath on "nations" (11:17–18); "thunders and earthquake" (11:19); world becomes kingdom of Christ (11:15–17).	"It [wrath] is done" (16:17). "Cities of nations" fall (16:19). "Thunders . . . great earthquake" (16:18). Babylon destroyed and Christ comes as King of Kings (17:1–19:21).

Any reader who takes time to compare the related passages soon sees that the whole variegated movement converges on Armageddon (or *Har-Megiddo*, or *Har-Magedon*, i.e., Mount Megiddo) where the Lamb, now spectacularly descending to earth as King of Kings and Lord of Lords, forever obliterates the alliance of the dragon and the beast and the false prophet, tramples underfoot all opposition, and brings in his global reign. This the following three passages show in parallel.

Revelation 16:12–13, 16	Revelation 17:12–14	Revelation 19:11–16
And the sixth angel poured out his bowl on the great river Euphrates; and the water thereof was dried up, that the way might be made ready for the kings that come from the sunrising. And I saw coming out of the mouth of the dragon . . . three unclean spirits . . . which go forth unto the kings . . . to gather them unto the war of the great day of God, the Almighty. . . . And they gathered them together into the place which is called in Hebrew Har-Magedon.	The ten horns . . . are ten kings who have received no kingdom as yet; but they receive authority as kings, with the beast for one hour. These have one mind, and they give their power and authority unto the beast. These shall war against the Lamb, and the Lamb shall overcome them; for he is Lord of lords and King of kings. And they also shall overcome that are with him, called and chosen and faithful.	I saw heaven opened; and behold, a white horse, and he that sat thereon, called Faithful and True: and in righteousness he doth judge and make war. His eyes are a flame of fire, and upon his head are many diadems. . . . And the armies which are in heaven followed him on white horses. . . . Out of his mouth proceedeth a sharp sword, that with it he should smite the nations. . . . He treadeth the winepress of the wrath of God. And he hath. . . a name written: KING OF KINGS AND LORD OF LORDS.

Armageddon culminates and exhausts the fearful but fully deserved vengeance of God. With that "wrath of the Lamb" the account is settled, the "controversy of Jehovah" is over, the vengeance of heaven is completed. In this final judgment we are given to see that the Lamb who has absolute finality as the race's Sin-Bearer and heavenly Administrator has also an absolute finality as the Executor of the divine wrath.

I believe that this world-staggering "wrath to come" is now near. The stage is being set for that last grim week of years in which the features of the Beast (666) and the False Prophet and the harlot will have become recognized beyond mistake by those who know the written Word of God. All eyes today may well be on the Middle East, which will be the center of that final act in the six-thousand-year drama, as it will also involve all the major nations of our time.

Finality of Rule

Despite all appearances to the contrary, this world of ours belongs to the Lamb. It is his as God the Son by creative right. It is his as the Son of Abraham and of David by messianic title. Crowningly it is his as the Lamb by redemptive purchase. It is also to be his by military conquest, as various prophecies foretell and the book of Revelation forepictures. It will also be his (I speak reverently) by popular vote. Ask the millions and millions of the saved now in heaven (who will return to earth with him) whom they want as king (Rev. 7:9). Ask the whole realm of created beings in heaven and on earth (5:13). Ask all the sealed of Israel (14:1-5) and the regathered millions of the earthly Israel after they "look on him whom they pierced," and recognize him (Zech. 12:10). Ask all the "meek of the earth" (Isa. 11:14; Matt. 5:5).

There will be depraved leaders and hordes of Gog who will hate and oppose, but they shall be crumpled into mute impotency, smitten with a sword of fire, and ruled with a rod of iron. Yes, for the first thing that our holy Lord will do, upon his lightning reentry from the outer spaces, is to "make war" (Rev. 19:11). That, at long last, will indeed be the war to end war. It will be sudden and final. After that overwhelming conquest he will reign as "King of Peace" in Salem. After that demolishing blaze of wrath he will rule all the nations (Rev. 12:5; 20:4-6).

Once again the seeming incongruity becomes conspicuous; that is, the titanic smashup of all evil powers on this earth is to be inflicted by the flaming fury of the little Lamb, who is now seen as King of Kings and Lord of Lords!

> *After these things I heard as it were a great voice of a great multitude in heaven, saying: Hallelujah; salvation and glory and power belong to our God. True and righteous are his judgments; for he hath judged the great harlot, her that corrupted the earth with her fornication; and he hath avenged the blood of his servants at her hand. And a second time they say, Hallelujah. And her smoke goeth up for ever and ever. And the four and twenty elders and the four living ones [the seraphs] fell down and worshipped God who sitteth on the throne, saying, Amen; Hallelujah. . . . Hallelujah: for the Lord our God, the Almighty reigneth. Let us rejoice and be exceeding glad, and let us give the glory unto him; for the marriage of the Lamb is come, and his wife hath made herself ready. And it was given unto her that she should array herself in fine linen, bright and pure: for the fine linen is the righteous acts of the saints. And he saith unto me: Write, Blessed are they that are bidden to the marriage supper of the Lamb (Rev. 19:1-9).*

This is the goal of all biblical prophecy: the return and reign of Christ. After the "wrath of the Lamb" comes the "marriage of the Lamb." The bride, as seems clear from the paragraph here quoted and from other references, is the transformed and transfigured city of Jerusalem—not that city, of course, merely as a city of magnificent architecture and incomparable elegance but Jerusalem as mystically representing our Lord's own blood-bought people, who now enter and share with him his millennial rule and endless reign. Indeed, the bride is plainly identified in Revelation 19:8 as "the saints," those already described in 17:14 as "chosen and called and faithful."

That city is the inheritance of all our Lord's "saints"—those of the true, spiritual church completed and raptured at his return and then on earth again in their immortalized bodies—together with all those of the earthly Israel—a nation that, by a nationwide spiritual eye-opening, will have become a restored, regenerated people (in fulfillment of such promises as Jer. 31:29-36; Ezek. 37:21-26) recognizing and adoring Jesus, at last, as Messiah-Savior (Zech. 12:10; 14:9, 20). New York, London, Moscow, Peking, Tokyo, Berlin, Paris—all will be eclipsed. There will be supernatural splendors about Jerusalem then that no other city has ever known, and the King of Kings himself will reign there in a visible presence radiating supernal light throughout the whole city. "Every eye shall see him" (Rev. 1:7), continuously around the whole world, by ubiquitous television, and all the earth's peoples will hear that wonderful voice "as the sound of many waters" speaking to them directly from Jerusalem, for "out of Zion shall go forth the law, and the word of Jehovah from Jerusalem" (Isa. 2:3).

Jerusalem will be the legislative and governmental center of the globe. It will be acknowledged as such by all nations. It will be a magnetic center where heavenly glory will be made visible to human eyes. Zion will be the citadel of omnipotence that allows not a breath of insurrection and tolerates no breach of commercial honesty anywhere on earth. From there the eyes of omniscience will continually survey all people, with benign comfort to the upright but deterrent warning to would-be evildoers.

A world-girdling Christocracy will be here, demonstrating our Lord's absolute finality of rule as the Lamb. That rule of warless tranquillity and unparalleled scientific progress, having crushed out the last vestige of earthly anti-Godism, will merge into the postmillennial reign of the Lamb through timeless aeons. In the book of Revelation there are certain phrases that are so recurrent as to be characteristic. One of these is the Greek *eis tous aionas ton aionon:* "to the ages of the ages." It occurs thirteen times—more than all other New Testament occurrences. So far as I know, the Greek language did not have any single word that expressed absolute eternity. It used the nearest possible phrase: "to the ages of the ages," meaning boundless perpetuity. That is the phrase used of our Lord's reign as the Lamb. See Revelation 11:15:

The world-kingdom of our Lord and of his Christ is come; and he shall reign unto the ages of the ages.

Finality in Judgment

In all the Bible there is not a more solemn paragraph than Revelation 20:11–15. It pictures the final, general judgment of human beings at the throne of God. Clearly this judgment is after the Millennium. The wording indicates that it is racial and that it settles individual destiny for ever. That judgment also marks the dissolution of the present cosmic system, for death (of the body) and hades (present detention place of the disembodied departed) are forever done away, and a new order ensues.

> *I saw a great white throne, and him that sat on it, from whose face the earth and the heaven fled away, and there was found no place for them. And I saw the dead, the great and the small, standing before the throne: and the books were opened; and another book was opened which is the book of life. And the dead were judged out of the things which were written in the books, according to their works. And the sea gave up the dead that were in it: and death and hades gave up the dead that were in them: and they were judged, every man, according to their works. And death and hades were cast into the lake of fire. This is the second death, even the lake of fire. And if any was not found written in the book of life, he was cast into the lake of fire (Rev. 20:11–15).*

The basis of the judgment is "according to their works." So no one will perish for Adam's sin, that is, for an inherited depravity that he or she could not escape. The One who sits on that throne is the omniscient Psychologist. His diagnoses are as infallible as his righteousness is inflexible and his verdicts inexorable. The blood of the Lamb, the atonement of Christ, covers all hereditary evil that we human beings involuntarily inherit in Adam. The sentence will correspond with exquisite exactness to individual responsibility. And there is something absolutely determinative:

> *Another book was opened, which is the book of life. . . . And if any was not found written in the book of life, he was cast into the lake of fire.*

The "book of life." Whose is it? Who decides the entries and deletions? The Apocalypse leaves us in no doubt. In 13:8 and again in 21:27 that book is called "the Lamb's book of life." His also is the hand that inscribes or excludes according to his own sovereign decision, for in 3:5 he says, "He that overcometh shall be arrayed in white raiment, and I will in no wise blot his name out of the book of life." Oh, the power of that nail-pierced hand! Oh, the tremendous meaning of the Lamb! The final judging and ultimate destiny of all humans are his!

Finality of Deity

At the present time a subtle and deceiving distinction is being drawn by certain movements and writers between our Lord's divinity and his intrinsic deity. Formerly, when our Savior's "divinity" was referred to, it was understood to mean his coequality and eternality with the Father. For instance, Canon H. P. Liddon's classic book *The Divinity of Our Lord* is a masterly survey of Scripture witness to our Lord's eternal Godhead. But today, the word *divinity* as used of him often means something less— infinitely less, for the difference between the Creator and any created being is infinite.

As already noted, the Apocalypse fittingly comes last in our Bible because of its completive additions to recurrent topics of scriptural revelation. Another instance of that completive function is its testimony to our Lord's true deity. Indeed, there is no part of Scripture that exhibits so repeatedly, side by side, our Lord's personal distinction from the Father and yet his indivisible oneness with the Father.

The following are instances of his being personally distinguished from the Father: Revelation 1:1, 6; 3:2, 12, 21; 5:7, 13; 6:16-17; 7:10, 17; 11:15; 12:10, 17; 14:1, 4, 12; 19:14. But traveling along with those, all the way through, there are the most definite implications of his coequal identification in Godhead with the Father. We cannot here refer to them all, but we point out a few examples. We turn first to chapter 1, verses 7–8:

> *Behold, he cometh with the clouds; and every eye shall see him, and they that pierced him; and all the tribes of the earth shall mourn over him. Even so. Amen. I am the Alpha and the Omega, saith the Lord God, who is, and who was, and who is to come; the Almighty.*

The natural thing is to take the words, "I am the Alpha and the Omega, . . . the Almighty," as spoken by our Lord Jesus of himself, as his signature to the preceding statement, "Behold, he cometh with the clouds." That is the more in keeping because of the twice occurring word, "cometh," that is, "Behold he cometh. . . . I am Alpha and Omega, who is, and who was, and who cometh."

However, there are those who insist that the words of verse 8 are spoken by God the Father, that he alone is the eternal Alpha and Omega, the Almighty. They strengthen their case by reference to verse 4: "Grace to you, and peace, from him who is and who was and who is to come; and from the seven spirits which are before his throne, and [as distinct from the Almighty] from Jesus Christ."

Yet all must agree that just afterward, in verse 18, it is our Lord Jesus who speaks: "I am the First and the Last [i.e., Alpha and Omega], the living One; and I became dead; and behold, I am alive unto the ages of the ages." Moreover, lest even a shadow of doubt should linger in any reader's mind, the book of Revelation settles the matter once for all in its closing paragraph. See 22:12 and following. It is our Lord Jesus speaking: "Behold, I come quickly, and my reward is with me, to render to each man according to his work. I am the Alpha and the Omega, the First and the Last, the Beginning and the End. . . . I, Jesus, have sent mine angel to testify unto you these things."

So there it is: the very phraseology that applies exclusively to absolute Deity is used of and by our Lord Jesus. Equally with the Father, he is the uncreated Alpha and Omega. In the most conclusive way it evinces his essential identity of being with the eternal Father. Utter marvel: the Lamb is none other than God!

Turning now to chapters 4 and 5, we find this same mystery of the Godhead expressed in another way. John sees the flashing, rainbow-circled "throne set in heaven," with the seven flambeaux burning before it and the four flamelike seraphs encompassing it, uttering their continuous antiphony, "Holy . . . holy . . . holy is the Lord God, the Almighty." Round about that central throne he sees the twenty-four subsidiary thrones occupied by the twenty-four white-robed "elders." Then amid the lightnings and thunders emanating from the throne, he hears the worship.

Worthy art thou, our Lord and our God, to receive the glory and the honor and the power; for thou didst create all things; and because of thy will they are, and were created (4:11).

The vision moves on to its climactic surprise—"the Lamb"! That little Lamb—slain yet living—approaches that throne of the "Almighty" and occupies it and does so with a propriety at once acknowledged by all the heavenly observers, for the guardian seraphs and royal elders now "fall down before the Lamb," with harp chords of praise and incense odors of prayer and prostrate worship, while the vast outer ring of angel myriads blends with them in ascribing to the Lamb the very same "glory" and "honor" and "power" that they ascribe (chap. 4) to the "Almighty." In other words, the Lamb is equally and inseparably one with the Father as the object of creature worship.

Strange as it seems, there are movements and writers today who call themselves Christian yet are bent on denying that enthronement of the Lamb. Seizing on triviality (as it seems to me) they ask how the Lamb could be at one and the same time both "in the midst of the throne" and yet "in the midst" of the elders. They would translate the Greek word to mean that the Lamb was "between" the throne and the elders. They also point to the end of the chapter, where all creatures sing: "Unto him that sitteth on the throne, and unto the Lamb. . . ."—which is supposed to differentiate between the one and only "Almighty" who alone sits on the throne, and the Lamb who is only before it. But they misplead the Scripture. The four seraphs and twenty-four elders are themselves all ranged "round the throne" (4:4, 6). To be "in the midst" of them is to be "in the midst" of it, the throne. Nor is that all, for our dear Lord himself says, "Even as I overcame, and sat down with my Father in his throne" (3:21).

Is even that not enough to convince the doubter? Then the book of Revelation will settle it for us conclusively in its closing vision where, in its last reference to that throne of the universe, it twice names it "the throne of God and of the Lamb" (22:1, 3). Yes, the Lamb is in that throne as being one in absolute deity with the Father.

We might usefully linger over several other passages in the Apocalypse where the deity of the Lamb is similarly denoted, but we mention only one more. It comes in the last and most sublime of the Patmos unveilings. John is privileged to see the New Jerusalem in the coming new heaven and new earth. It is a city of such surpassing splendor and beauty, filled with such delectable conditions, as earth has never known before. It blends the heavenly with the earthly and the celestial with the terrestrial. In a way never known before, it is heaven on earth.

But amid its pearly gates and jasper walls and golden streets and ivory palaces, there was something missing as John's ravished gaze lingered over it, something that John expected would be the center of everything and for which he apparently looked particularly. There was no temple or sanctuary! Then he perceived the reason. No temple was needed, for God himself was actually there in visible presence and therefore not needing to be either represented or approached by means of any emblematical building. In visible Shekinah God is seen and worshiped there!

How significant is the way John describes it! "A temple I saw not in it; for the Lord God, the Almighty, is its temple, and so is the Lamb." Similarly, as the Father and the Son are together the temple, so are they together the light: "The city hath no need of the sun, nor of the moon, that they should shine on it, for the glory of God lighted it, and its luminary is the Lamb."

Mystery of mysteries: when we see the Lamb we are seeing God! God is not only the Almighty. No, in his ineffably glorious, eternal Son, he is also the Lamb-Redeemer! Let all worlds wonder and all creatures adore! As we have seen, our Lord Jesus as the Lamb is coequally one with the eternal Father by identical designation as "the Alpha and the Omega" (1:8 with 22:12), then by joint enthronement in heaven (5:8–14), then by oneness with the Father as the temple and the light and the King and the glorious God worshiped in the New Jerusalem (21–22).

Well may we wonder and worship as we reflect upon those seven finalities of the Lamb exhibited to us in that last book of the Bible: (1) as Lord of the church, (2) as universal Administrator, (3) as Savior-Shepherd of his people, (4) in age-end retribution, (5) of ruling power, (6) as Judge of all, (7) of absolute Godhead. What a climax of revelation! What a Savior! What a God! Glory to the Lamb!

> Thou art the everlasting Word,
> The uncreated Son;
> God manifestly seen and heard,
> And Heaven's beloved One:
> Worthy, O Lamb of God, art Thou
> That every knee to Thee should bow.
>
> In Thee most perfectly expressed
> The Father's glories shine;
> Of the full Deity possessed,
> Eternally Divine:
> Worthy, O Lamb of God, art Thou
> That every knee to Thee should bow.
>
> True Image of the Infinite,
> Whose essence is concealed;
> Brightness of uncreated light;
> The heart of God revealed:
> Worthy, O Lamb of God, art Thou
> That every knee to Thee should bow.
>
> Of all the coming endless bliss
> The Center and the Sun;
> Our endless theme of praise be this,
> To Heaven's beloved One:
> Worthy, O Lamb of God, art Thou
> That every knee to Thee should bow.
> *Josiah Conder*

PART TWO

The Dimensions
of the Cross

8

The Cross As a Superlative Wonder

The Christ we worship and adore,
Though truly "Son of Man,"
Is God the Son for evermore,
Ere time and worlds began.

Both Son of God and God the Son,
From all eternity;
Lo, Father, Son, and Spirit, one
In threefold unity.

Sheer mystery? Would it be less
Were God but One, not Three?
His unbeginning endlessness—
Could greater mystery be?

Lo, mystery far stranger still,
The Son, our souls to save,
Once bled upon a sombre hill,
And lay within a grave!

Creator-Savior, Three in One,
We worship, praise, adore;
Redeeming love and grace have won
Our hearts for evermore.

THERE ARE THREE PERPETUALLY amazing mysteries in the incarnation of Christ that transcend all its other profound and towering meanings. Those three mysteries, indeed, not only transcend all other aspects of the Incarnation, they include them, and the center most mystery of the three is the

Cross, the "wondrous Cross on which the Prince of Glory died." In this present study, we ponder again those three superlatives of the Incarnation and the Cross, their central wonder.

First Superlative: God Became Human

The first stupendous meaning of the Incarnation is that God became clothed with our humanity. The more deeply we reflect upon this, the more staggering it becomes.

Four philosophic-scientific theories have been propounded to account for the phenomenal universe: (1) that it is an illusion and does not really exist at all, (2) that it is eternal, (3) that it is self-evolved, (4) that it was created. Of these four, the first, that the material universe is an illusion, is a mirage of unrealistic reasoning that modern exploration of the atom has surely dispelled. The second, that the universe is eternal, seems disproved more than ever today by the disparity between conservation and dissipation of energy in the nuclear processes of the universe. The third, that the universe is self-evolved, is utterly untenable without that imaginary fairy godmother, an "original protoplasm," for *ex nihilo nihil fit:* "out of nothing, nothing comes." The fourth, that the universe was created, has become the inescapable necessity. The universe was created. The origin of matter is Mind. There is a personal Creator, a Creator who must be eternal in his being and infinite in his attributes.

Thus far science can take us, but no further, at least not with any certainty. But at the point where science leaves off, the Bible begins: "In the beginning God created the heavens and the earth." That is the Bible "protoplasm" from which all its subsequent revelation develops. The Bible never argues God; it assumes him. That is because the Bible is not a series of human propositions but a progression of divine testimonies. Psalm 93:5 says, "Thy testimonies are very sure." There is a polarity of difference between a theory and a testimony. A theory is an interpretation of facts, whereas a testimony is a statement of facts themselves. It is vital to realize that the opening verse of Scripture is not merely the first postulate of a human philosophy but the first testimony of a divine revelation: "In the beginning God created the heavens and the earth." That which is the ultimate conclusion at which science arrives is the primordial testimony with which divine revelation begins.

That, then, is the point at which natural science and supernatural revelation meet—and part: "In the beginning God." The one works to it. The other starts from it. In both aspects it is stupendous. If God created all, then God must be before all and above all and beneath all and within all and around all, and beyond all. If anyone created him, then he is not God, for he did not create all. But if none created him, and he created all, then he must be eternal, for he could not have issued from blank nothing.

Mysterious and baffling as the eternality of God is to these finite minds of ours, there is simply no thinkable alternative. Science requires it. Scripture declares it. How can we but accept it?

But what or who is God? To know that, we must learn of the Bible. In its developing revelation the Bible discloses ten all-inclusive differentiae of the divine Being, three of them denoting the divine essence or substance, and seven of them denoting the divine attributes.

In essential being,

1. God is a spirit
2. God is light
3. God is love

In basic qualities,

4. God is personal
5. God is triune
6. God is eternal
7. God is immutable

In active attributes,

8. God is omnipotent
9. God is omniscient
10. God is omnipresent[1]

To see the Bible doctrine of God in this tenfold summary is easy and useful, but to grasp its baffling infinitude with these little minds of ours is about as possible as for a teacup to contain a million Atlantics and Pacifics. God is at once and forever the greatest of all realities and the deepest of all mysteries. Let him ever be named with awe and reverence. All that we know of him is by his own self-revealing as preserved for us in the inspired Scriptures. "Holy men of God spake as they were moved by the Holy Spirit" (2 Peter 1:21).

In our ten-point abstract of Bible doctrine concerning God, nothing is more wonder-evoking than article 5, the triunity of God. The ever-existing, all-creating, eternally unchanging God is not an indivisible single Unity but a hypostatic Triunity. That is, in the Godhead there are three coequally divine and personal Beings, distinguishable but inseparable and in such utter union that we can define it only as One in Three, and Three in One. It is not tritheism—a trio of Gods—but *triunity*—a divine Trinity in unity: one absolutely divine hypostasis in three distinguishably personal and reciprocal subsistencies.

The Bible nowhere reasons the triunity of the Godhead; it nowhere categorically states it, but it dimly foreshadows it in the Old Testament and clearly demonstrates it in the New. Whatever quality, attribute, majesty, or glory is appropriately ascribed to Jehovah as the one, true, all-sovereign God is equally and unhesitatingly ascribed to Christ as God the Son, also to the Holy Spirit as the Spirit of the Father and the Son, but absolutely to no other. In nothing is the New Testament more notably the crown of the Old than in this implication and demonstration of triunity in the Godhead.

The few thousand years of human history on this planet of ours and the millions of years that the earth itself has existed are as nothing compared with the beginningless, endless, eternal continuing of the triune God. Yet it is in connection with our Adamic race and its brief chapter on this orb that there took place in the threefold Deity a development surpassing all else even throughout eternity. It was a development greater than the calling forth of the whole universe from nothing. The One whom we now know as the second member of the ever-blessed Three-in-One became Human!

It seems almost too astonishing to be believed, and we may well be sympathetic toward those who sincerely shrink back with intellectual shyness or with frank incredulity from such a startling idea. There are those who object that such a transition in the Deity simply could not take place, while others aver that even if it could, it is unthinkable that it ever would. The only cure for such hesitation or doubt is to take a long, steady, thoughtful, unbiased look at Jesus in the four gospels. As to his being God manifest in the flesh, there can scarcely be honest denial that he claimed it.

Even more arresting is the guileless propriety with which he assumed it. Further to this, an open-minded survey of his moral character confirms it, for as someone has boldly said, "Even God could not be better." All this is reinforced by the mighty works that he wrought and the supernatural originality with which he taught and the sublime new picture of God that he brought. As we review Jesus as predicted by the Hebrew prophets, then as presented by the gospel writers, then as interpreted by the New Testament epistles, how can we but exclaim with John, "The Word became flesh, and dwelt among us, and we beheld his glory, the glory as of the only-begotten of the Father, full of grace and truth"?

Yet even as we say it, we are again overwhelmed by it, for it is not merely a daring idea but a reality. Humanhood has been incorporated into Godhead! There was nothing theatrical about the Incarnation. It was not merely that God occupied a human body, for that would have been nothing more than a prolonged theophany. Nor was it that God monopolized, as never before, a human personality, for that would have been no more than psycho-physical superimposition. Nor was it that God the Son took humanity in appearance only—a "docetic" incarnation—no, for he was actually born of a human mother.

Well, there it is, the real incarnation of God the Son: "very God of very God" but now also "bone of our bone and flesh of our flesh," and "in all things made like unto his brethren." Not two *personalities*—a divine and a human—in one earthly tabernacle, but two *natures*—one uncreated and the other created—now united in one divine-human person, Jesus Christ. This indeed is the miracle of miracles, the perpetual wonder from which the mind never completely recovers.

Second Superlative: God Became Human to Die for Human Sin

It would be overpowering enough if that were all. The fact is, however, that it is but the vestibule to further wonder and mystery. The Incarnation not only brought the eternal Son into our human relation of creaturehood and servanthood; he entered that relation after it had sustained a fearful shock, a fatal jar, a foredooming fall! He became one of us and one with us not at the original, pre-Fall level but in our present humanity, fallen, infirm, corrupt, guilty, and under condemnation. Hence, it is written in Romans 8:3, "God, sending his own Son in the likeness of sinful flesh, and for sin [i.e., as an offering for sin] condemned sin in the flesh."

That cannot and does not mean that there was any taint of sin in our Lord's human nature (see 2 Cor. 5:21), but it does mean that he was made one of us as we now are, except for inherited depravity. It would seem that human nature, in its original state and status, had regal superiorities and exquisite resplendences that now no longer adhere to it. Our first parents were not given clothing until after the Fall. It was only after the Fall that "they knew they were naked" (Gen. 3:7). Until then, from those two faultless bodies an opalescent glory-sheen had radiated which itself was a supernal mantle. If, hundreds of years later, the face of Moses shone with reflected Shekinah glow after his forty days of communion with God on Mount Sinai, how must the faces and bodies of Adam and Eve have shone with gentle splendor in Eden's garden of continual, sinless communion with God!

Alas, when disobedience disrupted that communion and estranged human nature from God, the pristine glory-light fell away. There was a suddenly realized nakedness. A sense of shame flared up, and a covering became necessary. Infirmities, weaknesses, restraints, and limitations also now began to beset human nature, some of these being directly inflicted and others incidentally permitted.

It was "in the likeness" of humanity at this lower level that our Lord became one with us. There was no halo or aura or luster, no immunity to fatigue or other physical infirmities, but a complete similarity of his human nature to that of mankind since the Fall. This meant, also, not only that he took the relation of a human subject to the divine law, but that of subjection to a condemning divine law that had been outraged by the species of which he was now a member.

Oh, how this heightens the marvel and deepens the mystery of the Incarnation! Yet how it lights up the purpose of it! Had the purpose of our Lord's incarnation been only ethical or revelatory, he could have come (far more impressively perhaps) in the likeness of unfallen man, but if he would be man's Redeemer, he must come in "the likeness of sinful flesh." That he did so come proves at once that his incarnation was not merely ethical or revelatory. Nothing but a redemptive purpose can explain his coming "in the likeness of sinful flesh." It is equally clear, too, that if he had come in the likeness of unfallen man, he could not have accomplished his redemptive work.

Thus it was, that in his incarnation the second member of the eternal Triunity entered our estranged human relation to God, a relation involving guilt to be answered for and curse to be endured. This is the centermost marvel of all, that the eternal sonship of God the Son should now, for a time, coexist with the relation of criminality and condemnation under heaven's righteous sentence. It may well amaze us that these two relationships could and did meet in the incarnate Son.

He must have been conscious of their acute meeting in him through all his ministry, but it was in Gethsemane that the two finally became a sheer agony of opposites that nevertheless must be blended into one on that tragic, ugly, triumphant, glorious cross which is the most inexpressible event in the history of the universe and even in the eternity of God. On that cross, "God was in Christ," (2 Cor. 5:19), and so was the whole of fallen humanity, for "If one died for all, then all died" (2 Cor. 5:14 RV)! As in that birth at Bethlehem his sonship stooped to subjectship, so in that cross of Calvary our subjectship was lifted up again into sonship. As he hangs there, see the perfect sonship, "obedient unto death, even the death of the cross"; see also the subjectship answering in him the just penalties of the outraged divine law, so that subjects might once again be righteously reinstated as sons!

Yes, every aspect of the Incarnation is wonderful, but the central wonder and glory of it is the Cross. The eternal Son was born to die! It is all mystery and wonder that he could be born. It is even more so that he could die. It stuns the mind that he could be born of a human mother. It melts the heart that he should die to save human sinners. Yet such was the purpose. The creaturehood was the gateway to Saviorhood. Let the poet Edward Young help us to express ourselves.

> And what is this?—Survey the wondrous cure;
> And at each step, let higher wonder rise!
> Pardon for vast, for infinite offence,
> Through means which speak its value infinite!
> A pardon bought with blood, with blood divine!

With blood divine of Him I made my foe!
Persisted to provoke! though wooed and awed,
Blessed and chastised, a flagrant rebel still:
A rebel, 'midst the thunders of His throne.
Nor I alone; a rebel universe!
My species up in arms—not one exempt:
Yet for the foulest of the foul He dies,
Most joyed, for the redeemed from deepest guilt!
Leap, every heart, and every bosom, burn!
O what a scale of miracles is here!
Its lowest rung, high planted on the skies;
Its towering summit lost beyond the thought
Of man or angel!

Third Superlative: God Remains Human for All Eternity

And now, finally, reflect for a moment on the third superwonder of the Incarnation. Is it strangely astonishing that the eternal Son should feed as a baby boy at the breast of a young human mother? Is it even more confounding that this infinite One who thus transferred himself from utter spirit being, deity, infinity, and eternality into union with our humanity should hang tortured, crucified, dying as a supposed blasphemer on that unspeakable cross? Then is it not crowningly wonderful that just as he could not undeify himself when he became human, so now, having become human, he remains human for all eternity?

See Hebrews 13:8 (RV mg) again: "Jesus Christ, the same yesterday, and today, and unto the ages"! Mark well that it does not say, "from the ages . . . unto the ages." No, for the second person of the Godhead has not been the Man Christ Jesus from all ages, even though from all ages he has been the Son of God and God the Son. As the now incarnate Son of God he has become also "Jesus Christ" from the wonderful "yesterday" of his birth in Bethlehem. Blessed be his glorious name, he is now God-Man, Redeemer-Revealer *"to the ages,"* even forevermore!

The Eternal Spirit, the Triune Deity, has found a perfect mode of sympathetic expression to all sentient creatures throughout the universe and a perfect objective link with all such creature intelligences for ever and ever. He needed not to incarnate the omnipotence and omniscience and omnipresence of God, for those divine attributes everywhere speak for themselves, but, as never before, and forevermore, he incarnates and exhibits the heart of God, the heart that broke itself on Calvary in sheer love!

Even the abysmal and tantalizing mystery of permitted sin in Satan and in angels and in humanity has been astoundingly overruled to express to the whole universe what had never found expression eternally hitherto—

"God is love!" The divine power and wisdom and righteousness and holiness and providence and goodness had always shone forth resplendently
throughout the universe, but now, in "Jesus Christ, the same yesterday
and today and unto the ages," the divine *love* had at last found perfect
expression. Oh, the wonder of it!

> The myst'ry of permitted sin,
> Unfathomable seeming,
> Reveals yet deeper deeps within
> Since Jesus came redeeming:
> For God Himself, all worlds above,
> In Jesus bled to save us,
> And proof sublime that God is love
> For evermore He gave us!
> Oh, love profound, to save us thus
> From sin and guilt and blindness,
> To weave from Calv'ry thorns for us
> A crown of "lovingkindness"!

"Jesus Christ, the same yesterday and today and unto the ages." At the
very sight of the words, all kinds of reflections leap to mind. If the eternal
Son of God has become permanently human, shall we believe the evolutionist who tells us that humanity is an inferior order of beings gradually
to be superseded by eventually evolving superior forms? Has the eternal
Deity indeed become linked to a low rank of intelligences? For every
Christian, let the Incarnation be the utter and final denial of such speculative evolutionary irreverence. No, indeed, it was because man, in the
beginning, was created "in the image of God" (Gen. 1:27) that the Son
of God could later be incarnated in the image of man.

In Adam we see what man first was. In Christ we see what man is yet to
be! Despite his overconfidence, the evolutionist has never yet found the
missing link that binds humans to the ape and the worm. The "missing
link"?—there are millions of links missing! But while evolutionary theo-
rists, like Bunyan's "man with the muck rake," have been scraping round
for their supposed missing link to the gorilla, the tadpole, the protozoan,
or the monad, God has lifted up before our human race the immaculate,
luminous, all-glorious God-Man link to supreme heights of human destiny in heaven, even to the ages of the ages!

Even in our present life, how wonderful to us is Jesus Christ, the same
yesterday and today and to the ages! As God the Son he has ever been
omnipresent, or, simultaneously everywhere, but it is only since his resurrection and ascension and Pentecostal return to us in the Holy Spirit that
he has been omnipresent as "Jesus Christ, the same . . . today." Yes, today

he is still Jesus Christ—unchanged in his sympathetic human oneness with us after his crucifixion and resurrection. It is not only as an all-pervasive divine Spirit that he indwells us, but as the warm, tender, sympathetic, divine-human, and personal Jesus Christ. He who became of us and then died for us now lives in us, as "Jesus Christ, the same . . ."

Of course, the body that he now has is not physiologically identical with the body that he had before his crucifixion, yet it is recognizably the same body transmuted to a higher form of existence, similar in structure though not identical in texture, interpenetrated by his own divine life, and thereby refined, supernalized, transfigured into a "body of glory" (Phil. 3:21 RV). It is the type and pledge of the resurrection body that is promised to his Spirit-sealed people at the coming Rapture.

There he is, in the glory: Son of God, Son of Man; Revealer of God, Redeemer of men; the express image of the invisible God; the sympathetic High Priest of all God-conscious creatures; the King of Kings and Lord of Lords; the center and source of heavenly bliss and blessedness; reigning in the "great white throne" high over flashing cherubs and seraphs, yet we may say with Ezekiel, "And upon the throne is the likeness of the appearance of a Man"!—Jesus Christ, the same yesterday and today and to the ages!

> And have the bright immensities
>   Received our risen Lord,
> Where light years frame the Pleiades
>   And point Orion's sword?
> Do flaming suns His footsteps trace
>   Through corridors sublime,
> The Lord of interstellar space,
>   The Conqueror of Time?
> The heaven that hides Him from our sight
>   Knows neither near nor far;
> Our prayer-room candle sheds a light
>   As surely as a star:
> Where'er in prayer with Him we tryst
>   We touch the All-Divine,
> And from a human Savior-Christ
>   All Heaven's splendors shine.

Let us say again with tears of unspeakable gratitude,

> Love so amazing, so divine
> Demands my soul, my life, my all.
> *Isaac Watts*

9

The Cross As a Raison d'être

> This earth too small
> For Love Divine? Is God not infinite?
> If so, His love is infinite. Too small?
> One famished babe meets pity oft from man
> More than an army slain! Too small for love?
> Was earth too small to be of God created?
> Why, then, too small to be redeemed?
> *Aubrey De Vere*

IS THE CAPABILITY OF wondering becoming strangely perverted in modern humanity? Are we so occupied with wondering at little things, which are only seemingly big, that we do not marvel anymore at the things that are really big? We are so in the habit of marveling at clever new human-made gadgets and machines that we are losing our marvel at the sunrise and the procession of the seasons. We are kept so marveling at airplanes whizzing through skies at supersonic speeds, guided missiles ominously screaming from continent to continent, outer-atmosphere rockets, spaceships, and other inventions of these days that we may be losing both the appetite and the aptitude to marvel at the truly great things, the things that are spiritual and divine. We think ourselves wonderfully superior and scientifically informed, when in fact it may be that we are fast becoming metallic-minded mechanics or mere children again, too busy playing with exciting new toys to have an adult sense of marvel at what is really marvelous.

A short time ago I picked up a pretty Christmas card in which the brief message ran, "Greetings and best wishes for the holiday season." That card represents the big tragedy. Christmas for millions is just "the holiday season." Are we losing our ability to be amazed at the Christmas miracle? Yet that event is the most stupendous and astonishing wonder that could ever engross the human mind—that the eternal, infinite Creator of the universe should enter our human life and assume our human nature by being born as the babe of a human mother!

The Never-Ending Surprise: The Incarnation

So far as we know, time, in the sense of days, weeks, months, years, decades, centuries, millenniums, began only some six thousand years ago. To our human review, what mighty developments have occurred in that long unrolling of time! To our little day-at-a-time existence, what a vast sweep six thousand years seems! Yet what is "time" but a very temporary concept? It is a purely accommodating way of making continuity intelligible to tiny, finite people. The earth itself is much older than time, the modern consensus of scientific opinion dating it as over four thousand million years old. Yet what are four million years compared with eternity? Earth and time are a mere infinitesimal parenthesis. Oh, that word *eternity*—without beginning, without ending. Yet, at that first Christmas, it was the Eternal who became born of a human mother, to become our Kinsman-Representative and vicarious Sin-Bearer!

If our Lord Jesus Christ were only a creature, as certain modern Unitarian sects aver, then, even though he may now be the most exalted of all creatures, there would be little if anything in the Christian message to command the utter astonishment of the human intellect, for the Creator and the creature would still be infinitely apart. But if Jesus is indeed Emmanuel—"God with us"—then there is a union of the Creator with the creature. Once you grant that the awesome power within and behind phenomena has parted the veil and appeared in fashion as human, then the proper reaction is that nothing else matters except in relation to that all-eclipsing event.

That union of the Divine and the human necessarily dwarfs all other facts and concerns. Indeed, all other phenomena, knowledge, events, and concerns must now be viewed in the light of it, for it not only dwarfs all others, it illumines and changes them all, whether natural, social, political, racial, or individual. All other appearances that have held humanity's admiring gaze, including all the trophies of art, philosophy, or science, are burned, as it were, in the unique white light of this superfact. As we have said, it is the continual surprise from which the mind never recovers, so long as the mind is awake and real and not torpid with unthinking acquiescence.

The Incarnation is the miracle of miracles, the meaning of meanings, which should rivet the attention of so-called Christendom today as never before. It is the fundamental interpretation of things, compared with which the splitting of the atom is a barely noticeable incident. As the angels of heaven look down upon this earthly scene, surely their biggest marvel must be the absence of human marvel at this eternal surprise—that Infinity has clothed itself with our humanity. With that first little baby breath of Bethlehem's chilly night air, the King of Ages had come from beyond the stars to dwell with us as our blood relative! He who gave the stars and suns their flash and flame had become the babe of a virgin!

Upon every new reflection, the Incarnation becomes more amazing. At all ordinary births a new personality is brought into existence. When a little babe is born, there is not only the tiny body, there is a new personality that absolutely did not exist before. Where there was a sheer blank there is now a new mind, a new being, a living, thinking, human entity. But this was not the case when Jesus was born in Bethlehem. In that supernormal conception and birth, an already existing divine person actually assumed our human nature, both physically and mentally.

Meaning for Human Nature and History

Let this be clearly realized that when our Lord was born of Mary, it was of the physical part only that she became his mother. He did not inherit his mind from Mary. As our Lord's manhood has no father, so his Godhead has no mother. What happened away back in Bethlehem was that the preexistent Son of God took our human nature to himself and entered our human family by the process of a supernatural conception and a truly natural birth. On that long-ago Christmas day the Son of God became humanly one with us. In his stainless life he became our accepted representative. In his Calvary death he became our vicarious Sin-Bearer and Savior. In his resurrection and ascension he flooded our dark sky with the sunrise of glorious new hope.

Think again what sacredness the Incarnation gives to motherhood. The eternal Son of God, brighter than the brightest of the morning stars, holier than the holiest of the flaming seraphs, lovelier than the loveliest of the anointed cherubs in the paradise of God, enters our race by a real human birth. If he was to become really one with us, so as really to represent us and redeem us, a real human birth was a necessity. It was also necessary that he should be born of a virgin. It was impossible that he should have a human father, for a Christ with a human father could not possibly have been the eternal Son of God. Yet he must not be born even of the Virgin until she has become a married woman, lest his incarnation should ever seem to countenance unmarried parenthood. How wonderfully, then, the Incarnation honors and sanctifies womanhood, wedlock, parenthood, childhood, and especially motherhood!

Again, what dignity it confers on human nature! Years ago Professor Dana of Yale raised the question as to whether some new and more noble order of beings might yet appear on earth and outrank humanity, as humanity now outranks the lower animals. Professor Agassiz partly answered this from a scientific point of view by observing that in the lowest vertebrates the spinal column is horizontal, in the next higher species it is oblique, while in humans it has reached perpendicularity. A well-known geologist argued that man must be the highest order of being that will ever stand on earth, because he crowns the long series of animal creations, the fossils of which lie embedded in the successive geological strata as we ascend from the fire rocks to the alluvium on which we now live.

Neither of these arguments seems conclusive to me. But what does settle it conclusively that there will never be a higher order than human is the incarnation of Christ. Our very Creator has taken our nature upon himself. This stamps our human constitution (apart from its present degeneration in sin) as of highest dignity, never to take second rank through the creation of a superior order, even though the earth should roll through its orbit ten billion years to come, for it is inconceivable that God would create a species outranking that to which the eternal Son is now united forever. It is the more inconceivable because when our risen Lord ascended, he carried to heaven our humanity in a far more glorious form than had been given to it even in unfallen Adam. The One who now shares the throne of universal government with the eternal Father is One who wears the human form! And in the ultimate consummation, all his redeemed people will be presented before that same throne as lovely replicas of that Man!

Think again what promise the Incarnation brings into human history. Would anyone seriously deny that the history of the human race, from the earliest records onwards, is stranger and sadder than the most pathetic fiction ever fabricated? Oh, this tragic tale of human sin and suffering, of war and woe, of evil-sowing and evil-reaping! Will the sinister lines never be ironed out? Ebenezer Elliott, a troubled poet, asks,

> Shall crime bring crime forever,
> Strength aiding still the strong?
> Is it Thy will, O Father,
> That man should toil for wrong?

Then, with pathetic bravery the poet answers his own question:

> No! say Thy mountains; No! Thy skies;
> Man's clouded sun shall brightly rise,
> And songs ascend instead of sighs.

But is the poet's sanguine deduction anything more than desperate optimism? Do the mountains and the skies guarantee any such eventual utopia? My own eyes do not always so interpret them. The one and only real pledge of an ultimate golden daybreak is the fact of Christ—his birth into our race, his espousal of our cause, his repulsing of our foe, his substitutionary atonement, his resurrection from death, by which he subdued Satan and the grave and hades, and, as the crowning touch, the promise of his second coming to our earth as global Administrator. That is heaven's sure token of earth's bright morrow. "Unto us a child is born, unto us a Son is given: and the government shall be upon his shoulders." Already he sits on the throne of universal sovereignty in heaven. His kingdom rules over all.

The mystery of permitted evil on earth has thereby assumed a new aspect and has almost run its course. The usurper shall be finally banished, and the now rebellious territory shall rest in warless, tearless quietude beneath the scepter of Emmanuel. It shall certainly be so, for he has really risen, and he really reigns, and he will really return. That promised day, as the philosopher-poet Tennyson puts it, is

> The one far-off divine event
> To which the whole creation moves.

The Deepest Reason

This brings us to the vital raison d'être of the Incarnation. Above all else, it was meant to bring eternal salvation to sin-cursed human individuals. The announcing angel said to Joseph, "Thou shalt call his name Jesus, for he shall save his people from their sins." Soon afterward the angels were singing over the fields of Bethlehem, "Unto you is born this day a Savior which is Christ the Lord." His very name defines him as Savior. His very birth was that he might become our Savior.

No lesser explanation of his incarnation is adequate. He did not need to become incarnate for any other reason. Theological philosophers have theorized that quite apart from the grim fact of human sin, God would have become incarnate, because (they contend) it is inconceivable that he should have remained forever invisible and unrevealed. But why, then, in all his eternal continuity did God not assume permanent visibility at some point long before the Bethlehem miracle? And why, in thus becoming linked forever to visible creaturehood, did God choose this astronomically infinitesimal planet and this short-lasting Adamic race of ours? Why did he not assume permanent visibility in some other way? And why did he need to endure that ugly, awful cross on Golgotha?

We are far wiser to keep to the forthright testimony of the Scriptures: "Thou shalt call his name Jesus, for he shall save." "Unto you is born this day a Savior."

We are foolish when we try to explain the Incarnation on other grounds, and we are equally foolish when we try to explain away the fact of human sin. We have listened to the evolutionists telling us that sin, so-called, is but an animalistic barbarity from which evolving humanity is gradually freeing itself—until two world wars of cultured, scientific brutality laughed that pathetic nonsense out of court. We have listened to aesthetic psychologists and humanistic poets telling us in technical or decorative phraseology that sin is not really the evil thing that it used to be thought—while all the time conscience, conscience, conscience, that solemn sentinel within us which neither evolution nor any of our humanistic philosophies has ever satisfactorily explained, keeps on telling us with unsilenceable authority that sin is indeed sin.

Our wisdom is to accept the united witness of human nature and divine Scripture: we are sinners, and there is a Savior. Sin is humanity's tragedy. Jesus is God's answer. "God so loved the world that he gave his only-begotten Son"—gave him to become one with us through his holy incarnation at Bethlehem, gave him to become one of us, so that he might offer up from within humanity and on our behalf, a sinless life, a perfectly obedient will, and an infinitely meritorious atonement culminated on the Cross.

Of all kinds of salvation this is the most wonderful—a salvation for sinners. It is not just a salvation from poverty or from sickness or from war or from ignorance or from bad government. For the greater part of their lives, many people think that those are the things from which we most need to be saved, but eventually they come to see differently. They perceive at last that there is a deadlier evil that lies behind all other evils and is their originating cause, an evil that the Bible calls *sin*. Yes, sin, not in our lighter, modern, psychological sense but in the plain, stark, old-fashioned Bible sense of the word.

We are living in a disillusioned age. The dreams of humanitarian poets and the fond fancies of evolutionist philosophers, with which our twentieth century dawned, have been mocked by world wars of such staggering vastness and educated vileness that the brave notion of a future human-made utopia has become inane. The world today is in a state of political and social upheaval. Society has been shaken to its foundations. And behind all our twentieth-century brutalities, calamities, and agonies is sin. Yet the world is still vainly pinning its hope on the big reformer, the big business leader, the big diplomat, the big combine, or the dictator-wizard, when all the time what it really needs is a Savior, *the* Savior, whose name is Jesus. He alone can save individuals from sin and nations from corruption and our world from atomic self-destruction.

It is comic, tragic, pathetic, how thinking people will bluff and shuffle and pretend that this is not so, when all the time, deep down in their hearts, they know that it is so. Sometimes it takes a spurt of candidness on the part of some newspaper editorial to express it. The other day we came across this: "The materialism born of the industrial revolution, and which has found its apogee in the terrible conception of the totalitarian State, has brought neither inward peace nor outward security. Never did we more need the Christian message of a Savior." That, from a modern newspaper editor! And why not? Nothing could be truer.

The Incomparable Condescension

In 1934 the following incident was narrated in a British magazine.

The young Prince Edward, heir to the British throne, was visiting a small hospital where thirty-six hopelessly injured and disfigured veterans of the First World War were tended. He stopped at each cot, shook hands with each veteran, and spoke words of encouragement. He was conducted to the exit, but he observed, "I understood you had thirty-six patients here; I have seen only twenty-nine." The head nurse explained that the other seven were so shockingly disfigured that for the sake of his own feelings he had not been taken to see them. The prince insisted that he must see them, and he stayed long enough to thank each soldier for the great sacrifice he had made and to assure each that it should never be forgotten. Then he turned to the nurse again, "But I've seen only six men. Where is the seventh?" He was informed that no one was allowed to see him. Blind, maimed, dismembered, the most hideously disfigured of them all, he was isolated in a room that he would never leave alive. "Please do not ask to see him," the nurse pleaded. The prince, however, could not be dissuaded, and the nurse reluctantly led him into the darkened room. The royal visitor stood there with white face and drawn lips, looking down into what had once been a fine man but was now a horror. Then the tears broke out, and with lovely impulse the prince bent down and reverently kissed the cheeks of that broken hero.

There is one who has stooped far, far lower, to kiss a far, far worse ugliness—not the physical disfigurement of a broken hero whose brokenness called forth reverent gratitude, but the leprous, evil ugliness of corrupt sinners and hard rebels against infinite love! Oh, there never was a story to equal it! Calvary is the gracious, compassionate, redeeming kiss of the condescending Prince of heaven upon these sinful hearts of ours. "Christ Jesus came into the world to save sinners"! Is not that worthy of all acceptation? And if we refuse that love, is not our refusal the most unworthy behavior we could indulge?

Years ago, a worker was eating his lunch high up on the huge glass roof of the famous Crystal Palace in London, when a curious thing happened. For weeks this man had been in deep concern about his soul and wanted to be saved. Suddenly, and apparently from the sky, a sonorous voice rang out, "This is a faithful saying, and worthy of all acceptation, that Christ Jesus came into the world to save sinners!" To that solitary man up there on that high roof, it was the voice of God direct from heaven. He lay full length on the roof, accepted Christ into his heart, and became saved. The fact was that the great Victorian preacher C. H. Spurgeon had gone into the Crystal Palace to test his voice for a meeting there and from the main transept had called out that gospel text with that wonderful, resounding voice of his.

Let us never cease ringing it out, for it expresses in immortal syllables the raison d'être of Bethlehem and Calvary:

> *This is a faithful saying, and worthy of all acceptation,*
> *that Christ Jesus came into the world to save sinners.*

10

The Cross As a Culmination

Father, over all exalted,
By Thy Son to us revealed,
In His manhood Thy true Godhead
Is for evermore revealed:
In His life and death and teaching
'Tis Thyself we see and know;
Love divine we see outreaching
To Thy creatures here below.

Hast Thou made us merely creatures
Who a servile homage bring?
Can we bring no nobler features
Than mere vassals of a king?
Nay, Thy father-heart intended
We should Thy dear children be,
Heart-to-heart forever blended,
Gracious Father-God, with Thee.

And in Christ Thy wondrous union
With our fallen humanhood
Now restores our true communion
With Thy glorious fatherhood:
Oh, for childlike heart-affection
Answ'ring Thine own father-love,
Till we love Thee with perfection
In that sinless world above!

FROM WHICHEVER ANGLE THE Cross of Christ is viewed it is evermore the
supreme expression of divine love and wisdom. This arises from the fact
that in certain profoundly significant ways it is a predetermined culmina-

tion. It is always salutary to review it as such. That is how we here recontemplate it: the Cross as an infinitely significant culmination.

A Culmination of Testing

The Cross is a culmination in a dispensational sense. This is of mighty significance although few perhaps seem clearly to grasp it. Indeed that very word *dispensational* is out of favor in some quarters today. Yet to shut one's eyes to the fact that God has tested human nature in different ways during different periods of history is to ignore one of the plainest disclosures of Scripture. Surely all can see that God could not (and did not) deal with humanity after the Fall in the same way as when human nature was in its original state of sinless innocence and perfect moral harmony. It is equally clear that when the nation Israel was put under the Law of Moses, the covenant people were being tested under a new form of probation or, as some would say, by a new "dispensation."

The truth is that human nature since the Fall has been tested in several successive forms, and this process of probation reached its culmination at Calvary in such a way as to make it the world's crisis. Today things move on such a scale of immensity and at such a pitch of intensity, we are repeatedly told that the greatest crisis of history is impending. We Christian believers, with our eyes on biblical prediction as well as on the evolution of our twentieth century, concur that a super event is looming, and we believe it will occasion the return of our Lord in world empire. Yet even that, globally revolutionary though it will be, is not in the supreme sense the world's crisis. Two thousand years ago our Lord Jesus said, as reported in John 12:31, "Now is the judgment of this world." The Greek word translated "judgment" is *krisis*.

> *Now is the crisis of this world. Now shall the prince of this world be cast out: and I, if I be lifted up from the earth, will draw all men unto me.*

In the most decisive sense the world's crisis was then and there. Not only did that Cross defeat the world-deceiver and provide the world-Redeemer and atone for world-guilt and supremely reveal the love of the world's Creator, it climaxed and ended the divine testing of Adamic human nature. This may be illustrated from our Lord's parable of the vineyard (Luke 20:9–16).

> *A certain man planted a vineyard and let it out to husbandmen, and went into another country for a long time. And at the season he sent a servant to the husbandmen that they should give him of the fruit of the vineyard, but the husbandmen beat him and sent him away empty. And again he sent another servant, but they beat him also and entreated him*

shamefully and sent him away empty. Again he sent a third, and they wounded him also, and cast him out. Then said the lord of the vineyard: What shall I do? I will send my beloved son; it may be they will reverence him. But when the husbandmen saw him they reasoned among themselves, This is the heir; let us kill him, that the inheritance may be ours. So they cast him out of the vineyard, and killed him. What therefore will the lord of the vineyard do to them? He will come and destroy those husbandmen, and will give the vineyard to others.

Just as the owner of that vineyard sent to those wicked farmers a first servant, and then a second, and then a third, and finally his own "beloved son," hoping each time that the farmers would dutifully respond, but only finding out more and more certainly their incorrigible infidelity, so God has repeatedly tested human nature since the Fall. First he made man responsible to him through obedience to individual conscience. We know the result of that testing. It brought on a racial corruption that precipitated the Flood. After that there came a testing of man under human government, that is, the government of humans by humans for God. This began in its simplest form with Noah and the early post-Flood peoples.

The failure under that scheme of testing soon displayed itself and is now patent to all. People have ruled for human greed and aggrandizement instead of for God. That is why Bible prophecy often symbolizes world powers as beasts. Next, God intervened by way of specialized test, using one chosen nation for the experiment. He gave new revelation of himself, of his holiness, righteousness, love, to that covenant people and amid many benefits placed them under obedience to his law through Moses. We call it the dispensation of the Law, and we all know its outcome.

Finally God came in the person of his beloved Son, saying (in the words of the parable), "It may be they will reverence him." In the incarnated Son, God was no longer merely represented; he was visibly embodied for man to see. In the only-begotten Son the love of God took human hands and feet, beat through a human heart, looked on us through human eyes, and listened with human ears. His holiness and love and sovereignty clothed itself in the meek and lowly Jesus. Now, at last, man will respond and prove the innate goodness of his nature! But does he? No, he says, "This is the Heir! Let us kill him!" Man not only slew his incarnate Maker but also crucified him in naked shame—the most awful repudiation conceivable!

Now as it was in the parable—that is, the wicked farmers were under successive testing until they slew the beloved son, but after that were tested no longer, being pronounced finally reprobate and under death penalty—so likewise up to the event of the Cross, Adamic human nature was successively under testing, but since then it is no longer so; verdict has been reached. That Cross finalized and settled it: human nature, as it is by heredity in Adam, is incorrigibly reprobate, rejected, judged. "Now is the judgment of this world"—and that Calvary judgment is by its very finality the crisis of this world. Judgment is passed; albeit the stroke of judgment is graciously delayed so that there may be this present, intervening age of grace, out from which there is to be saved a "multitude which no man could number, of all nations and kindreds and people and tongues" who through regeneration, sanctification, bodily resurrection, and glorification are to constitute the new and immortal humanity in Christ Jesus, the second Adam.

At this point we need to make a sharp distinction lest there be misunderstanding on a very important aspect. We have said that since the Adamic race representatively crucified the incarnate Son of God on Calvary, Adamic human nature is no longer under probation. That indeed is true, but it does not mean that we human beings as responsible individuals are no longer under probation. On the contrary, it is as true as ever: "So, then, every one of us shall give account of himself to God" (Rom. 14:12). The whole of this life on earth is a probation of us as accountable human individuals, and it will register its fateful results in that big destiny that awaits us on the other side of the grave. It is human nature itself that is no longer under probation. In the judicial reckoning of God, when our Lord Jesus died on Calvary, Adamic humanity—the "old man" and the "body of sin" (Rom. 6:6) was judged, crucified, put away, even though judgment on the race as individuals awaits a solemn day yet to be. Or, in the words of 2 Corinthians 5:14, "One died for all; therefore all died in him." Yes, indeed, the Cross was a culmination dispensationally. In the fundamental sense it was the world's crisis.

A Culmination of Identification

But the Cross is also a culmination of identification, the identification of the Son of God with the sons of men. In the biblical revelation, God is made known not as a unity absolute but as God inwardly interrelated by reciprocal subsistencies denoted as Father, Son, Spirit. The relation of Father and Son is innate and uncreated, and it is in the coeternal Holy Spirit that this paternal-filial reciprocity, with all its ineffable endearment, is eternally realized. It must always remain a depthless wonder that the uncreated Son could or would or should become incarnated in creature flesh, yet even that depthless wonder becomes the more astounding when recognized as the portal to a culmination greater with significance than the universe itself. Let me open this up a little.

At his human birth, the Son of God became one of us. Other than the Virgin Birth, no miracle, however psychophysiologically exquisite, could have made him so. If he was to be really one of us, he must be born one of us.

But if by his human birth he became one of us, by his human life he became one with us. He became one with us in our toilings and testings, in our nervous system and sensory reactions and emotional susceptibilities, in our temptations, sicknesses, and sorrowings. Matthew 8:17 declares him to be the living enactment of Isaiah's prediction, "Himself took our infirmities and bare our sickness." It is observable that in Matthew 8:17 (a favorite proof text with modern faith-healing movements) the Greek word translated "bore," that is, "and bore our sicknesses," is not *anaphero*, the word elsewhere used for our Lord's vicarious bearing of our sin, but *bastazo*, a word that rather indicates a sympathetic sharing, indicating his having become one with us. Although he himself did not have any physical sickness (his body being as diseaseless as his soul was sinless), he entered with such exquisite empathy and sympathy into the sickness of those whom he cured that the sorrow of it all entered into him.

But if in his birth he became one of us, and in his life one *with* us, in his death he became Sin-Bearer *for* us. The *of* and the *with* find their ultimate meaning in the *for*. The incarnation at birth and the identification by life lead to substitution in death. First, he wears our humanity. Then he shares our infirmity. Then he bears our iniquity. The first two are climacterics that culminate in the superclimax of the third, that is, the Cross. Take away the first two and the third becomes impossible. Take away the third and the first two become inexplicable. Apart from the Cross, the birth and the life have no redemptive consummation and no decipherable rationale.

> The universe's God, in flesh! But why?
> How could it be, God born, and born to die?
> Yet if 'tis not to rescue souls from hell,
> What reason big enough can any tell?

A Culmination of Obedience

And third, the Cross is a culmination of obedience, the obedience of the eternal Son to the heavenly Father. The Pauline *kenosis* passage in Philippians 2:5–8 is the classic epitome of this:

> *Have this mind in you, which was also in Christ Jesus: who, existing in the form of God, counted not the being on an equality with God a thing to be grasped, but emptied himself, taking the form of a servant, being made in the likeness of men; and being found in fashion as a man, he humbled himself, becoming obedient even unto death, yea, the death of the cross.* (ASV)

This passage is often said to exhibit "the humiliation of Christ." It does no such thing. What it silhouettes for us is his self-humbling. There is a wide difference between humiliation and self-humbling. The former is something that comes through no choice of our own and is often endured unwillingly. The other is a movement of voluntary choice throughout. The key to Paul's *kenosis* passage is in verse 8: "He humbled himself." See now the four levels distinguished in Paul's kenotic stratograph:

1. God—"being in the form of God"
2. Man—"in the likeness of men"
3. Slave—"and the form of a bondman"
4. Felon—"yea, the death of the Cross"

In these four levels there is a threefold movement of descent: (1) from the "form of God" to the "likeness of men"; (2) from the "likeness of men" to the "form of a bondman"; (3) from the "form of a bondman" to the death of a criminal, even the "death of the cross." In this vast self-abnegation from that unthinkable height to that unthinkable depth, the Cross is the culmination of the Son's obedience. It is this culminated obedience of the incarnate Son that gives the Cross its supreme moral virtue and saving value. The first two movements make Jesus time's most arresting character and example, but the culmination at Calvary—and that alone—makes him our eternal Savior. Well may we say to him,

> To die for me, I oft reflect,
> Yet be the God Thou art,
> Is mystery to my intellect
> But sunshine to my heart.

A Culmination of Union

Fourth, the Cross is a culmination of union, the union of the believer with Christ. I know only too gratefully that in the conversion and salvation of a soul, the Cross is the starting point not the culmination; nevertheless, in that connection we need to distinguish between the Cross considered objectively and the Cross considered subjectively. When we first come to Christ as awakened and penitent sinners for salvation from the guilt and penalty and power of sin, we view that Cross objectively, that is, as something outside us, on which something was done for us. But, once we are Christ's, the Cross is meant to become something to us subjectively, that is, to induce something inwardly experiential. It is in this subjective, inward, experiential sense that the Cross is a culmination or, at least, is meant to be a culmination, a culmination in our communion with the Father, in our approximation to Christlikeness, in our experience of Spirit enduement, a culmination in our developing union with Christ.

This may be graphically illustrated from our Lord's birth and life and death on earth. First, he was born into our human life by a supernatural birth. Second, he shared our human life, dwelling and serving among us. Third, he took that life and all that he was to the Cross, where he yielded it up to God in culminating sacrifice and allowed the nails to crucify all that part which belonged to the Adamic creation.

Even so is it in the progress of our spiritual union with him. First, we are born into newness of life in him through a supernatural birth effected in us by the Holy Spirit. Second, we share his life, having become "new creatures" in him. Third, in virtue of that, we are meant to take all that we now are to the place of utter surrender and allow the nails to crucify all that is of egoistic selfism. That is what Paul refers to in Galatians 5:24, "They that are Christ's have crucified the flesh with the affections and lusts."

Going to the Cross in that sense and crucifying "the flesh" there is indeed a spiritual culmination. Remember, it was immediately after the Calvary culmination that our Lord Jesus ascended to the "heavenly places" in a communion more wonderful than ever with the Father, a communion now made even more ineffable by its baptism in the Calvary flood surge of utter devotion. Similarly, when we Christian believers reach our Calvary in a spiritual sense, when we yield ourselves utterly, crucifying "the flesh" with all its ambitions and appetites, we find as never before our ascent into "heavenly places in Christ Jesus," to sit with him there, in a rest and joy and victory high over the world and a communion with him that is the very borderland of heaven.

> A rest where all our soul's desire
> Is fixed on things above;
> Where doubt and guile and fear expire,
> Cast out by perfect love.
>
> Fair fields where peace and love abound,
> And purest joys excel,
> And heavenly fellowship is found,
> A lovely place to dwell.

A Culmination of Relationship

Again, the Cross is a culmination of relationship, of relationship with God. It was so for the Lord Jesus, and in a parallel spiritual sense it is so for us as Christian believers. When the Son of God became the Son of Man, he thereby linked himself with creaturehood. Not in any sense or degree did he or could he cease to be God. There may have been the temporary suspension of certain divine attributes, but he simply could not "empty himself" of what he eternally was and is, even "very God of very God." Nevertheless, by incarnation he became linked forever with our creaturehood through his assumption of a created human nature, and he therefore took the position of the creature in relation to the heavenly Father.

But if in his birth he took relationship with the creature, in his life he accepted the relationship of a subject, a human and earthly subject of the divine and heavenly King. Hence, when the Tempter first approached him with the disguised flattery, "If thou be the Son of God, command that these stones be made bread," our Lord replied, "It is written: Man shall not live by bread alone, but by every word that proceedeth out of the mouth of God" (Matt. 4:3-4). In that reply to the Tempter, our Lord took the lowly place of a creature and a subject. There is no need to give other quotations; his humble, grateful, obedient, and perfect honoring of his relation as subject is stamped on every page of the records.

Still further, however, his acceptance of the creature relationship by birth and of the subject relation in life was culminated in his expression of the sonship relation in his death. He had expressed the sonship relation, along with the creature and subject relation, all the way through, but the sonship relation received its culminant revelation in the Cross, for his going to that Cross was neither a necessity of creaturehood nor the compulsion of subjecthood; it was the voluntary, loving, trusting, uttermost response of glorious sonship. Now they are the three relationships that you and I, as human beings and more especially as born-again believers, sustain toward God—(1) creatures, (2) subjects, (3) sons (let it be understood that the word *sons* in this sense includes believers of both sexes, for in the basic spiritual oneness that is ours in Christ, there is "neither male nor female"). Our first two relationships, as creatures and subjects, are meant to find their culmination in the consciousness and loving consecration of sonship.

God never created us merely to be creatures nor to be only responsible subjects. He created us to be sons. In willing us into life, he did not intend mere recognition by creatures nor mere service by subjects but the responsive communion of intelligent, volitional, affectionate sons. Sin has wrecked our sonship, but in Christ divine grace restores it by blood-bought forgiveness, reconciliation, and regeneration. Yet regeneration is but the beginning of the restored sonship. The culmination point is always the Cross. When we allow the once crucified but now ever-living Jesus to link his arm through ours and persuasively lead us to a place called Calvary, when we bow low enough with him there to say, "Not my will, but thine be done," then we find the true, deep, rich, wonderful meaning and glory of sonship flooding upon us. It is then, and only then, that we break into singing such sacred ecstasies as,

> Oh, this is life! Oh, this is joy!
> My God, to find Thee so!
> Thy face to see, Thy voice to hear,
> And all Thy love to know.

This fullness of life begins where all other life ends—at death. The Cross that culminated our Lord's union with us culminates our union with him. When we love him deeply and dearly enough to give him the crown and scepter of complete dominion over us, when our self-will really abdicates in favor of his will for us, when, in an abandon of adoring worship, we welcome his utter subjugation and monopoly of us, then we suddenly discover that such death to self is the gateway to life more abundant, and that this utter yieldedness is widest freedom!

Some years ago, when certain repairs were being made in Pevensey Abbey, England, part of an ancient stone wall was taken down, and behind it there was found an old Saxon crucifix. Experts estimated that it dated back to around the year 1000. All through the intervening centuries it had lain protectively sealed behind that wall, preserved from wind and weather.

But the main interest of that crucifix is the witness that it bears as to the kind of crucifix in use during earlier times. It is not like the crucifix that in more recent times has been impressed on large areas of Christendom—the figure of a pain-racked victim on a cross. The later Middle Ages, the dark age of papal domination, forced that crucifix continually before people's eyes. The old Saxon crucifix discovered in that old English abbey represents the earliest kind of crucifix—not a dying or dead figure, but a living, regnant Jesus, attired as our High Priest and crowned as King! His eyes, instead of being agonized by suffering or closed in death, are wide open in calm serenity, and from that crucifix he reaches down a hand, *manu Dei,* the hand of God, which is mighty to save!

How eloquent that ancient crucifix is! When we really get down at the foot of that Cross, we find that the place of death is actually the place of life. When we really die in his death, we really begin to live in his life, yes, even to reign with him (Rom. 5:17) as "more than conquerors through him that loved us" (Rom. 8:37).

> Thus prostrate, may I learn of Thee
> What now I dimly prove,
> That Thou, my Lord, canst be to me
> Unutterable love.

11

The Cross As the Ensign of Creation

I do not wonder that some men whose whole strength is given to the investigation of the phenomena and laws of the vast material universe refuse to believe that little man can be the object of any special interest on the part of God. The Most High, as a great philosopher has said, does not seem to manifest Himself in particular volitions, but by universal and unchangeable laws. . . . He destroys in the same storm the ships of an aggressive and tyrannical empire and the fishing-boats of an obscure, harmless and industrious village; smites with the same lightning the churches erected to His own honour and the temples of false gods; permits drought and famine and pestilence to desolate whole nations, so that the virtuous and the wicked perish in a common misery. . . . This is the gospel of science—a gospel harder, sterner, more appalling than the law which came from the thunders and lightnings of Sinai. . . . The Incarnation ("Emmanuel," God with us) is the final answer of God to the natural fear of the human heart that God must be too great and high to have any close and permanent relation with our race.

R. W. Dale

HAVE YOU EVER BEEN afraid of the universe? I know at least one who has! It can be terrifying. There is its frightening immensity that smothers one's imagination and from which there is no escape and that makes our hung-on-nothing little earth seem less than a speck of dust beneath a dinosaur's foot. There is its awesome, depthless, mysterious ocean of seemingly never-ending space, in which even the myriads of colossal stellar galaxies are mere spots of spray on immeasurable billows of an invisible something that cannot be described. There is the ugly look of cruelty on the face of Nature in our own little earthly cosmos: the deadly lightning, the erupting volcano, the frenzied tornado, and that liquid cemetery with its countless victims, the sea. There is the indispensable but inescapable sun, which not only calls forth life but also blazes out torturous death in pitiless desert and forest fire, prodigally destroying plants, insects, birds, animals, humans. There is the horrifying law of fang and claw among the beasts, with its unabating savagery and suffering. To all these may be added drought, famine, flood, earthquake; also narcotic and poisonous plants that allure, deceive, drug, hurt, and demoralize; also the never-ending scourge of pestilence, plague, sickness, disease, deformity, pain, death, bereavement, sorrow, heartbreak.

Beside all those, there is the stark, even more unnerving fact of human sin—hate, lust, violence, murder, war, with all their toll of physical suffering and accompanying mental agony. Far back as we may travel in history, sin is already there. What is most frightening of all is that sin did not begin at the beginning of human history; it came in from somewhere outside and beyond and before. The Bible definitely teaches so. See that startling word "came" in Romans 5:12, "As by one man sin came into the world." Human sin is not a slowly developed racial malignancy from an original microbe in Adam. Sin sprang into the world full-grown. The first son ever born of a human mother was a murderer! And his murder was of the most awful kind—fratricide!

But if sin thus "came," from where did it come? The mystery grows yet more perturbing. There is no disguise in the Bible. It says there is sin outside the world as well as in it. There is sin in eternity as well as in our cosmic time. There is an already existing prince of evil who with clever trickery brought sin into this world of mankind. Nor is he one on his own. He is the "dragon" whose tail draws a third even of "the stars of heaven"; and there is "war in heaven" (Rev. 12:4, 7). There are fallen angels (2 Peter 2:4; Jude 6) and "unclean spirits" or "demons" (Matt. 8:16) that prey on human government, on society, and on individuals (Eph. 2:3; 3:10; 6:12; 1 Tim. 4:1; Rev. 16:14). Rather than veiling this, the Bible exposes it, and human history endorses it with a pen dipped in blood.

I can never forget how the awfulness of it all floored me during the Second World War. Revelations of the scientifically sadistic horrors perpetrated in the Nazi concentration camps were stunning and shocking to us all. Those, along with all the other highly educated savageries and prodigal slaughter in the biggest war of all history, plus history's six thousand years of sin, hatred, greed, cruelty, crime, war, suffering, and death, plus the reflection that such sin, hatred, strife, ugliness existed before ever the first man breathed and in realms of intelligences outside our own little world—all this swept over my mind with desolating effect, the more so because, Sunday by Sunday, as a Christian minister I had to stand up before large congregations and represent the God who allowed it all.

Are Evil and Pain Basic Necessities?

This brought on an ordeal of prostrating doubt. I found myself asking: Are sin and evil, conflict and suffering, an integral and unobliterable part of the universe? Have they always been?—and must they go on forever? Is there some basic necessity for them and their resultant agony? Are they constituents in the very being of the Creator or else inherent in the very nature of things, as the old Gnostic philosophy averred?

Such contemplations may well make any mind shudder. Nor, apparently, was I alone in such thoughts at that time, for just when I was in my own dark and boggy valley of pessimistic groping, I read of an American minister who had suffered a nervous breakdown through such cogitations and had retired from the ministry.

But even before World War II was on us the stark problem was already painfully present to many a troubled thinker. A most brilliant woman, cultured, scholarly, deeply versed in philosophy, and a gifted writer on philosophic-scientific subjects had to be placed under the care of a mental institution. When the specialist asked her family how the trouble began they answered, "She became obsessed by a strange fear—a fear of the universe."

Perhaps it may seem a transition from pathos to bathos, but that unfortunate woman reminds me of another woman—a learned member of a philosophy circle who, in a group debate on the nature of phenomena, eventually conceded, "Well, I am prepared to accept the universe." To many who never soar among the vapory clouds of speculative or dialectical philosophy, that abstruse "acceptance" of the universe may seem like comic nonsense or juvenile naïveté—as though she was condescending to "accept" some legacy from a rich uncle—but to her it was serious enough, and she meant, of course, that she now accepted the universe as being a reality and not an illusion.

That is what we all have to do, that is, accept the universe as a reality. To think that it is an illusion does not make it so. To deny the reality of everything outside our own individual self-consciousness is highbrow inanity. It is the theory itself that is an illusion, not the universe. The rational universe corresponds to the rational human mind as "deep calleth unto deep."

The Philosophy of Omniscience

But the only fully coherent and finally authentic philosophy of the universe is the teaching that we find in the Bible. That is because the Bible presentation of realities is the philosophy not merely of human reason but of divine omniscience (i.e., *omni*, all, plus *science* means the all-science or all-knowing of God). If the Bible is indeed the written Word of God, given by supernatural inspiration, and if our Lord Jesus Christ is verily God the Son incarnate, then six tremendous facts of measureless meaning and comfort are certified to us.

1. Sin and pain have not always been.
2. Sin and pain will not always be: they are not an integral part of the universe.
3. In Christ, God himself has entered into and become one with our human suffering.
4. God has overruled permitted sin and pain to give his universe the supreme revelation: God is love.
5. God overrules present suffering to eventuate in blessing that apparently could not otherwise be.
6. In Christian believers the Holy Spirit witnesses that the present "groaning" creation shall yet be finally "delivered" from all bondage to "corruption" (Rom. 8:20–30).

These six disclosures of biblical revelation will be referred to again, at one point or another, as these studies proceed, but without delay I call attention to number 3—namely, that God himself has become one with our creature suffering—for it transforms the whole question. God has suffered! The demonstration of this in terms of earthly time and visibility is given to us in Christ and, culminatively so, at Calvary. See there the threefold identification of God with us.

1. God suffered for man—bearing our human guilt.
2. God suffered as man—wearing our human nature.
3. God suffered with man—sharing our human sorrow.

That God should thus suffer for man and as man will always be as unspeakably precious to us as it is unspeakably mysterious, but the older I grow, the more do I gratefully marvel at that third aspect—that somehow, with such sweat and tears and blood as were never known elsewhere, God suffered with us. Our sin and suffering hurt him—hurt him that much! And, remember, that staggering revelation of God's heart on Calvary has a continuing present tense. The marks of the nails and the spear, do they not still show in our Lord's resurrection body? Are not the marks still there in his heart? Up yonder, in heaven, is he not still "the Lamb, as it had been slain" (Rev. 5:6)?

In the shortest verse of our New Testament we read, "Jesus wept" (John 11:35). Those tears were with human mourners at a grave. But the tears of Jesus were not just then and there. They are a present-tense reality. Does he not weep at many a human grave today? And are not the tears of Jesus the tears of God through human eyes? Oh, the deep, deep comfort of it! God is no mere distant and unmoved spectator of our human suffering. He is in it with us! Calvary is not only the gauge of his redeeming love for us, it is the gauge of his suffering sympathy with us.

Outside the Bible: No Real Certainty

Of course, if the Bible is not the unique and authentic Word of God, then (let us be blunt) we have no real light of certainty on the problem of human sin and suffering. We are only guessing. Outside the Bible there is no conclusive explanation, no solution.

Furthermore, if our Lord Jesus Christ is not absolutely God, but a creature, as is taught by modern Unitarian sects, then on Calvary it was not God himself who suffered for man, and as man, and with man. The distance between a wriggling earthworm and the very seraphs that flash around the throne of God is as nothing compared with the infinite gulf between those highest of all creatures and the uncreated Creator himself. If Christ is not absolutely God, then the infinite vast between Creator and creature has not been bridged. Nor is there any real sin atonement, for no finite being could ever make the necessarily infinite atonement for infinite transgression and rebellion against an infinite God. Nor have we any proof that God loves us.

If our Lord Jesus Christ were only a creature—even though one of the highest ever created, his death on Calvary (however pathetically beautiful it might be as a martyrdom) could not be a revelation of the love of God. Nay, for an infinite Creator, who at will can create worlds and angels by the million—for him to give a mere creature to that death on Calvary, what revelation of infinite cost or agony or sympathy or love in the heart of God himself could that be? That is ten million leagues away from what really happened on Calvary, namely, that in the person of his uncreated Son, coeternal and coequal with the Father, God gave himself for us!

All this becomes the more wonderful as we survey it in the full biblical revelation concerning the Cross and the universe. God, the greatest of all mysteries but the greatest of all realities, is before all and above all and beneath all and within all and around all and beyond all. Therefore the universe must be a creation that reflects its Creator. It does reflect him, and that is the most reassuring of all guarantees that it is a good universe.

According to the Bible, the universe is *theocentric,* or God-centered. As a corollary of that, the universe is *Christocentric,* or Christ-centered, for the glorious Being now known to us as our Lord Jesus Christ is none other than Immanuel, "God with us" (Matt. 1:23)—even the eternal "Word," or Divine Reason, become "flesh" (John 1:14). The Scripture says that in a startlingly unique way the universe centers in him and in such a way that it is redempto-centric. Strange as it may sound to some ears, our whole cosmic[1] system, indeed the whole universe, is evangelical.

Of all the universe's endless wonders, that is the biggest and the best. It makes the universe safe as well as good.

Where Is the Universe's Center?

From earliest times people have sought to ascertain the center of the phenomenal cosmos surrounding them. Outside of and prior to biblical revelation, primitive people apparently assumed that the place where they lived was the center of everything. Then, as people spread ever more widely over the earth and realized something of its bigness, they concluded that there must be one place on it which is the world's center. Comical as it now seems to us, as late as the fifteenth century A.D., when Columbus sailed out west across the Atlantic, people in Europe were sure that he would float too far from the center and then fall over the earth's edge into a nameless void.[2]

Fortunately for Columbus, however, Nicolaus Copernicus, the founder of modern astronomy, was proving (just in time!) that the earth was round—a ball swinging in space and rotating on an axis. Along with that, people presumed that our earth itself was the supremely important center, around which the sun and moon and stars circled respectfully.

Next, about a century after Copernicus, came Galileo Galilei, the father of the modern telescope. Christendom was shocked to learn that our earth is not the most important world God made. It is not the center of everything. Like the other planets, it swings round the sun. So the sun now becomes the great center of creation!

Copernicus (1473-1542), who was the real originator of the revolutionary new ideas, and Galilei (1564-1642) and his brilliant contemporary Johannes Kepler (1571-1630) all had a bad time of it at the hands of the stultified ecclesiastical authorities of the times. Copernicus knew how hostile the church (i.e., the Roman church) would be to such a revolutionary new concept of our world and solar system. Recognizing that hostility, he left his monumental work unpublished for forty years (the first printed copy was issued on the very day he died). Seventy years later the work was officially banned because it "degraded" the earth to a subordinate position in the solar system! Both Galilei and Kepler were summoned before the Inquisition. Galilei was forced to abjure the new "science." Kepler's writings were publicly burned. For fifteen hundred years Christendom had remained unquestioningly tied to Aristotle's dictum: "Planets move in circles round the earth, for the circle is the paramount shape of all shapes."

But when the real truth about things is uncovered, no power on earth can prevent its eventual release. The new learning proved stronger than the old prejudice. Science was not only discovering new dimensions but also was dispersing medieval fogs. Bewildering though it was, it soon became apparent that our solar system was outclassed by titanic suns and revolving systems enormous distances away in a seemingly illimitable ocean of space. Where, now, was the center of the universe? Science answered that there must be some colossal superstar, inconceivably magnitudinous, with such centrifugal force and centripetal magnetism as to give the whole vast totality of phenomena a centric coherence.

The Goal of Discovery

Even that idea had to give way to further discovery. Stronger and stronger telescopes swept around a bigger and still bigger universe. There was no end in sight anywhere. Twenty million "light years" away—and still an endless profusion! Where, now, is the universe's center? Or is there a center? Is the universe actually endless, boundless, infinite? For a time that idea held a tentative sway, but it was too fantastic to be valid. Absolute boundlessness would mean a universe infinite and eternal, but that is unthinkable in view of the universe's fluxionary processes such as the continual interplay between conservation and dissipation of energy. The universe does not run on its own uncreated, self-perpetuating dynamo. Energy replenishes it from somewhere outside itself. So, since it is not self-sustaining, it cannot be either self-created or eternal. The universe had a beginning. It has both boundary and center. And if matter could not create itself, much less could it invent cosmic law and order with all their intricate, reciprocal processes. The center of the universe is Mind!

Yes, science at last got there! The center of the universe is Mind. Startling confirmation of this has recently come in the splitting of the atom. The old concept of matter as having a concrete solidarity is gone forever. Matter, so-called, is energy in visible, tangible extension. The atom is no longer an ultimate, indivisible particle but is itself an infinitesimal universe of intense energy in motion, in the form of nucleus, protons, neutrons, and electrons. The "solid universe" is not strictly solid at all. The whole, utterly vast, systematic, and rational operation of things that we call the phenomenal universe receives its constant energy from a prior, uncreated, all-transcendent, immanent, omnipresent Intelligence, an absolutely ultimate Mind; or, in other phrase, a personal Creator. That (or, rather, He) is the center of the universe.

Of course, the Bible has been saying this in nonscientific, beautifully simple words for ages, but if people now please to call it a discovery of modern science, let them say so, for the Bible says much more than that—more than telescopes, spaceships, or any other contrivance of clever technology could discover in aeons. For two thousand years our New Testament has been telling us who this center Mind is, and modern science will yet bow its knee to him in recognition and obeisance.

At the center of the universe, says Holy Writ, is the One who is now known to us as our Lord Jesus Christ, and this has an infinitely profound bearing on the mystery of permitted sin, war, and woe. It throws a flood of revealing light on why God created our present world and mankind even though he knew in advance the devastating havoc that would be caused by sin. Let me quote a couple of superb New Testament affirmations pertaining to this.

John's Prologue

Take first the opening verses of the gospel according to John. See chapter 1, verses 1–4, 14:

> *In the beginning was the Word, and the Word was with God, and the Word was God. The same was in the beginning with God. All things were made through him, and without him was not anything made that hath been made. In him was life, and the life was the light of men.... And the Word became flesh, and dwelt among us (and we beheld his glory; glory as of the only-begotten from the Father), full of grace and truth.*

These verses tell us that our Lord, as the divine Word, or Logos, was eternally preexistent before ever he "became flesh" and walked this earth. They do not say merely that he was from the beginning (i.e., of "all things," v. 3), but that he already "was." It is not even that in the beginning he did something. No, the Greek is unmistakably plain that in the beginning the Logos already "was"—indicating an uncreated, eternal priority such as can belong only to God.

Observe, next, that he is called the "Word," or, in the Greek, the Logos. Whether in classical Greek or in Gnostic philosophy or in New Testament usage, *Logos* means always and only that which expresses. How exquisite a designation it is of the preexistent Lord who in this same context is also called the "Son" (vv. 14, 18)! With fine differentiation it indicates inside the Godhead personal distinction and yet essential oneness. "The Word was with God" (distinction). "And the Word was God" (oneness). You can separate a thought from a word (distinction), but you cannot separate a word from a thought (oneness). A person born deaf and dumb has thoughts but no words. The same is true of the more intelligent animals lower than humans. A thought, therefore, is separable from a word. Yet a word is inseparable from a thought, for the very fact that a word is spoken implies the thought that speaks it. Even so, Christ, the eternal Word, is distinct from the first person of the divine Triunity, yet inseparable from him.

Those two designations, the "Word" and the "Son," in John's prologue, protect each other from misunderstanding. To think of our Lord only as the eternal "Word" might suggest, to some, merely an impersonal quality or attribute of God. On the other hand, to think of him only as the "Son" might suggest to others a personal but created being. The two titles together safeguard us from both errors. Our Lord, as the eternal "Word" and the "Son" who is "in the bosom of the Father" (v. 18) is both eternal and personal.[3]

Enter, the Universe

See, now, John's further statement about the Logos. It takes little space to say it, but it staggers one's imagination: "All things were made through him, and without him was not anything made that hath been made." The phrase translated as "all things" is the Greek equivalent of our own word *universe*.[4] Here, then, through Christ as the expressive divine "Word," the whole universe finds its originating and continuating expression! Therefore, not only is he prior to all things but also is bigger than all things. He is the originating source and life of the whole universe. Indeed, that is what John's Spirit-guided pen immediately adds: "In him was the life; and the life was the light of men." So, he is the "life" of all human beings, and the "light" of all intelligence.

How some of our newfangled Unitarian cults today can make such Scripture statements mean no more than a mere creature-Christ passes my comprehension. If ever carefully chosen words had clear meaning, those in John's prologue have. Our Lord, as the eternal Word, is the First Cause and sustainer of the universe.

This is the mysterious, preexisting, all-glorious Being who by incarnation entered our humanity and its history. See verses 9–10, 14 again:

> *He was the true light . . . coming into the world. . . . He was in the world, and the world was made through him, and the world knew him not. . . . And the Word became flesh, and dwelt among us; and we beheld his glory; glory as of the only-begotten from the Father; full of grace and truth.*

Here is conclusive further evidence that the eternal Word is personal. No mere impersonal attribute could be born of a human mother and walk the earth. Here, too, is further corroboration that the eternal Word is distinct from the Father. See verse 18: "The only-begotten Son, who is in the bosom of the Father, he hath declared him." As the eternal "Word" he comes to express the truth of God. As the eternal "Son" he comes to express the heart of God. Observe: he is "full of grace and truth," that is, full of grace to redeem man and full of truth to reveal God. Yes, the God-Man, Revealer-Redeemer has come! Gaze on him. If he is the origin and life force of the creation, then God is good, and the universe is safe.

The Pauline Version

For the second of our New Testament quotations turn to Colossians 1:14–20. In it we have the Pauline version. Who can measure its breadth and length and depth and height?

> *In whom [Christ] we have our redemption, the forgiveness of our sins: Who is the image of the invisible God, the firstborn of all creation. For in him were all things created, in the heavens and upon the earth, things visible and things invisible, whether thrones or dominions or principalities or powers: all things have been created through him, and unto him. And he himself [emphatic] is before all things, and in him all things consist [i.e., hold together, ASV mg]. And he is the head of the body, the church: who is the beginning, the firstborn from the dead; that in all things he might have the preeminence. For it pleased the Father that in him should all the fulness dwell, and through him to reconcile all things unto himself, having made peace through the blood of his cross; yes, through him, whether things on the earth or things in the heavens.*

Here again see the universal Christ. He is the "image of the invisible God; the firstborn of all creation." Under a strange misunderstanding, Unitarian sects have overliterally pressed that word "firstborn" to mean that if Christ was "born," even though the firstborn, he had a beginning, and therefore cannot be God. But they have failed to grasp the difference between John's prologue and this Pauline passage in Colossians. John's prologue shows the eternal "Word" and "Son" in his preexistence, that is, before he "became flesh, and dwelt among us": whereas in Colossians Paul is showing us that same supercosmic Christ in his now-glorified humanity. It is as the glorified God-Man that he is now the visible "image" of the invisible God, for all to see. And it is as the glorified God-Man that he is the "firstborn" of all creatures. His now glorified humanity was born, and did have a beginning (so let Unitarian expositors press that word *born* to the full, if they will); and his then-beginning humanity was conjoined to his eternally preexisting divinity.

Obviously Paul does not mean that our Lord was the first to be born of a human mother (that distinction belongs to Cain). He uses that expression "firstborn" in just the same way as he reemploys it in verse 18, where he says: "And he is the beginning, the firstborn from the dead." Our Lord was not the "firstborn" from the dead in the sense that he was the first to come back from death (there are six prior instances given in Scripture), but he was the first to come back in a life that death can never touch again (all others who were brought back to life died again).

The eternal but now-incarnate and now-glorified Lord is indeed the first-born of all creatures by a real birth and resurrection such as no one ever had before him, a birth and resurrection into a life and immortality that nothing can ever destroy! Also, in the coming resurrection of the saints, he will be consummatingly revealed as literally the firstborn of the new humanity, the "firstborn from the dead" of countless millions of others who through him are "begotten from the dead" to a life of similar immortality and glory.

Now note again how Paul here identifies this glorified God-Man with the eternally preexisting Logos.

> *For in him were all things created, both in the heavens and upon the earth, things visible and things invisible, whether thrones or dominions or principalities or powers, all things have been created through him and unto him. And he himself is before all things, and in him all things cohere.*

Here is the infinite Christ, the all-preceding, all-surrounding, all-centering, all-sustaining, all-governing One in whom the whole universe holds together!

But the staggering supersurprise is that this infinite God-Man, with his glorified human body, has nail prints in his hands and feet! He once wore a crown of thorns and hung in naked shame and depthless suffering on a felon's cross! And because of who he is, that cross has universal outreaches. See verse 20 again: "It was the good pleasure of the Father through him to reconcile all things to himself, having made peace through the blood of his cross; through him, whether things on earth or things in the heavens"! So the universe is not only theocentric and Christocentric, it is redempto-centric. Were it not so, God would never have created.

Incomprehensible Magnitudes

We are now on the fringes of immense meaning that our finite minds can only dimly grasp. The Cross of Christ is no mere event of earth and time. It is the crux of the whole creation and the focus point of eternity. That Cross was in the heart of the Deity ages before it was erected on the hill of Calvary. Ponder well these further statements of Scripture.

> *Ye were redeemed, not with corruptible things, with silver or gold, from your vain manner of life handed down from your fathers, but with precious blood, as of a lamb without blemish and without spot, even the blood of Christ, who indeed was foreknown [or predecided] before the foundation of the world [kosmos] but was manifested at the end of the times for your sake (1 Peter 1:18–20).*

> *And all who dwell upon the earth shall worship him [the beast] whose names are not written in the book of life of the Lamb slain from the foundation of the world (Rev. 13:8).*[5]

So, then, away back before ever mankind and the present cosmos began on this planet, the Lamb was there; the Cross was there! Yes, the Evangel was there! The Gospel of redemption was anticipatively there, in the prognosis and purpose of our Maker! The Cross of Christ is no afterthought or emergency measure of a surprised Creator after catastrophe has struck. It is the precosmic forethought, the very aegis, or ensign, under which the world and its environ were created. See Paul's flash of light on this in 2 Timothy 1:9, and again in his letter to Titus (1:2–3):

> *Who [God] saved us, and called us with a holy calling; not according to our works, but according to his own purpose and grace, given us in Christ Jesus before the ages began [lit., before the ages of time].*

> *In hope of eternal life which God, who cannot lie, promised before the world began [lit. before the ages of time], but manifested in its own season, even his word, in the proclamation [or message] with which I was entrusted, according to the commandment of God our Saviour [lit., of our Savior-God].*

The Gospel of divine grace, then, was singing in the mind and heart of God long before sin set the world weeping. And (gladdest sunshine that ever broke on human minds) the Creator himself is here named by the Holy Spirit through Paul, "our Savior-God"! His very Godhead is saviorhood, which is the sublimest of all possible guarantees that the universe is beneficent.

The usual idea behind Christian evangelism and missionary enterprise is that of carrying salvation tidings to a lost world. We do not here criticize that. On the contrary, oh, for more voices to tell people! But we are closer to Scripture if our message is good tidings to a world that was redeemed even before it fell. To present the message in that way, would, I think, have much more influence on many intelligent minds to whom God and his lost world are a problem rather than a Gospel.

When we preach the Cross of Christ as being only, or even mainly, a thing of time, an event in history, an act of wicked men, we greatly impoverish and constrict its appeal. That Calvary crucifixion (real and awful though it was), perpetrated by people but overruled by God, was but the momentary concentration into dramatic earthly visibility of a supercosmic reality preceding all time, outbounding all history, bigger than the world, extensive as the universe, the profoundest, sublimest reality in the heart of "our Savior-God"!

12

The Cross As the Rainbow of Government

When God said, "Let us make man in our own image," He had in view, not the mere rudimental man of Eden who He knew would fall into sin, but the new man in Christ and as glorified with Him for ever. It was that consummate ideal which moved God to creation as a whole and to every feature embraced in it. . . . It was the ground purpose of the universe and therefore God's forethought for mankind. . . . Every child born into this world, therefore, is born not only of the fallen first Adam, but also under the aegis of the redemptive system. Every child is a potentially redeemed being because of this antecedent purpose and provision of God's grace.

Henry C. Mabie

ALL THAT WE HAVE been saying thus far about the universal dimensions of the Cross ties in with the wonderful disclosures that the Bible makes concerning the throne of the universe. One of the most magnetic and meaningful names for that throne occurs in Hebrews 4:18: "Let us therefore come boldly unto the throne of grace."

The throne of God is often referred to in Scripture, but specially there are two passages in which it is actually described by the use of physical symbols or appearances that make intelligible to us its holy splendor and governmental nature. Those two passages are the book of the prophet Ezekiel, chapter 1, and the book of the Revelation, chapter 4. Look first at that opening vision of Ezekiel.

Out from the fiery heart of a whirling storm-cloud, Ezekiel sees those four living creatures, that is, the cherubim (1:5), each with four faces— lion, ox, man, eagle (symbolizing strength at its greatest, service at its meekest, intelligence at its highest, and spirituality the most soaring). Of the four lion faces, one looked north, another south, another east, another west; so was it with the ox and man and eagle faces. Therefore each four of each kind saw everything, everywhere, all the time. Thus the four heavenly beings had no need to turn (v. 12). Each had four wings and four hands, for swiftness and service in undeviating prosecution of the divine will. Their appearance was as "burning coals of fire, like the appearance of torches" (v. 13)—utter holiness. Beside were four vast, awesome wheels (v. 15), which reached from earth to heaven: a "wheel within a wheel," that is, one running east-west, and the other north-south, therefore never needing to turn either left or right in order to be at any spot on earth with lightning speed. Moreover, those gigantic wheels, which connected those flaming seraphs of heaven with earth, were full of eyes that looked simultaneously in every direction from their crosswise rims (v. 18).

Those flaming beings and those vast wheels full of eyes, moving by a power from above, vividly express the divine holiness, omnipotence, all-seeing omniscience, and omnipresence. Ezekiel gazes and wonders. Then, suddenly, the climax of the vision breaks upon him. A voice calls from the expanse above the seraphs and those earth-patrolling wheels. Ezekiel looks up and sees "the likeness of a throne as the appearance of a sapphire stone." On the throne is a fire-enveloped Figure having "the likeness as the appearance of a Man."

The language is cautious, the final picture necessarily having the vagueness of the indescribable. The Figure is wreathed in fire. There is a center glow as of luminous or molten metal, "amber," and a "brightness round about." The symbols are again expressive of awe-inspiring holiness and unapproachable glory. Ezekiel at once recognizes in it "the appearance of the likeness of the glory of Jehovah" and falls before it in prostrate adoration.

What is the main purpose of the vision and its overwhelming climax? We are meant to see in it that over all permitted events on earth and over all supernatural powers in the heaven is the sovereign throne and all-controlling directive of the infinite Jehovah himself. Beyond all doubt, Ezekiel was seeing in that flame-clad "likeness of a Man" the preincarnate God the Son, even as did Isaiah when he cried out in awed subduement, "Mine eyes have seen the King!"[1]

But even that is not all. Ezekiel suddenly catches sight of something after and beyond everything else, something that he can never forget. He has seen a rainbow round about that throne: "As the appearance of the bow that is in the cloud in the day of rain, so was the appearance of the brightness round about."

The Patmos Vision

Significantly enough, in the only other Scripture passage that describes heaven's throne of thrones, that is, Revelation 4, that encircling rainbow appears again. From that apocalyptic vision we quote just verses 2–3.

I was in the Spirit: and, behold, there was a throne set in heaven, and One sitting upon the throne. And he that sat was, to look upon, like a jasper stone and a sardius; and there was a rainbow round about the throne, like an emerald to look upon.

That rainbow around the throne immediately connects back to the rainbow and its meaning in Genesis 9:12-16:

This is the token of the covenant which I make between me and you and every living creature that is with you, for perpetual generations. I do set my bow in the cloud. . . . And I will look upon it that I may remember the everlasting covenant between God and every living creature of all flesh that is upon the earth.

That rainbow sign of perpetual mercy and everlasting covenant was given just after the destroying judgment indicted by the Flood. Ezekiel was given to see it arching the ineffable throne just as the desolating final stroke of divine judgment fell on Israel and Judah. Later, on Patmos, John saw it just before the culminating judgments (in vision) at the end of the present age. In each case that rainbow still gleams, yes, outshines the thunders and lightnings of judgment storm. Finally, as if to show us yet once again the meaning of that rainbow for us we find, in the Apocalypse, that just before the seventh angel sounds his trumpet, bringing on the earth the very last woe of the divine wrath, this happens:

And I saw another strong angel coming down out of heaven, arrayed with a cloud; and the rainbow was upon his head. (Rev. 10:1)

Then, even as that last woe breaks loose, with its thunders and earthquake and great hail (11:19), to "finish the mystery of God" (10:7), that is, his dealing with permitted sin on earth, "great voices in heaven" began to sing: "The kingdoms of the world are become our Lord's and his Christ's; and he shall reign to the ages of the ages" (11:15). Once again, and now forevermore, the rainbow outrides the storm!

The Rainbow and Divine Grace

Now it is the thunders and lightnings and that gleaming rainbow which together make the throne of the universe a throne of grace. How? And why? It is because of what that *grace* really is. What is divine grace? The usual idea is that grace is love in action, love reaching out to save the lost, or some kindred idea. But no, divine grace is a composite. We realize, of course, that abstract mental and moral qualities or states such as goodness, hate, hope, fear, cannot be dissected, yet in a true sense grace is a union of two such qualities or attitudes. It is a blend of divine justice and divine love. That rainbow overarching the throne of the Deity expresses this—as becomes clearer the more we reflect on it.

We must not fall into the old error of departmentalizing the moral being of God—one part holiness, another part love; one part justice, another part mercy. If we do, it is easy to imagine a dissension inside the divine mind, with justice on the one side fiercely demanding that sinners be punished and love on the other side begging that they be leniently absolved. God must never be thought of as thus inwardly divided against himself. The will of God is always the activity of his total being.

Yet even so, if we may put it this way, when sin originated among freewilled creatures in God's universe, it provoked into existence an *antinomy,* or operation of self-opposites, in God. It accentuated certain qualities of the divine mind into polarities. It not only accentuated them, it called them into new exercise. The divine holiness must necessarily condemn sin, and it immediately reacted with demand that the evil be judged, that such treason against such benign government of the universe be requited absolutely and the broken harmony atoned for. Simultaneously the love that is also God reacted with outreach to redeem and restore.

The Lamb, slain "from before the foundation of the world," is the answer. The Cross, first in the heart of God and later on the brow of Calvary, expresses those two seemingly antagonistic polarities—holy justice and holy love in perfect union. The very justice that passes the sentence on us endures the penalty for us. The very holiness that inflexibly condemns us itself vicariously suffers to restore us. The very government that dooms us sides with us to deliver us. It is fact as well as paradox that we are saved just as much by the divine judgment as from it. On the other hand, the divine love that reaches out to forgive and embrace will do so only as the divine holiness is honored and the moral law of the universe is vindicated even though the cost is Calvary.

Grace, a Synthesis

Grace is the synthesis of this sin-abhorring divine holiness and this compassionate divine love. It is the two united as one in cooperative action—to redeem and reclaim. Both holiness and love are mental and moral qualities, yet they are not the same kind of quality as each other. Holiness is a state or condition in one's own being. Love is an outreach to others. Holiness is intransitive: it does not require an object outside itself; love is transitive: it always has an object. In other words, holiness is a condition, whereas love is a disposition. We do not *holy* anyone, but we do *love* someone. Holiness and love, however, are vitally necessary to each other. They must infuse each other. Holiness apart from love is frigid. Love apart from holiness lacks highest motive and safeguard. In God both holiness and love are perfect. They unite utterly, to honor the demands of the broken moral law yet to save the fallen creature. The concentration point of their union is Calvary, the Cross, the Lamb. The result is grace. This therefore means that grace is not merely a movement to save us from an angry God; it is that Savior-God himself, inwardly self-propitiated by self-suffering, calling us back to our true home in his bosom.

Simultaneously with the beginning of sin in his universe, the ages-long expiation began in the infinite mind of the Creator. This timeless reality, we repeat, became historically and visually objectified, focalized, and culminated on Calvary. In that Calvary deed, as Dr. A. H. Strong puts it, the eternal "telescoped into moments of time"; as another has said, in that "one eternal moment of time, God himself in Man was forsaken by God." Without in any sense palliating the guilt of our Lord's slayers, we may say that, in the deepest meaning of all, on that cross hangs a self-crucified God. The blood that sprinkles the throne of God and transforms that governmental tribunal into the mercy seat is his own blood! Yes, indeed, for in Acts 20:28, the Holy Spirit through Paul uses that very expression of God: "his own blood"!

It is that cross which puts the rainbow round the throne in heaven. It is because that rainbow gleams there that it is the throne of *grace*. And that radiant rainbow remarkably symbolizes grace. Remember: the rainbow is "in the cloud." It is the storm and the sunshine together that produce the rainbow, even as it is the divine holiness and love together, or the divine justice and mercy together, that issue in grace. In the words of Psalm 85:10, "Righteousness and peace have kissed each other." So, in Revelation 4, the "lightnings and thunderings" still "proceed" from the throne, but together with that overarching rainbow of the "everlasting covenant." They belong together in grace.

What is the rainbow? It is light refracted in its seven constituent colors—all seven distinct yet in such exquisitely perfect blend that no one can quite discern where one hue shades into another. So is it with the moral attributes of God. If we think of any of those moral attributes as being separate from the others or as being the principal or as being the center of a circle around which the others subsidiarily rotate, we are wrong. In their indivisible totality they are the moral being of God.

Those attributes must never be thought of as mere abstractions. It is utterly important to grasp that they are realities in the infinite divine consciousness, for they add up to this wonderful meaning, that God feels. However, the point that we are here reemphasizing is that the appearing of sin in the hitherto sinless universe immediately vivified into contrastive reaction the outflowing divine holiness and the outreaching divine love, that is, the one demanding atonement, and the other providing it. Calvary is the synthesis that brings to us the Gospel of saving grace.

The Inevitable Target

That throne of grace, reflect, is the administrative center of the universe, and the preexistent Christ, as the Father's coequal and infinitely beloved Son, sits there by eternal propriety. Everything inevitably centers in him. With this in mind look again at that Pauline passage in Colossians.

> *In him [Christ] were all things created, both in the heavens and upon the earth, things visible and things invisible; whether thrones or dominions or principalities or authorities; all things have been created through him, and unto him; and he himself is before all things, and in him all things hold together.*

He is not only prior to all and bigger than all; he is center to all. Both centripetally and centrifugally the entire universe functions round him. All the concentric circles of phenomena and sentient beings, from the distant circumference to the innermost ring, converge to their focus point in him. All the glory, all the sustaining energy, all the administrative control, and all the moral meaning of the whole creation meets in him and emanates from him.

In Isaiah 53:6 we read: "All we like sheep have gone astray; we have turned every one to his own way; and Jehovah hath laid on him the iniquity of us all." Note that verb, "hath laid." So far as I can find, nowhere else is the Hebrew verb so translated. Its truer sense is to "meet" or to "meet together." So read it: "Jehovah hath made to meet together in him the iniquity of us all." That universal Christ who is the center of all is necessarily the target of all. A world has gone wrong—our world. Immediately it registers in him. There is sin—Satanic, angelic, demonic,[2] human. It has to "meet in him." There is but the one center, where all "meet." Isaiah 53:6 is even bigger than it looks! There is no other who could be our race's Sin-Bearer. Long before he is born of Mary into our humanity, he calls to us through the pre-Christian Hebrew prophets: "Look unto me and be ye saved, all the ends of the earth: for I am God, and there is none else."

Oh, the vast, ungraspable mystery of divine response and suffering that lies behind Gethsemane, Gabbatha, and Golgotha! Think of it: the very throne of the universe sprinkled with that blood of atonement and therefore overarched by that rainbow—the rainbow of grace! See that Cross anew, hid in God through ages before ever human history began, and, in Pauline phrase, the Creator himself our Savior-God!

> Higher than heaven; deeper than hell;
> Wider than sin's wide curse;
> Deeper than creature-minds can tell,

Vast as the universe;
Bigger, and bigger still it grows,
That Cross on Calvary,
Till God alone who hung there knows
Its full immensity.

Coextensiveness of the Cross

The rainbow round the throne of God means that the message and operation of the Cross are coextensive with the government exercised from that throne. Far as that government reaches, the Cross is in it. This means that it is coextensive, yes, more than coextensive, with the sin that necessitated it. As the extent and the problem of sin are far bigger than this human world of ours, so also is the salvation and solution. The extra-terrestrial inclusiveness of the Cross is definitely stated in the latter part of the Colossian passage quoted earlier:

> *In him [Christ] all the fulness of the Godhead was pleased to dwell. And [God] having made peace through the blood of his cross, by him to reconcile all things unto himself; through him, whether things upon the earth, or things in the heavens (Col. 1:19–20).*

According to Bishop J. B. Lightfoot (there was never an abler or truer interpreter of New Testament Greek) this passage teaches "an absolute and complete reconciliation of universal nature to God." Does that sound too strongly stated? Read the text again. Let the scope and sweep of its last phrase really hit the mind. There it is: "all things . . . on earth and in the heavens." It does not do away with a coming Judgment Day or with gehenna, but it tells of a final harmony between every part of the universe and that rainbow-circled throne. Whatever may be the ultimate destiny of a seemingly incorrigible monster of evil such as Satan and of other finally impenitent evil beings, this is made sure: evil will be so banished from all possible further contact with the myriads of other intelligences in God's universe that the restored full harmony can never be broken again.

The Preaching of the Cross

I know, of course, that in preaching the Cross, especially to the unconverted and unenlightened, we must mainly keep to those aspects of it that bear directly upon the unsaved sinner. We must present it as a propitiation, as an expiation, as a vicarious and substitutionary atonement—as a ransom, a redemption, a reconciliation—and in all those aspects it must be exhibited as the means through which divine forgiveness and restoration come to us human beings. I realize, too, that far more often than otherwise we must needs keep to the simplicities rather than expatiate on the profundities.

Yet what need there is today for a worthier, ampler setting forth of the Cross! In much that goes by the name of Gospel preaching, if the Cross is prominent at all, it is presented solely as a means of escape for the guilty sinner and with a comparative paltriness all too unworthy of the full-orbed New Testament doctrine. There is great need today to set forth what the Cross means to God and the kind of God it reveals.

Do not many of us need to start all over again to preach the "wondrous Cross"? Are we not needing to uplift it anew, in its expansive New Testament aspects, until Christian believers, and others too, marvel with subdued minds at its immeasurable span and transcendent moral glory? We need to be astonished at it again as the precosmic and supercosmic event eclipsing all others, as indeed the biggest thing that even Deity ever did. Yes, and it needs preaching by those who live continually in a vivid awareness of its sublime immensity.

How many there are today, among well-educated or reflective persons, who are turned away or even repelled by a constricted or deficient or warped presentation of the Cross! How many there are who seriously yet quite aberrantly suppose that what happened at Calvary was no more than a shocking human atrocity or bad blunder that God, in an emergency countermove, opportunely adapted to his own purpose and used as a propitiation! Even worse, there are more than a few who think that God himself predestined that crime and then in due time actualized it through men preordained to commit it—thus making God a party to their vicious perfidy, even indeed the instigator of it! How many there are who see the Cross merely as a long-ago local crucifixion without recognizing it as a timeless and universal atonement! How few there are, comparatively, who see the real Cross!

God certainly did foreknow what was to happen on that "green hill outside the city wall," and he accordingly foreplanned that it should become the altar on which "the Lamb slain from the foundation of the world" should be offered. Such foreknowing, however, is very different from predetermining. God never predestined Judas to betray Jesus or Pilate to sentence him or Israel's leaders to slay him—any more than he ever predetermined that anyone shall now reject him (fearful vagary of hyper-Calvinism!). But the omniscient God, to whom the past and the present and the future are an eternal though successive "now," did see, before ever time began, the Eternal Son, the Word, become flesh; God did see freewilled human beings freely acting (though under Satanic incitement) to bring about that Calvary death, and God did plan accordingly. Without in any way overriding the freedom of the human will, God superimposed an overruling of it. He anticipated and overruled it in such a way as to make it the eternally decisive climacteric of collision and contrast between sin and holiness, between the serpent and the Savior, between the dragon and the Lamb, between God and archrebel Lucifer—so that all the world, indeed, all the worlds, might see how ugly sin really is and what it costs the divine love to redeem.

The Indestructible Guarantee

I could not easily put into words what it meant to me when the bigger, pretemporal, preterrestrial, supercosmic meanings of the Cross really broke through into my own thinking. It gave a new poise of reassurance to my mind that nothing since, either outward or inward, has disturbed.

Everything began to look different. God and the universe, time and history, permitted sin and suffering, the future of our world, and destiny beyond the grave all took on a new complexion. It did not suddenly answer all the interim questions relating to permitted troubles and injustices now, but it utterly answered that deep-down question beneath all others as to the integrity and safety and beneficence of the universe—and of God. Problems of providence, painful enigmas, poignant puzzles of permitted injustice, and other mysteries still remained, but now I saw the light of that guaranteeing Cross streaming with prophetic promise through them all. In William Cowper's words, behind every "frowning providence" there was the "smiling face" of temporarily hidden good purpose. Through every dark cloud I saw that gleaming rainbow of evangelical covenant which overarches the throne of grace.

With deepening adoration I began to discern more surely that in a way that only the crimson of Calvary could express it, God had given himself not only for me, but to me, if my loving trust would have him! I began to see, in Calvary's boundless dimensions and unobliterable guarantee, the love that would never give me up and never let me go. All fear became inexcusable, except the fear of grieving such a God, who had now made me so willingly his again, and himself so dearly mine. It set my heart singing with richer gratitude, Wade Robinson's words:

> Heav'n above is softer blue,
> Earth around is sweeter green;
> Something lives in ev'ry hue
> Christless eyes have never seen!
> Birds with gladder songs o'erflow,
> Flow'rs with deeper beauties shine,
> Since I know, as now I know,
> I am His, and He is mine.
>
> Things that once were wild alarms
> Cannot now disturb my rest,

> Closed in everlasting arms,
> Pillowed on the loving breast!
> Heav'n and earth may fade and flee,
> First-born light in gloom decline,
> But while God and I shall be,
> I am His, and He is mine.

The Language of Calvary

In a language that all the worlds understand, the cross of Calvary spells out this fundamental wonder, that when God punishes he suffers. It hurts him to hurt. We catch echoes of this in different parts of Scripture. We hear it in Isaiah 63:9: "In all their affliction he was afflicted." When Pharisee Saul was fanatically distraining the disciples of the Nazarene, the risen Lord accosted him with "Saul, Saul, why persecutest thou *Me?*" Long ago, when Patriarch Abraham took his beloved Isaac up Mount Moriah, which of the two suffered the more—the handsome young Isaac as he let his father bind him[3] on the altar to be killed, or his agonized father as he lifted up the knife, not knowing that God would at that moment intervene to spare both of them?

Years ago, in Mississippi, I had a meal with an elderly farmer who was widely esteemed for his acts of brotherly help to both blacks and whites and also because of his seven sons, all of whom had acquitted themselves with notable distinction and high ideals both at school and in the community. Many a father, I told him, would be grateful to know the secret of rearing such sons. He replied, "I always followed the scriptural principle that if you spare the rod you spoil the child. I've used the rod on all of 'em—and wept every time. When I used it, I always tried to let fairness equal severity, and it always hurt me far more than them."

Yes, when God punishes he suffers. Away with that travesty of the Atonement which makes Calvary the high-tension point between God as the Judge and God as the Father—with the Judge insisting on vengeance and the Father purposing free pardon. At Calvary the Judge is the Father, and the Father is the Judge—which is no mere play on words but the expression of an inconceivably precious truth. Strictly speaking, a judge has neither love nor hate, neither hardness nor tenderness, for law does not feel. The more rigidly a judge identifies himself with the law that he administers, the less can he have within himself either anger or pity, for law in itself is as impassive as it is impartial.

Yet suppose for a moment that a judge does feel anger against the lawbreaker. Which is the more awful, the anger of a judge or the anger of a father?—that of transgressed law or that of outraged love?

When "the day of wrath" (Revelation 6) comes at the end of the present age and people cry to the mountains and rocks, "Fall on us, and hide us," what is it from which they seek cover? Is it the roaring of the lion? No, it is "the wrath of the Lamb," the wrath of abused and long-suffering love! The old Puritan theologians used to play off the two aspects of Judge and Father against each other in the being of God so as to emphasize the necessity that despite God's love sin must be judged, but they were in error in that their concept of the divine fatherhood was deficient. Actually, it is because God is the Father that he must be the Judge. The fatherhood does not grow out of the judgeship, but the judgeship does grow out of the fatherhood. That which makes the coming "wrath of God" so crushingly unanswerable, so awesome, is its being the anger of a Father, the anger of love—an anger through tears.

The Moral Glory of God

All this and more gleams from that rainbow round the throne, and is included in that magnetic phrase, "the throne of grace." No one has ever really seen anything until he or she has seen that cross on Calvary in its deeper, wider meanings. Once we really see it, we are never the same again.

I remember when my own eyes first began to see that cross within the Cross, that infinite Cross above and beneath and around the rough, wooden cross on Golgotha. I can say with deepest reverence that it was then that I first saw the sublime loveliness of the Eternal One who made us and then redeemed us! Oh, the mystery of that ineffable holiness and love that together bled on Calvary! Oh, the moral splendor and boundless compassion of that heart which both demanded and then became the propitiatory sacrifice—"the Lamb slain from the foundation of the world"!

Remember: all the triune Deity was there at Calvary. As Paul says in 2 Corinthians 5:19, "God was in Christ, reconciling the world unto himself." The nails that pierced those hands and feet of Jesus went straight through into the Father's heart. Every pang that Jesus suffered quivered on in the cosuffering mind of the Holy Spirit, for as Hebrews 9:14 says, our Lord "offered" himself "through the eternal Spirit."[4] In that Cross, therefore, we see not only the love of Christ or the love of the Father but the love of the triune God. Is our Lord Jesus, in his beautiful character and redeeming self-surrender, the altogether lovely One? Then truly that loveliness describes God.

When we begin to see more clearly the profound divine act behind the circumstantial externals at Calvary, it changes our attitudes toward ourselves. That is what happened in my own experience. As I surveyed the holiness and love that both demanded and provided that unspeakably costly reparation—not only requiring but enduring such penalty in order to clear me—I hated, as never before, the sin that drove those nails into the unresisting Emmanuel, God incarnate. In my deepest mind I took sides with God against myself. With sharpest clarity I saw that for the moral safety of the universe the ugly thing, sin, must be judged, and how lucid it became to me that what God did at Calvary was no obligation of creatorship to rebels but the spontaneous compulsion of love! My surprise and shame were that until then I had considered the Cross mainly as a propitiation offered to an angry God, without seeing in it also, and supremely, God's welcome of the fugitive sinner back to his gracious, caring, waiting heart!

Calvary rewrote in capital letters that every noble deed, every high aspiration, every unselfish, forgiving, generous, loving thought, everything of physical and moral and spiritual beauty on earth, is from God and reflects God. Everything of beauty was, in fact, representatively concentrated at Calvary, where gloating sin drove the nails through it. At Calvary we see vividly the ugliness of sin and the "beauty of holiness." I saw that the loveliness of Christ is in reality the loveliness of God, and I marveled that for so long I had run away from such a God instead of running to him, that for so long my eyes had been blind to the divine loveliness that looked out on me through the eyes of Jesus. How could I but side with such a God against myself? It was from myself that I might well wish to run away!

Long ago, in Eden, on that fateful day of man's Fall, when God came in some visible form, "walking in the garden in the cool of the day" (Gen. 3:8), Adam and Eve, instead of eagerly hastening to him as formerly for pleasant fellowship, now slunk away and tried to hide amid the shrubbery of the garden. And when God called, "Adam, where art thou?" Adam replied, "I heard thy voice in the garden, and I was afraid . . . and I hid." With the first sin came the first fear and the first evasion of God.

The superlative tragedy and most pitiful irony of human history is that ever since then people have been running away from such a God, from the purest, kindest, most gracious, adorable, and beneficent Being in the universe, from the God of all true loveliness, from the Savior-God of Calvary—instead of running to him. Sin not only binds people; it blinds them.

I say it again: when once we "see" the real Cross, we never recover from the wonder—and never want to. It becomes our theme forever. There at Calvary we see united in one both the Judge and the Father, both holiness and utter love, both justice and mercy, both penalty and pardon, both the vindicated law and the flood-point of compassion. That Cross honors the divine law equally as it releases the divine grace. It is the one absolutely necessary and eternally all-sufficient atonement. It fulfills every moral obligation of governmental righteousness and effects an eternal security. It is a salvation outbounding the farthest ravages of sin, and its solution is as extensive as creation. That, indeed, is what Paul says of it in

Colossians: a reconciliation covering not only this world of ours but also "all things in the heavens." It rings the very throne of God with that rainbow and makes it the throne of grace. It saves the penitent sinner here on earth; and, in a way at present surpassing human comprehension, it saves the universe!

> Vaster and vaster the universe grows
> To our wondering human eyes;
> Farther and farther its boundary goes
> As new telescopes sweep the skies;
> Wider and wider its nebulae gleam
> As the scientists "probe" and "find";
> Deeper and deeper its mysteries seem
> To our questioning "modern mind."
>
> Sadder and sadder the evil and grime
> In this "age of enlightenment";
> Bolder and bolder the format of crime
> Which the clever young "mods" invent;
> Deafer and deafer to biblical truth,
> Men are dazzled by lies that degrade;
> Blinder and blinder our rioting youth
> To the penalty yet to be paid.
>
> Richer and richer grows Christmastide
> In its God-given pledge to our race;
> Bigger and bigger the Cross where He died,
> The Creator, as Man, in our place!
> Hid in God's heart ere creation began,
> Heaven's answer to sin and the curse;
> Bigger that Cross in its infinite span
> Than the whole immense universe!

13

The Cross As the Victory of God

Pride, self-adoring pride, was primal cause
Of all sin past, all pain, all woe to come;
Ambitious pride, the first, the eldest sin,
Great fountain-head of evil, flowing still!

• • • •

Hence man's perpetual struggle night and day
To prove he is his own proprietor,
Quite independent of his God; that what
He has might be esteemed his own, and praised
As such. He labors still and tries to stand
Alone, unpropped; to be obliged to none;
And, in the madness of his pride, he bids
His God farewell, and turns away to be
A god himself; resolving to rely,
Whatever comes, upon his own right hand:
Oh, desperate frenzy! Madness of the will!
Inebriety of heart which nought can quench
But floods of woe poured from the Sea of Wrath!

Pollok

IF, THEN, AS SCRIPTURE teaches, our Savior is the Lamb "foreordained before the foundation of the world," how far back in the pre-Adamite ages do we find the Cross in the heart of God? The answer is: At least as far back as the inception of sin in the universe. Scripture does not say when that was, but from a correlating of various passages we know where and how sin originated. Those passages may also seem to suggest that it was not so long (in the flight of ages) before this present Adamic period of our earth.

Sin had its origin in the extraordinary mind of Satan. That the arch-fiend was originally a resplendent excelsior among the angel hosts, also that he is still an intelligence of immense power and scope, seems very evident from various Scripture references to him. With awesome frankness, in John 8:44, our holy Lord exposes that once-glorious but now hideous mind of Satan as the foul first-spring of evil.

1. He "abode not in the truth."
2. He lies "from his own [self]."
3. He is "the father of it [lying]."
4. He is a "murderer from the beginning."

There is an echo of this in 1 John 3:8. "The devil sinneth from the beginning." Also, there are subtle but unmistakable anticipations in Old Testament passages, particularly Isaiah 14:9–17 and Ezekiel 28:12–14. I appreciate all that scholarly commentators say in trying to restrict the startling phraseology of those two passages, respectively, to the king of Babylon and the King of Tyre. I allow for the extravagantly vainglorious self-exaltation uttered by those long-ago royal despots. Yet even so, there are clauses and phrases that go far beyond them and clearly refer to Satan.[1]

> How art thou fallen from heaven,
> O Lucifer, son of the dawn!
> Thou hast been cut down to the ground,
> O prostrater of nations!
> Thou saidst in thine heart,
> I will ascend into heaven,
> Above the stars of God
> I will exalt my throne;
> I will ascend above the heights of the clouds;
> I will make myself like the Most High.
> Yet thou shalt be brought down to Sheol,
> Even to the lowest recesses of it.

If that is not a vivid snapshot of the superangel who became the archfiend, some of us are strangely mistaken. It surely sounds like that coming Antichrist who "exalteth himself above all that is called God . . . showing himself that he is God" (2 Thess. 2:4). It certainly reminds us also of our Lord's word in Luke 10:18, "I beheld Satan as lightning fall from heaven." We may say the same of Ezekiel 28:12–17:

> Thus saith the Lord Jehovah; Thou sealest up the sum—full of wisdom, and perfect in beauty. Thou wast in Eden the garden of God. Every precious stone was thy covering. Thou wast the anointed cherub that covereth; and I set thee so that thou wast upon the holy mountain of God.

> *Thou hast walked up and down in the midst of the stones of fire. Thou wast perfect in thy ways from the day that thou wast created, till perversity was found in thee. . . . I cast thee as profane out of the mountain of God: and I have destroyed thee, O covering cherub, from the midst of the stones of fire. Thy heart was lifted up because of thy very beauty; thou hast corrupted thy wisdom by reason of thy resplendence.*

Even allowing for poetry and symbol, can those words be limited fairly to any mortal human? Remember, this original perfection and cherubic splendor and wisdom in that pristine paradise are not said to be high-flown ideas in the mind of the Tyrian king: they are all declared as actualities by God himself, for the passage begins, "Thus saith the Lord Jehovah."

Again and again in the Old Testament we find passages that, while having a first reference to contemporaneous place and circumstance, have a latent or esoteric and far bigger reference. Some things are purposely worded in enigmatic form until the appointed time for events to unlock their far-reaching meaning. For instance, who could have guessed, in Isaiah's day, the greater reference of Isaiah 7:14, "Behold, a virgin shall conceive, and bear a son; and they shall call his name Immanuel"? Who could have divined that in Psalm 16:10–11, David was latently foretelling our Lord's resurrection and ascension?

As for this cryptic addressing of Lucifer-Satan through the kings of Babylon and Tyre, were not both of them vainglorious types of Satan, even as was the Egyptian pharaoh of Moses' day? And when God addressed the deceptively beautiful serpent in the Garden of Eden, is it not plain that he was speaking through that originally beautiful creature to Satan himself? Both in Isaiah and in Ezekiel the fall of the exalted heavenly being is attributed to pride, and is not pride spoken of as peculiarly the sin of Satan (1 Tim. 3:6)?

Those two Old Testament paragraphs tie in with the whole biblical testimony as to Satan. He is the progenitor of evil. That first treasonous "I will make myself like the Most High" marks the origin of sin in the universe.

But why should Satan be concerned, in particular, to deceive and dethrone the first father of our human race? That question lies in the same region of strange mystery, yet here again, in obvious accord with its full teaching about Satan, Scripture comment shoots revealing light shafts into the deep shadow.

That Satan has some special relationship with this earth seems evident. Three times our Lord Jesus names him "the prince of this world" (John 12:31; 14:30; 16:11). That was no merely casual title expressing nothing more than a foolish ambition in Satan to become what he never could be.

No, it uncovered a background reality. Apparently, Satan was formerly, in his unfallen excellence, the divinely delegated vice-regent or "prince" over the system of things on this earth. Although later deposed as the "wicked one," he seemingly refuses to surrender his claim, as is indicated in his first major temptation of our Lord Jesus. When he showed our Lord "all the kingdoms of the world" and said, "To thee will I give all this, for it hath been delivered unto me," our Lord did not contradict the claim as a lying absurdity of fantastic make-believe. On the contrary, his nondenial tacitly implied concurrence.

That administrative authority which was formerly held by Satan explains his special interest in this world of ours and also why he jealously contrived the ruinous downfall of Adam as soon as God gave the "dominion" on earth to man, putting "all things under his feet" (Ps. 8:4–6).

Satan determined that what was formerly his by delegation should still be his by usurpation. How far he has been permitted to succeed the Bible makes pretty clear. Behind all the moral evil of this world's kingdoms or ruling powers is the mastermind of the archrebel, aided by participating evil spirit-beings who are one with him in his anti-God insurrection. For instance, in Daniel 10 there is an eye-opening paragraph in which an angel appears to Daniel, and explains:

> *Then said he [the angel] unto me: Fear not, Daniel, for from the first day that thou didst set thy heart to understand, and to humble thyself before thy God, thy words were heard: and I am come for thy words' sake. But the prince of the kingdom of Persia withstood me one and twenty days; but, lo, Michael, one of the chief princes, came to help me; and I remained[2] there with the kings of Persia. Now I am come to make thee understand what shall befall thy people in the latter days; for the vision is yet for many days. . . . And now will I return to fight with the prince of Persia: and when I go forth, lo, the prince [an angel or spirit power][3] of Greece shall come. But I will tell thee that which is inscribed in the Scripture of truth; and there is none that holdeth with me against these [i.e., against these evil spirits operating behind earthly ruling powers] but Michael your prince (Dan. 10:12–21).*

The following comment on the above passage is worth noting. "The intimation is clear, that as the holy angels are sent forth in behalf of the heirs of salvation, so demons are concerned in behalf of the world-system of Satan" (see John 7:7; Rev. 13:18).

Just how "fight" (v. 20) or warfare is conducted in the nonphysical and (to us) invisible spirit-realm we do not know, though perhaps it is a battle of minds for the furthering or hindering of good or of evil, respectively, on earth through human beings. In Revelation 12:7–9, we read:

> *And there was war in heaven: Michael and his angels going forth to war with the dragon. And the dragon warred and his angels; and they prevailed not, neither was their place found any more in heaven. And the great dragon was cast down, that old serpent, he that is called the Devil and Satan, the deceiver of the whole world [note: how like Isaiah 14 and Ezekiel 28 all this indeed sounds],[4] he was cast down to the earth, and his angels were cast down with him.*

How Satan at present operates against the outstandingly godly is seen in his (humanly undetected) oppression of Job. How he operates against the liberating message of the Gospel is uncovered in 2 Corinthians 4:3–4: "If our gospel is veiled, it is veiled in them that are perishing, in whom the god of this age hath blinded the minds of the unbelieving." Or, again, the machinations of Satan behind and through the governing powers of "this present world" are exposed in Ephesians 6:11–13:

> *Put on the panoply of God, that ye may be able to stand against the artifices of the devil. For our wrestling is not against flesh and blood, but against the principalities, against the powers, against the world-rulers of this [world's] darkness; against the spirit-hosts of wickedness in [and operating from] the heavenly spheres.*

No Gospel preacher or Christian worker gets far without realizing that behind every form of evil on this earth, behind all anti-Godism and opposition to Christian truth, lies the ugly hatred and scheming of Satan.

Big-Scale Rebellion

It is equally clear that Satan is commander-in-chief over a large confederation of evil spirit-forces. This is dark mystery indeed. He is "the prince of the demons" (Matt. 12:24–27). There are references, also, to "the devil and his angels" (Matt. 25:41; Rev. 12:7). Who, then, are those "demons," and who are Satan's "angels"?

As for the demons, nowhere is any of them called an "angel," nor in the plural are they ever classified as angels. Alternate names for them are "evil spirits" and "unclean spirits" (Mark 5:2–12; Luke 8:2; Acts 19:12, and other references). They are shown to be very numerous. The demoniac in Mark 5 was swamped and tyrannized by a "legion" of them (about six thousand soldiers comprised a Roman legion). Here we have a very large plurality of demons in military unity—a regiment! How many more such "legions" of demons are there? Evidently Lucifer-Beelzebub-Satan, in pitiful copy of God, has made himself a "lord of hosts"! However, in Mark 5, as in other places, the demons at once recognize our Lord Jesus as the true Lord, even "the Holy One of God" (cf. Mark 1:24), and cower before him.

There seems to have been an abnormal eruption of these demon spirits in Palestine synchronizing with our Lord's incarnation and probably provoked by it into concentrated opposition. They inflict both physical and mental maladies (Matt. 12:22; 17:14-18; Luke 13:11, 16).

But if these demon spirits are not "angels," who are they? One peculiar feature that marks them off from angels is that they seek all the while to traffic with human beings, and, where possible, to occupy human beings, whereas that is nowhere indicated of angels. Some fifteen times in the Old Testament they are called "familiar spirits." They are also called "evil" and "lying" spirits. They are "unclean" and "defile" the humans whom they indwell (Lev. 19:31; Zech. 13:2). All contact with them was banned in Israel (Lev. 20:27; Deut. 18:11; et al.). Spiritism, or traffic with demons, was evidently rife among the Canaanite nations (Deut. 18:11). It would seem from Matthew 12:43 and 8:31, and so forth, that these demons are tantalized by a strange restlessness in their bodiless state, hence their craving for covering and physical media of expression.

It is remarkable that although they had never seen our Lord before in the flesh, they all, without exception, immediately knew him as the Son of God. They knew that he could "destroy" them, or send them into the "deep"—literally, into the abyss, that is, of hades (Luke 4:34; 8:31). Their purpose in controlling humans is to dement, pervert, injure, torture, and deprave them—as we see in many references. They pervert the truth through "false prophets" (1 John 4:1) and seduce people's minds by deceptive error (1 Tim. 4:1-2). In the end time of the present age some of these demon spirits will work marvels that will affect the whole world (Rev. 16:13-14). Peculiarly enough, as we see from several references in the Synoptic Gospels, the demons have advance knowledge of their doom (Matt. 8:29; Luke 8:31).

Few of us today realize the widespread hold of demon worship and the extensive misery of demon possession in the pre-Christian centuries. Beyond doubt, since the coming of Christ and the dissemination of Gospel enlightenment the invasion of humans by demons has been greatly curtailed. Scripture seems to indicate, however, that there will be a recrudescence of demonism along with the anti-Godism that is to mark the closing decades of this present age. Indeed, we see sudden new signs of this around us today. The demon spirits are finding new opportunity as the present-day movement develops away from the Bible and from Christian moral standards. Spiritism, occultism, black magic, and demon possession are again greatly on the increase.

Moreover, there is a subtler Satanic strategy than visible demon possession. There is a widespread invisible infiltration by demon minds today that takes the form of interference in the thinking of governments and peoples. Guerrilla ravaging of human individuals here and there by

154 • Part Two: The Dimensions of the Cross

demon possession is not nearly so pervasively successful as the mass psychology tactics of disseminated error or the demoralizing of human society through the popularizing of permissive sensualism or the glorifying of vice and violence.

In Ephesians 2:2 Satan is called "the prince of the power [a collective aggregate] of the air, the spirit now working in the children of disobedience." That is no mere figurative language. The demon forces of commander Diabolos operate from the air and are just as invisible. They cannot actually take over any human mind, except where there is human consent through witchcraft, necromancy, or some abnormal mental condition, but they unsuspectedly prey, all too really, upon human thinking and behavior. It is a concerted campaign of incitement, and the three main incitements are: (1) to anti-Godism, (2) to extramarital sexualism, (3) to demon worship, for those three things most basically demoralize human nature.

But we are still asking who are these demon spirits that are so cooperatively under Satan's leadership, so hatefully interested in mankind, and so strangely desiring embodiment? Is it not plain that they have some common interest with the fallen Lucifer? And was not Lucifer-Diabolos, in a pre-Adamite era of the earth, the divinely appointed "prince of this world"? And are not these disembodied spirit beings, now known to us as the demons, the beings who long ago occupied this earth in bodily form, under the overlordship of Lucifer? We are miles away from dogmatism on such a matter, yet are we not bordering on strong probability?

What about some of those puzzling fossils that scientists tell us are from thousands of years before the time when, according to our Bible, Adamic mankind appeared on earth? May not these fossils be the skeletal remains of an anterior race of beings more or less similar to man in physical structure, though not necessarily identical in other respects?[5]

The German scientist F. L. Boschke, of Heidelberg, has published (1962) an engaging book, *Creation Still Goes On*, in which it is made clear that modern science no longer believes that the present condition of our earth was reached by one long unbroken process of slow evolution. The evidences are that our earth has known cataclysm(s). Thus does geology come closer again to what we believe Genesis teaches. Neither the present cosmos on this earth nor the human race is the product of a thousand million aeons of evolution. Man is very recent, and the occupation of this planet by our Adamic race was immediately preceded by a cataclysm as indicated in Genesis 1:1-3.

In the beginning God created the heavens and the earth. And the earth was without form (tohu) and void (bohu); and darkness was on the face of the deep. And the Spirit of God brooded upon the face of the waters. And God said: Let there be light: and there was light.

If, as some say, those words "without form and void" describe the earth's condition immediately after its creation or separate existence, that is, an original chaos, an inchoate, slowly shaping orb, with a slow dissipation of darkness by a gradually penetrating light, why should the inspired Genesis account indicate that the end of the enswathing darkness and the flooding of the whole scene with light was a sudden divine intervention? For that is what the report clearly implies, just as much so as it also indicates that the creation of the animals and man was a direct divine act.

In Isaiah 45:18 it is didactically stated that God did not create the earth "without form and void," that is, *tohu,* the Hebrew word used in Genesis 1:2.

> For thus saith Jehovah who created the heavens, God himself who formed
> the earth and made it. . . . he created it not without form [tohu].

If, then, God did not create it so, it must have become so at some subsequent stage. The Scofield note on Genesis 1:2 is much to the point:

> Jeremiah 4:23–26, Isaiah 24:1, and 45:18, clearly indicate that the
> earth had undergone a cataclysmic change as the result of a divine
> judgment. The face of the earth bears everywhere the marks of such a
> catastrophe. There are not wanting intimations which connect it with
> a previous testing and fall of angels. See Ezekiel 28:12–15 and Isaiah
> 14:9–14, which certainly go beyond the kings of Tyre and Babylon.

It is more than surprising to find how many people there are, even today, who still think of the Bible as teaching that the earth was created only six thousand years ago and that God then created it in six days. Yet the Bible is not responsible for such misapprehension. Nowhere does it teach that God created our earth in those six days. Except in Genesis 1:1 ("God created the heavens and the earth") the word, c*reate* is not used again in the Genesis account except in the creation of the animals and man.

What those six days tell us is the reconditioning of the already existing (and interveningly disordered) earth to become the home of mankind. If those six days were, as some assume, six long geological ages of evolution from an original chaos into our present cosmos, with each "day," as Genesis says, having its "evening" and its "morning" (i.e., half dark and half light) then during those six ages-long periods of unbroken darkness and six ages-long periods of unbroken light, neither vegetable nor animal life could have survived.

Why, then, that cataclysmic interference denoted in those words, "without form and void"? Does it not strongly suggest the result of a judgment on some former race and system on this earth—over which, with its millions of inhabitants, Lucifer was the illustrious vice-regent of the Creator?[6]

Satan's Angels

We are not postulating that all the members of that pre-Adamite race of beings fell in the outbreak of rebellion instigated by Lucifer; we are presuming that only part of them did. But what about "the devil and his angels" (Matt. 25:41)?

These, of course, are not to be confused with the "angels that sinned," spoken of in 2 Peter 2:4 and Jude 6, for they are penally chained and interned in Tartarus, the deepest abyss of hades, reserved "unto the judgment of the great day." Those angels may not have been many. In neither passage are they called "the" angels, as in our King James Version, but simply "angels," thus: "God spared not angels having sinned, but, casting them into the abyss, delivered them to dens of darkness in custody unto judgment" (2 Peter 2:4). "And angels, those who kept not their lordships, but left their own dwelling, he hath kept in unending bonds and darkness, unto the judgment of the great day" (Jude 6).

The correspondence between those two texts is obvious. It is the same angels who are referred to in both. Whether many or few is not stated, though the word "angels" without the definite article, and without any intimation that they all defected at the same time, may perhaps suggest individual default rather than Lucifer's collective and organized mutiny. At any rate, those angels definitely are not present participants in Satan's warfare, for they are imprisoned in hades.[7]

Scripture makes clear that there are apostate angels who are not yet interned in hades and who were active myrmidons in the Luciferian revolt. They operate under Satan's command. One such evil angel was specifically assigned to harass the apostle Paul. In his second epistle to the Corinthians he tells how, fourteen years earlier, he had been "caught up to the third heaven" and had been given such visions as were beyond divulging. Then he adds that immediately afterward, lest he should be wrongly elated by such privileged vision of the heavenly realm, there was given to him a "thorn in the flesh," which he thus describes:

> *And by reason of the surpassingness of the revelations, so that I should not be exalted overmuch, there was given to me a stake [no mere "thorn"!] in the flesh, an angel of Satan to buffet me, lest I should be exalted overmuch (2 Cor. 12:7).*

To get the full force of it, we do well to read it in Weymouth's translation: "There has been sent to me, like the agony of impalement [i.e., like being pinioned on a cross] an angel of Satan, dealing blow after blow." What sharpness of suffering that expresses! And at the time of Paul's writing that letter it had been going on for fourteen years already! Dear, brave, wonderful Paul, who turned even that into riotous triumph through Christ (see vv. 9-10)!

The immense number of these renegade angels of Satan is clear from Revelation 12, where the tail of the "great red dragon" (specifically identified as Satan in v. 9) dragged down "the third part of the stars of heaven." That is, when their mighty leader himself is finally "cast down," his whole host of co-rebel angels falls by involvement with him. This is stated beyond misunderstanding in that ninth verse:

> *And the great dragon was cast down, the ancient serpent, he who is called the Devil and Satan, he who deceiveth the whole inhabited world; he was cast down to the earth, and his angels were cast down with him.*

In an incidental yet remarkable reference to the final, general judgment, Paul asks, in 1 Corinthians 6:2-3, "Know ye not that the saints shall judge the world? . . . Know ye not that we shall judge angels?" These must be the angels now in league with the archrebel, for there will be no judging of the unfallen angels. It is a part of the final irony that they will be judged by redeemed humans whom they, as Satan's accessories, have sought to drag down to their own perdition but who now, in Christ, have been made "kings and priests" unto God, and have "reigned with Christ for the thousand years" of his messianic empire—that is, have "reigned with him" as coadministrators of that global rule.[8]

Let it be emphasized again that these angels are not disembodied minds, for they never had bodies. Nor are they the demons. They are bodiless, sexless spirit-beings. There are no male or female angels no father or mother angels no son or daughter angels. There is no procreation among them, no heredity, and therefore no transmitted sin-nature. Each is a directly created intelligence. Each was created sinless in moral nature, perfect in mental faculty within the limit of designed capacity, and constitutionally freewilled. None of the angels who have sinned did so because of any inward proneness but despite its absence. Each disobeyed by deliberate choice and thereby incurred direct culpability.

Perhaps this may in part explain why, so far as we know, there is no divine plan for the redemption of the fallen angels as a whole. The fact is, they are not a "whole." As there is no reproduction among them, they are not an organic unity by heredity, as we human beings are. They are not a race. The heart of God yearned over the millions and millions of Adam's posterity who, through no personal fault of their own, were hereditarily involved in the fall of that first man, the father of our race. Yet although the fallen angels are not a collective unity such as we flesh-and-blood human beings are, and although, therefore, there cannot be a redemption plan covering a fallen angel "race," the Cross of Christ does have out-reaching, superterrestrial ramifications through those vast spheres of spirit beings, as we shall shortly reflect.

Consider again the magnitude of Satan's power, intrigue, empire, des-potism, and havoc-working operations—billions of human beings cheated of immortal paradise, alienated from God, spiritually dead, morally lep-rous, physically diseased and dying; a whole world of intelligent creatures in chains of sin and ill that drag them, million after million, into a gaping, ravenous grave; a world revolving through six millenniums of hatred, vio-lence, vanity, rivalry, war, woe, sickness, weeping, and beauty despoiled by vicious ugliness.

Besides this, the atmosphere that surrounds our earth is at present infested by those aforementioned polluting demon spirits, who exercise invisible pressures upon people and through governments to delude and degrade still further the race to which God gave such an exalted begin-ning. And more, even in those heavenly spheres, the nature and extent of which are beyond our imagination, there is a widespread insurrection involving a myriad of once-immaculate but now hate-ridden angels.

Yes, think of this monstrous, age-long, hell-creating upheaval in God's universe, a titanic agony conceived and masterminded by the infidel Luci-fer; think of it all, and then ponder 1 John 3:8 again: "The Son of God was manifested that he might destroy the works of the devil"!

Challenge and Answer

According to scientific calculations, based upon meteorite evidence, that is, on radioactive isotope xenon-129, the minimum possible age of our universe is some five thousand million years; though possibly it might take only one other eloquent meteorite to double that figure! Who knows? But from the beginning of the universe itself, however many thousands of million years ago that was, this was the greatest thing that even God ever had to do—to "destroy the works of the devil"—and God's means of doing it is the Lamb, the Cross, the precious blood, the virgin-born, crucified, resurrected, enthroned, victorious, God-Man-Savior!

That Cross is the biggest wonder in the universe. It is the sublimest perfection in the being of God himself. It is bigger than all the sin that was ever conceived or committed by Lucifer, angels, demons, humans. The infinity of love that it released outmatches all the intense hatred of all the incited anti-Godism on earth or in extraterrestrial spheres. The Cross so proves and demonstrates the holiness, love, grace, and suffering savior-heart of God that the glamorous mask of anti-God hate is torn away once for all, and the stark ugliness of Satan is exposed for a universe to see.

That Cross means salvation for "a multitude which no man could number," and the utter doom of Satan.

But if Satan and his confederate hosts know in advance, as they do, that their doom is certain (Matt. 8:29; Rev. 12:12), why do they still persist in their hopeless warfare? The answer is: for the same reason that King Saul, even though he knew that the kingship was "departed" from him and that David was the God-appointed successor, continued hunting David with insensate hatred and intent to slay him. For the same reason many a military leader has fought on even the more desperately, because he knew that he could not win and was therefore the more determined to inflict as much damage as possible on a hated but stronger enemy.

We see this most vividly in Revelation 12:12, in connection with the "tribulation" at the end of this present age: "Woe to the earth and the sea, because the devil is come down to you, having great fury, knowing that he hath but a short time"! The more sinful sin becomes, the more does it detest that which is beautiful. The more inveterate evil becomes, the more fiercely it hates that guileless holiness which exposes and condemns it.

In the ultimate analysis, the two greatest moral powers in the universe are love and hate. What will not love suffer? What will not hate do? What cannot love achieve? What cannot hate perpetrate? Thank God, of the two, love is the stronger! Calvary has settled that forever and ever.

> O Love of God, O monster, Sin,
> In this dread act your strength is tried;
> And victory remains with Love,
> For He, our Lord, is crucified.

The Master Deceiver

Does that raise a further question? If all those now-fallen angels and demon spirits were once sinless beings without any inward compulsion to sin, how has Satan become so expansively successful in dragging others down into infidelity? Perhaps the answer to that may be gleaned from two passages of Scripture—one at the beginning of the Bible and the other at the end.

Away back in Eden, how was Eve duped? See Genesis 3:1-4 again. It was by the sowing of doubt ("Hath God said?"), then the injecting of a lie ("Ye shall not surely die"), then the casting of a slur ("God knoweth that your eyes shall be opened"), then by inducing pride ("Ye shall be as God, knowing good and evil"). All that time, remember, Eve was a sinless being with absolutely no proclivity to sin. Why then did she sin? It was because she was cleverly deceived. In the words of 2 Thessalonians 2:11 (see also 1 Tim. 2:14) she "believed a lie." Disobedience to God was so skillfully camouflaged that it seemed something to be "desired"; a way to "make one wise."

There is a loud, final echo of this in the last book of Scripture, where Satan is branded as "the old serpent; he that is called the Devil and Satan, the deceiver of the whole inhabited earth" (Rev. 12:9). If Satan could so mesmerically trick a sinless human mind amid Eden's unsullied paradise and continuously trick a whole race through millennia and dupe a whole creation of beings, presumably, when he was "the prince of this world" over a pre-Adamite cosmos on our earth, it is not too difficult to believe that this resplendent "son of the morning," this flashing paragon of duplicity, this beautiful-looking apotheosis of consummate deception, could mislead even angel dignitaries.

The "Mystery of Iniquity"

Such, in Scripture phrase, is the "mystery of iniquity," in which we see the gigantic dimensions of the sin problem in God's universe. Having originated in the vainglorious ingenuity of Lucifer, it now involves myriads not only in time but in supratemporal ages; not only on earth but in the heavens. Over against this mystery of iniquity (2 Thess. 2:7) is the "mystery of Christ" (Eph. 3:4; Col. 4:3), the mystery that "from the beginning of the ages has been hid in God" (Eph. 3:9) but is now divulged by the Holy Spirit (3:5), with this intent or purpose: that "now" (since the resurrection and heavenly enthronement of the crucified Christ) there might be made known to the "principalities and powers in the heavenly spheres" (i.e., to Satan and all his hosts and to all other intelligences in those spheres) the "manifold wisdom of God" (3:10–11).

God's answer is Calvary—not Calvary considered only as a Palestinian happening of two thousand years ago but the Calvary that has been "hid in God" for ages. Over against the self-exalting Lucifer is the meek and lowly Jesus. Over against the vaunting rebel who said, "I will ascend above the heights! I will make myself like the Most High!" is One who, with sweat of blood, became "obedient unto death, even the death of the cross." Over against the serpent is the Savior.

The Divine Victory

The more we look at that Cross on Calvary, the more wonderful it becomes. That which, to all appearances, seemed to be the pathetic defeat of Christ by Satan is the decisive overthrow of the outmatched deceiver and the everlasting victory of God. This is graphically pictured to us in a further passage of the Colossians epistle:

> *God . . . having blotted out [or canceled] the against-us handwriting [or bond written against us] which was adverse to us, in its ordinances [or*

decrees], hath taken it out of the way, nailing it to the Cross. And, having despoiled the principalities and the powers, he made a show of them openly, triumphing over them in it. (Col. 2:14–15, my translation)

The "handwriting" *(cheirographon)* or "written bond" which was against us is, of course, the Mosaic Law. That Law inexorably condemns us as transgressors and debt-defaulters. Through the Atonement, God has publicly canceled the bond, "nailing it to the cross"—possibly an allusion to the old-time custom of abrogating a decree by running a nail through it and hanging it up in public. Or maybe the allusion is to the common old-time practice of writing on wax tablets with a stylus. When a written and signed bond was canceled, the flat end of the stylus was drawn over the writing, smearing it out to indicate that it was now dealt with and done away.

The Law is here called the "handwriting" (Greek, *cheirographon*) in allusion to the famous singularity that it was directly written by God himself on two tables of stone (Ex. 32:14–15). Notice carefully: it is the Law itself, the cheirographon, or "handwriting," that is done away, which beyond all dispute means the Ten Commandments. Seventh Day Adventists tell us that it was only the ceremonial law that was done away, but that is not what this Colossians text teaches—and in any case the ceremonial law was never "against us," for it pointed to the coming Lamb, the Savior. It is the moral law itself (the Commandments) that condemns us and is rightly "against us." Accordingly, it is that which is here plainly said to have been nailed to the Cross. Observe the grammatical singular all the way through: not *them*, plural, the ceremonials, but "it" which "was" against us, and he "took it out of the way, nailing it to the cross."

God, to whom the vast debt is due, and against whom the bankrupt debtors pitifully default, now pays off our debt himself, answers all obligations, and publicly nails up the canceled bond on Calvary! It is not at all that God, in a sudden mood of clemency, winks at the grievous offense and says, Let's forget all about the big debt. No, it is that God himself, as our blood relative by incarnation through real human birth, now bears the full vengeance of the Law in our stead and himself pays off our debt, as our Kinsman-Redeemer. The canceled bond is nailed up there, on Calvary, because the debt is paid—paid on our behalf at a cost that brought blood and tears into the triune Deity and at a price that astonished the spheres. With all such bonds, the only one who could sign it into cancellation was the one to whom the debt or obligation was due. Calvary is God's public signature of nullification. On that "wondrous cross" we may read, in large crimson letters, the words of Romans 8:1: "There is therefore now no condemnation."

The voided bond is nailed up there by the nails that fasten Jesus there!

It is torn in two by the spear that rends the Savior's side! It is signed by God himself in the crimson ink of his own self-sacrifice, so that we human defaulters may see it and leap for gladness of heart at such a cancellation. It is nailed up there, also, in order that all the powers of evil may see it and recoil confounded. Yes, in that Cross of gory tragedy and sublime submission, the legions of Lucifer suddenly see their sheer discomfiture, for the text says:

> *Having stripped off the principalities and powers, he publicly [or boldly] exposed them, triumphing over them in him [Christ].*

It is not, as is commonly supposed, our Lord Jesus who strips from himself these spirit powers. The subject all through the paragraph is God, and the fact that the participle, "having stripped off" is in the Greek middle voice makes it the more remarkable. The full sense in English is, "Having stripped off from himself." The meaning is that in Christ and climactically through the Cross God has once for all flung away from before him those evil powers that accuse fallen man as transgressor and debt-defaulter and impugn the divine government. Calvary answers and silences them forever, for it honors the broken Law, and by full payment wipes out the defaulted debt.

The spirit powers thus decisively repulsed are Satan and his dark hosts of coconspirators, as the wording makes clear. Through the Cross God has "publicly exhibited" them, that is, shown them to his universe as they really are, with all disguise torn away, "triumphing over them in him"— that is, in our Lord Jesus. With unanswerable finality that Cross drags Satan and his perverted allies into a white blaze of torturing exposure, while countless myriads of angels and other spirit intelligences behold. The Cross does this because it exposes sin in three main ways. It says:

1. This is how the sin of his creatures affects God. It hurts him to the point of heartbreak, to the measureless pain and shame and cost of Calvary.
2. This is the kind of God sin hurts. He is the kind of God whose very heart is laid bare before humans and angels, in the guileless, gracious, meek and lowly, self-sacrificing Jesus.
3. This is the real nature of sin. It takes that meek and lowly Jesus, the most beautiful, harmless, noble, loving-hearted Being ever seen on earth, and mocks him, scourges him, nails him up in naked shame, and gloats over his agonizing humiliation.

God allowed it and overruled it, but it was Satan who engineered it, and in doing so the false "angel of light" utterly and finally lost his aura of deceptive charm. For through doing what he did at Calvary he was seen by a million million watchers "in the heavenlies" to be the ugly beast that he really is. Satan has never been able to get over that reverse. That Cross forever broke his deceiving power in God's universe.

We all know that if God had so willed, he could have trodden Satan into instantaneous non-existence ages ago, but that would have been no moral victory for God and good. Nor would that have given to his universe the revelation of God that would forever answer sin and make the universe safe against any further such ugliness. Through Calvary God has beaten Satan morally. Remember: it was as *human* that Jesus overcame Satan. In the person of Jesus it was the creature who proved stronger than the vaunting prince of darkness. Calvary was the crisis point. There the fuming powers of evil proved strangely powerless against a human heart utterly pure and a crucified love that never answered back.

Satan is still allowed active operation on and around this world, because the human story is not yet fully written, and the revelation of God through permitted evil is not yet completed. The archfiend has no answer to Calvary; therefore, his main strategy now is to prevent people from seeing it. Paul tells us in 2 Corinthians 4:3–4, that the Gospel is "veiled" by Satan wherever possible, so that perishing people cannot see it. The "minds of the unbelieving," says that text, are "blinded, so that the illumination of the gospel of Christ, who is the image of God, should not shine upon them."

As people are kept from the light of the Cross, they are kept in the dark, where Satan can the more effectively damage them. At the end of this now-closing age of grace, Satan shall be interned in the abyss of hades for the thousand years of our Lord's messianic empire, which climaxes the history of Adamic humanity on this earth.[9] After that, he will be "loosed for a little season," whereupon he at once goes forth and again "deceives the nations."

This finally demonstrates two things: (1) the utter incorrigibility of Lucifer-Satan, and (2) the failure of Adamic humanity even after a two-thousand-year age of grace and a millennium of perfect government. The time will thus have come for Satan's final banishment and for the winding up of the present racial order and for the new humanity in Christ and for the heading up of "all things in him," and the New Jerusalem into which "there shall in no wise enter anything unclean."

The Ultimate Triumph

What triumph for God there is in that "great multitude which no man could number, out of every nation, and of all tribes and peoples and tongues, standing before the Throne and before the Lamb, arrayed in white robes [symbol of perfected holiness], and having palms in their hands [symbol of final victory]" and exultantly saying "with a great voice, Salvation to our God, who sitteth on the throne, and unto the Lamb!"

There they are, that innumerable host who have "washed their robes and made them white in the blood of the Lamb," who "serve God day and night in his temple," whose tears have been forever "wiped away," and whom the heavenly Shepherd leads to "fountains of life-giving waters"! Yes, there they are, and they keep breaking into song before the throne, saying, in effect: "This is our God! In our Lord Jesus, the Lamb, we have seen him and have recognized him and have wanted him and have come to know him. We have seen him to be the holy, loving, gracious God that he is. He has suffered to save us and make us his own. We have learned to love him. We adore him, and of our free choice we glory to call him our God, to love and adore and worship and serve him for ever."

Surely Paul must be anticipatively thinking of that when in Ephesians 1:18 he speaks of God's "inheritance in the saints." I used to wonder how the infinite God could ever have any such "inheritance" in us poor, weak, little mortals and shame-faced sinners, but when I see those millions and millions yonder, with those robes and palms, exulting to avow their adoring love and singing, "By our own eager choice, this is our God forever and ever," then I think that perhaps just a little I begin to understand.

That is not all, however. Around the throne are angels to the number of "ten thousand times ten thousand [i.e., one hundred million] and thousands of thousands [i.e., endless millions more]." Calvary has done something to them, for all those vast hosts of angel intelligences break into singing their sevenfold perfect ascription: "Worthy is the Lamb that was slain, to receive [1] power, [2] and riches, [3] and wisdom, [4] and might, [5] and honor, [6] and glory, [7] and blessing!" Even those angel myriads, since Calvary, have seen in God what they never saw before.

That "wondrous Cross" reaches out its reconciling arms to encircle all worlds and beings and ages. It cost God more to hang nail-suspended on Calvary than to create ten million stellar thoroughfares. The redemptive meaning of that Cross, which first grew in the heart of our Savior-God and then in visible history was erected on the green mound outside old Jerusalem, will still be shining through the universe when the biggest alpha star has burned itself to a cinder. It writes God's sublime *V* sign over the whole universe.

14

The Cross As the Divine Answer

Men say, "I don't like your God. He is an unethical God. You represent Him as a cold, immobile, far distant, onlooking Being, who by a freezing edict makes a victim of Jesus the innocent." Men also say, "You evangelicals preach a tri-theism. You seem to represent that God and Christ are two different kinds of Deity. You seem to have one God to damn the world and another One to save it from the God who damns it." The real truth is that God, the all-loving, the infinitely compassionate, of Whom Christ is the Self-expression, became His own victim. It is the whole triune Deity that is vicarious and redeeming. In the depths of His triune being there is a "Lamb slain from the foundation of the world." The supreme court of this universe is itself vicarious and atoning . . . long before this became visual on Calvary's mount.

Henry C. Mabie

WHEN WE SEE THE Cross of Christ in its tremendous, precosmic, and universal dimensions it at once gives answer to various popular but superficial objections to our Christian message.

One such objection frames itself into the question, How can a crucifixion save us? The answer is: The Cross viewed only as a crucifixion cannot save us, but the Cross as an act of God does. Matthew 16:21 says, "From that time Jesus began to show unto his disciples that he must go to Jerusalem and suffer many things of the elders and chief priests and scribes, and be killed, and be raised again the third day." The next verse tells how Peter stoutly protested, "This shall never be unto thee!" By "this" he meant the slaying of Jesus at the hands of those wicked leaders. "This" so held and shocked his mind that he failed to hear and grasp the later clause in our Lord's disclosure—"and be raised again the third day." His eye was so taken by the human tragedy that it blinded him to the divine victory. We find the same in 17:22, "While they abode in Galilee, Jesus said to them:

The Son of Man shall be delivered into the hands of men, and they shall kill him; but the third day he shall be raised up. And they were exceeding sorry." They were so sorry at the tragedy, they could not see beyond it to the triumph.

Down through the centuries the same tendency has persisted. The Cross as a human tragedy, the Crucifixion as such, has predominated in the organized church and its teachings. This was most notably so during the mediaeval centuries, but in variant forms it still clings tenaciously around us since the Reformation. It has been observed, "In spite even of Luther and his Reformation, the crucifix occupies the high place in the sanctuary." That is less so, of course, in distinctly Protestant areas, but it is certainly true that the crucifix "is at this hour the central object-lesson in the State church buildings of continental Europe" and in other large areas too.

Dr. Henry C. Mabie says, "What the crucifixion, as such, denotes is the depth of humiliation to which Jesus went in submission"; therein exhibiting (so contrary to the expectation of the Jews) the "paradox of a humiliated Messiah, who, through such voluntary humiliation and correlative exaltation, would conquer the world. It was not the act of man's criminality (i.e., the crucifixion) which constituted the Atonement. The Atonement is God's act, and deeper than the crucifixion—a reality which none of the crucifiers saw."

Immense as was the enlightening liberation that came through the Reformation, yet to this day, even in soundly evangelical evangelism, the tendency is so to preach the Cross as a crucifixion that in emphasizing the human and external we obscure the divine and eternal. The Atonement was divinely predetermined, but not the crucifixion. God no more predetermined that dastardly human deed of outraged justice than he predetermined the wicked rebellion of Lucifer-Satan or the betrayal of Jesus by Judas or the massacre of innocent millions by Hitler. God is never the author of moral evil.

In his control of the human race and its history, God never suppresses or denies or violates the free operation of the human will within its divinely appointed limits. His control is a supercontrol that, at the same time it allows human free will unfettered movement, operates above it and amid it and beyond it. God foreknows all the responses and activities of the human will, individually, nationally, racially, to the end of time, and in his omniscient foreknowledge, he anticipates, foreplans, adapts, and overrules, to the accomplishment of his ultimate purposes.

God foreknew the crucifixion and even foretold it through certain of the Old Testament prophets, but let us never blunder into thinking that because God foreknew it, he foredesigned it. The truth is that God knew the mind of Satan, the archfiend antichrist, and the minds of his willing human tools. He foreknew how his self-revelation in Christ would be abused. That is, he foreknew the crucifixion, permitted it, anticipated it, and overruled it to the accomplishment of his mighty purpose to make an infinite atonement for the sin of his creatures. Moreover, through his thus permitting and overruling that uninhibited operation of free will, the Cross became the most utter exposure of the ugliness of sin at the same time as it effected the all-sufficient divine atonement for it.

Let it be said again: the Cross as a crucifixion is a human act. The Cross as an atonement is an act of God, and that is needing strong rearticulation today. We are not saved by a crucifixion but by the atonement to which that crucifixion gave concentrated visibility in the overruling wisdom of God. We are needing to emphasize more than ever that in and through the Calvary crucifixion God did something for our human race that is of infinite significance for every human being.

Historical Versus Timeless

Another objection to the Christian message is: How can something that happened two thousand years ago save us now? But, as we have been underscoring in these studies, the Scriptures clearly teach us that the Cross is timeless. Although chronologically it certainly did occur two thousand years ago because it had to happen in human history somewhere, what then happened gave focalized temporal expression to a reality that surrounds time—both before and after. In other words, the Cross on Calvary is the historical manifesting of an activity that originated ages ago in the infinite bosom of God. It is the self-revealing of that sympathetic, vicarious atoning nature which is God. It is no emergency afterthought to catch up with the tragedy of Satanic and human sin, as though sin had taken God by surprise. On the contrary, the Cross is the great antecedent, the all-controlling prior factor in the creating of mankind. There are two New Testament texts that it is well to see parallel with each other.

> "Sin came into the world," Romans 5:12—the most tragic thing that ever happened to our world.
> "Christ Jesus came into the world," 1 Timothy 1:15—the most glorious thing that ever happened to our world.

Both "came," so both preexisted. Both therefore came into this world from pre-Adamite cosmic mystery which already was, before time itself began. Sin was a movement from outside and before our cosmic system; so was redemption. The Cross is no mere temporal episode. Both sin and salvation were in full divine view before ever the evolutions of the temporal order began.

We are needing to proclaim with new insistence today that the Cross is not merely an event of two thousand years ago. The Lamb of God, then visibly and historically slain on earth, was already slain in the anticipative decision of God "before the foundation of the world" (1 Peter 1:20; Rev. 13:8).

During the past century there has developed in Christendom (most of all in Germany, and especially in our universities) an agnostic reaction away from all evangelicalism. I believe that in no small degree it was provoked by a seeing in the Cross of Christ only or mainly a tragic execution on a Roman cross. What atoning efficacy could there be in a criminal execution of long ago? That question may well be asked if we keep looking only at the human and external aspects of the Cross. But if we keep our eyes on the full testimony of Scripture, then time itself is not big enough to hold that Cross, and its efficacy is vast as the universe.

There is another reason why Calvary must not be thought of only as a happening of two millenniums ago. That cross is a continuing, present-day power because the One who died on it is a living, contemporary reality. Jesus is no mere figure of past history as all others are. As truly as he descended into the strange abyss of the grave and went beyond the discarded physical senses into hades, so just as truly he tore apart the bars of death's prison and demonstrated his victory by bodily resurrection. His last word before visibly ascending to heaven was, "Lo, I am with you every day, even to the end of the age."

You can no more imprison that risen Christ in the dusky past than you can do so the sun that broke over our hemisphere this morning. He is the living Contemporary of all generations. Just as truly as he ascended visibly to heaven in resurrection victory, so has he come back to us invisibly but now omnipresently in the outpoured Holy Spirit, a Savior who saves people today.

I hope this does not sound like hairsplitting, but in the strictest sense it is not the Cross by itself that saves us. We are saved by the living Christ himself through his cross and resurrection. A merely historical Christ can be no more than an object of memory, but this risen and ever-living Savior is the object of faith—faith that finds in him a blood-bought forgiveness, reconciliation with God, spiritual rebirth, new life, and sure hope of heaven.

Is the Cross Necessary?

Another common objection asks the question: Why cannot God forgive sin without any such sacrifice as the Cross? In other words, why was the Cross necessary? Do not earthly fathers forgive without demanding such penalty and pain? Is God less noble and forgiving than they are? Yet however plaintive and plausible that may sound, it is a product of sentiment rather than of clear thinking. The question itself is badly out of focus. It has an astigmatic view of fatherhood, both human and divine, and of the universe and of human nature.

Do human fathers always forgive without penalty? They do not. There are cases in history where judges and kings, in agony of heart, have passed death sentence on their own sons rather than violate the law of the realm and thus undermine the safety of its citizens. What they could forgive as fathers they could not condone as administrators. Without being any less fathers, they could not allow even fatherhood to override justice and honor. Their fatherhood could not act unilaterally; it had to operate in conjunction with other relationships. So is it with God. Because of who and what God is, his fatherhood cannot and does not act in isolation, although it is basic in his infinite being. All the qualities, attributes, and relationships of God necessarily express themselves in exquisitely perfect coordination. The fatherhood, without being any less gracious and benign, cannot act in any way that contradicts the divine holiness and justice.

But even where human fathers are not judges or kings but are fathers and only so, in relation to their sons, even then does human fatherhood always forgive without penalty? It does not. I recall the grief with which a father said to me: "I cannot forgive him any more after all he has done—not without clear proof of repentance and some restitution. The first time he played the prodigal and shamed our family name I forgave him and welcomed him back. Even after the second outrage, when as a deliberate rebel he flung away all we had ever taught him and done for him, I forgave him again and eagerly reinstated him. But then he went to even worse lengths, deceiving us with meanest hypocrisy. Years of savings that were meant to give his mother and father at least some ease and comfort in their later years he has deceptively filched from us. His wickedness has prematurely aged his mother and is bowing her silvered hair to the grave with sorrow. I am still his father. I still feel as a father. But I know, deep down, that what he now needs is not forgiveness, but punishment. I can still forgive, but I cannot and will not condone. There must be a thorough change in him, and he must make some restitution before we can forgive him any further." One has only to think of such cases to know how cursory, how paltry, is the view of fatherhood in the questions: Why cannot God forgive without the Cross? Do not earthly fathers forgive without penalty?

But the question is also out of focus in its view of the universe. The optically visible universe, with its teeming thoroughfares of worlds, and (to us) inconceivable myriads of thinking beings, is itself surrounded and interpenetrated by a moral universe. The outward and so-called material universe is conditioned and governed according to the divine ethics of that invisible moral and spiritual universe—of which the visible universe is but the counterpart. As earthly kings and judges must bear rule and administer law, penalizing saboteurs and criminals in order to preserve the safety of all the law-abiding, so, in the very nature of the case, God must administer righteous law throughout his universe.

Think what sin has done in human history! See what sin is doing in our world today! It is a mystery to us that God permitted it, but it is no mystery that he must deal with it for the safety of the universe. Something more than forgiveness is required! Basically, sin is cruel, ugly treasonous mutiny against purity, light, love, peace, and beauty in the universe. Even the simplest mind can see that if there were nothing but forgiveness without judgment, penalty, subjugation, and restitution, forgiveness would become nothing but a wide-open door to cosmic anarchy. All difference between heaven and hell would disappear, and the universe would become a colossal inferno.

We may well thank God that there is no forgiveness except through the honoring of that moral law which guarantees the safety of the universe. Look at the question again: Why cannot God forgive without exacting penalty? The further answer is that when I come to God as a contrite sinner, trusting in Christ Jesus as my Savior, he does forgive without demanding penalty, because (transcending the love of all earthly fathers) in order to save me he himself, in the person of his incarnate Son, bore the penalty in my place!

And there is still another fault in the question: Why cannot God forgive without any such sacrifice as the Cross? It misunderstands what fallen humanity really needs. Let me illustrate. Two men leave the wharf of a shipping company for their midday meal. One of them is a stevedore from the loading dock; the other is a young clerk from the warehouse. After a few paces the former falls from the pier into the water and would drown, only the clerk, flinging off his shoes and jacket, dives to the rescue, eventually getting the drowning man to a wooden jetty, and thence safely back to land. The stevedore thanks his rescuer, who replies, "I am only too glad I was able to save you." But what is the young clerk to think when the same man falls into the water the next day and has to be saved again? And what does he say when that same man does the same thing day after day? He says, "That poor fellow needs to be saved not just from the water but from himself! There's something wrong with the man."

Just as truly, what we human sinners need is no mere excusing of our sins or forgiveness for the past. We are spiritually dead and need new life. We are morally diseased and need a deep-going renewal. We are mentally defiled and need inward cleansing. We are sin-prone and sin-weakened, and we need divinely imparted new strength. We are alienated from God and need a "new heart" to know and love and serve him. We need all those and more, besides forgiveness.

Why cannot God forgive without the Cross? It is because, by the Cross, he brings us not only forgiveness, but regeneration to new spiritual life and the eternal salvation of ourselves. Also, by taking our place on that mysterious Cross and substitutionarily bearing the fearful judgment due to our race's sin, so that he might righteously absolve us from penalty, he reveals his infinite love for us, which could never be revealed by any casual, "I'll let you off." When once we truly see that Cross, with our very Maker hanging there as our suffering Sin-Bearer, we begin to loathe our sin and to take sides with God against ourselves. Never again, after that, do we ask why God cannot forgive without the Cross.

Without the Shedding of Blood

Another objection to the Christian message asks, But why should God demand blood before he will forgive? If I remember correctly, it was this supposed demand for blood that turned the late Sir Arthur Conan Doyle, author of the Sherlock Holmes stories, against Christianity. Modernist theologians, too, have contemptuously derided and denounced the biblical emphasis on the blood. I shuddered when I heard one of them—a "scholar" if you please—publicly declare: "This primitive Bible idea of salvation through the blood smells to me of a butcher's shop." Inwardly, I echoed the prayer of my bruised and broken Savior, "Father, forgive them, for they know not what they do"!

Such "scholars" of the liberal school sneer at "the blood" as if they were people of superior refinement—as if they were so modernly genteel that this idea of salvation through blood-shedding is utterly barbaric and repugnant to them. Yet they readily forget that the highest civilization and progress and refinement in the great Protestant nations (of which they themselves are inheritors) has come through that doctrine of the precious blood that they now disdain.

I recall a comment in one of Spurgeon's printed sermons, that throughout the history of Christendom, whenever the church has preached morality instead of the Cross, morality has badly deteriorated, but wherever the precious blood, or salvation through the slain Lamb of Calvary, has been most clearly proclaimed to people, the vilest of the vile have been lifted from the gutter of sin and transformed into holy nobility.

I remember another preacher, a dear old prince of the evangelical persuasion, one of the most scholarly and refined and sensitive people I ever knew. This is what I heard him say: "I have always had a horror of hurting anyone, either human or animal. I could never tread on a worm or set a trap for a mouse. The very sight of blood from a wound would turn me sick, so much so that I have often been ashamed of myself that I should have such an unmanly inability to render help. Yet there is one exception. The most glorious and infinitely precious wonder in time or eternity or in the whole universe to me is the 'precious blood of Christ.'

His birth, his life, his teaching, his miracles, his example—all are dearer to me than words can say, but beyond and above all, it is his precious blood that is everything to me. It is that which makes him my Savior, the divine Lover of my soul, my supreme Treasure, the all-eclipsing object of my heart's love and devotion. That 'precious blood' writes out in crimson capitals for me, 'God loves you.' Those nailprints in Jesus' hands and feet shine with a brighter luster and beauty to me than all the stars God ever made."

But where does this idea come from, that God demands blood? Where did Arthur Conan Doyle get it? Where do our liberalist teachers and others get it? The Bible does not teach it. No, this mistaken idea comes from not reading the Scriptures carefully enough. Now and then on my travels I meet persons who have the idea (supposedly from the Bible) that God "demands blood." As often as not they claim, "Oh, but the Bible itself says, 'Without the shedding of blood there is no remission.'" Well, those words are a correct quoting of Hebrews 9:22. Yet they are incorrect inasmuch as they are incomplete. Hebrews 9:22 does not say, as an independent statement: "Without the shedding of blood there is no remission." Read the whole verse carefully:

> *Moreover the tabernacle and all the vessels of the ministry he [Moses] sprinkled in like manner with the blood. And according to the law, I may almost say, all things are cleansed with blood, and apart from shedding of blood there is no remission. (vv. 21–22)*

So the words "without the shedding of blood there is no remission" are not an independent statement, nor should they ever be treated as such. They are qualified by the attached words "according to the law." It certainly was true, provisionally, under the Mosaic Law, that without the shedding of blood there was no remission, but it is not a fundamental law of the universe.

The basic truth is not that God demands blood, but that sin requires atonement. The former is a repellent misconception; the latter is at once understandable, as any unprejudiced mind must surely see. If the anti-God monstrosity that we call "sin" is to be dealt with in such a way as honors the moral law, which makes the universe safe, then somewhere there has to be a gigantic appeasement, reparation, reconciliation: an atonement. It must be an atonement in which God is consistent with himself and in which sinful man is saved from himself.

Can anyone tell us how such an atonement and salvation could have been effected apart from the infinite atonement made on Calvary by the incarnate Son of God? And are those who say they cannot believe in a God who "demands blood" prepared to face the utterly sublime fact that it was God himself who, in the person of his incarnate Son, shed his own blood for the sake of saving man?

As for those Old Testament sacrifices apart from which, "under the Law," there was no "remission," certainly they seem repulsive to the refined thinking that we owe to the influence of the Christian Gospel. Part of the very purpose in those animal sacrifices was to impress on the human conscience the ugliness and costliness of sin, as well as emphasizing the sin-abhoring holiness of God and pointing ahead typically to the all-sufficient atonement that our Lord Jesus would later make for human reconciliation.

A "Criminal" Doctrine

A somewhat similar objection voices itself in the words, Why should God lay our sin upon the innocent Jesus? In my own hearing one disapprover put it like this: "To me, the idea that God, an offended first Person, should take the sin-penalty of man, a guilty second person, and put it on the head of Jesus, an innocent third Person, is patently unjust; it is a criminal doctrine, and I reject the book that teaches it."

This is another case of turning away from the Bible because of something that it is presumed to teach but does not teach at all. What that critic said is an ignorant caricature of the truth. The Scripture teaching, in reality, is that "God himself was in Christ, reconciling the world unto himself" (2 Cor. 5:19). Admittedly, in the words of Isaiah 53:6, "Jehovah laid on him the iniquity of us all," but behind and underneath that necessary aspect of the Cross is the mysterious reality that the One on whom God laid our sin and guilt is himself God. The Sin-Bearer is the "Word made flesh," God the Son, which means that in its deepest meaning the Cross was not so much God's laying our penalty on another; it was God himself shouldering our burden and bearing the damning load as our Substitute!

All too often, perhaps, we evangelicals have presented God the Father and God the Son in apparent antithesis to each other: one the Judge and the other the Savior, as though they were two Gods in a trinity of Three. It was that distorted presentation that caused a child to say, "I love Jesus but I hate God." To many ears we may often have sounded as though we were preaching a Tritheism (three Gods) instead of a Triunity (one God in threefold personal unity). It is always important for us evangelicals to emphasize that God is not merely a Trinity (three), but a *Triunity*, that is, Three in One. One of the saddest yet one of the sweetest harp-strings in the music of the Gospel is that the heavenly Father himself suffered in all that his "only-begotten Son" suffered to save us. The whole triune Godhead was on that Cross and in that atonement: the most titanic mystery and miracle in the history of God and the universe!

"One for All"—How?

We refer to just one more of these common misunderstandings. It presents little if any problem to many, but to others it seems a baffling peculiarity. They ask: How could one bear the sin, the guilt, the penalty of all? The first part of the answer to that question, of course, is that no single "one" ever could bear the sin-penalty of all, except the One who actually did so. But when we take into consideration all the millions of sins committed by each human being and then all the billions of sinning human beings from the beginning to the end of history and then the whole astronomically stupendous aggregate of guilt and penalty involved, how could even that One substitutionarily bear it all?

In just the way that a boy's mind could grasp it, the answer to that question was unforgettably illustrated to me when I was in my early teens. I was a Lancashire laddie, living in Ashton-under-Lyne, near Manchester, England. A Sunday school field day was in the offing, and hundreds of pennies were needed by a generous patron of the school who wanted to climax the games by throwing those hundreds of pennies in all directions for the scholars to hunt and find. It was an exciting idea. A penny meant something in those days!

I accompanied another boy to a commercial bank to change a ten-pound note into pennies for that purpose. It happened that the bank did not have the usual five-shilling or ten-shilling packets of pennies made up, so the ten pounds' worth of pennies had to be weighed and packaged while we waited at the counter.

I can see it again even now. The cashier weighed all those hundreds of pennies out and poured them on to the counter, ready to be put into the usual packets. There they all were: twenty-four hundred copper pennies. Never before had I seen such a pile of them. My own spending money at that time was two pennies per week—and I thought even that was a weekly fortune! As I looked at that bank counter, at that one bit of crinkled paper called a "ten-pound note" and at the mountain of coins now piled beside it, I found myself thinking, "How strange it is, that one small paper 'note' should be worth all those two thousand four hundred copper coins!"

I think the deputy cashier must have been something of a seer as well as a Christian believer, for he suddenly said, "Yes, that one bit of paper is worth all those two thousand four hundred pennies: and in just the same way, boys, that is how the Cross of Jesus is equal to save all the sinners of the human race. He was given the name 'Jesus' because he was a real human baby, a real human boy, a real human man, but the prophet Isaiah told us his other name, which is Emmanuel, 'God with us,' and because Jesus is God's own eternal Son in human form, that life and death of his have more value than all the millions of us human beings put together!"

How could I ever forget it? Simple and impromptu though the illustration was, how much to the point! Our Lord Jesus could be the more-than-equivalent Substitute and Savior of all because he is the infinite Creator of all. There is a divine infinitude of value and merit in his Calvary self-offering for us that boundlessly more than covers all the millions of us sinning creatures.

Yes, in that as in all other aspects the Cross is the all-sufficient divine answer to our human need and problem. Not only does it save us legally from the guilt of sin and judicially from the penalty of sin and inwardly from the power of sin and ultimately from all impairment by sin, but the more honestly and deeply we ponder the various congruities of it, the more satisfyingly it answers us intellectually. There must always be mystery about it, for the Cross is nothing less than the profoundest act even of God himself. But from it, like golden light-shafts of the rising sun, there break upon us those glorious simplicities of the Gospel that all of us can understand and receive and whereby we become eternally saved.

> Can I be saved, or any man,
>   By Jesus' Cross so long time past?
> Yes, for that Cross, ere time began
>   Embraced our race from first to last.
>
> Yet, even so, could One alone
>   Bear all our world's iniquity?
> Yes, He, as God-Man, could atone
>   With endless all-sufficiency.
>
> But can that outward fact apart
>   Save me from inward fault and sin?
> Yes, when I ask Him to my heart,
>   His presence changes me within.
>
> Come, wondrous Saviour, in my heart
>   Give saving truth its vital glow;
> Reveal within how real Thou art,
>   Thro' all my days on earth below.

15

The Cross As a
Behavior Standard

Lord Jesus, loveliest and best,
    Example human and divine,
Thou art alone the pattern-test
    Adjudging all this life of mine.

No other mode of test can bear
    The scrutiny of Heaven above;
Thine is the life beyond compare,
    Incarnate holiness and love.

And dare I vainly flattered be
    When judged by human test alone,
While in my life I plainly see
    Dismaying contrast with Thine own?

Oh, joy exceeding power to tell,
    That Thou Thyself, my high Ideal,
Wilt all my yielded life indwell,
    To make the longed-for image real!

Let me repent, tho' not despair
    That I have failed so oft before;
These dismal ruins, Lord, repair,
    To be Thy dwelling all the more.

Environment be what it may,
    Let all I am so yielded be
That through my living, every day,
    My Savior's impress all may see.

IN THESE LINGERINGS TOGETHER at the Cross of our dear Lord we have reflected on it as a superlative wonder, as the only adequate explanation behind the Incarnation, as a mighty culmination dispensationally and in other ways, as the divine ensign emblazoned over the creation of the world and mankind, as the rainbow overarching God's government of the earth and the universe, as the victory of heaven over Satan and his insurrection movement, and as the only, but all-sufficient, divine answer to the prodigious sin-problem. We are painfully conscious of much poverty in our comments on those profound aspects of the Cross, as also of our inability in a limited book like this to survey other features. But there is one further link that must be added to our chain of studies. It so belongs here that we cannot think of omitting it, even though our consideration of it will be much too brief. It is the Cross as an example.

The Cross is the supreme revelation of moral sublimity. Enoch, Abraham, Joseph, Moses, Hannah, Samuel, Elijah, Hezekiah, Daniel, and others move before us in the pre-Christian literature of the Old Testament, each exemplifying traits of noble character that we may well observe and emulate. Yet at best what are they and what are all others, whether prophets, apostles, or martyrs, compared with the all-transcending example of Christ? They are mere flickering candles lost in the splendor of the meridian sun!

For sheer moral glory or sublimity of character who would ever conceive of putting Confucius or Buddha or Muhammad or any other religious innovator alongside Jesus? They lived remarkable lives, but who would ever put their highest doings against that "wondrous Cross on which the Prince of Glory died"? In Tennyson's words, what are they but "broken lights" of him who is "the true Light which lighteth every man coming into the world"? That awful Cross, however outwardly repellent, in its inner meaning is the enshrinement of all the purest idealism of which the purest human hearts are capable.

Despite the blight of sin, human history has its noble character statuary, but never was there a greater delineation of moral grandeur than we have in Philippians 2:5–8. Already in these studies we have halted at that passage, but there is always new reason for returning to it, particularly to linger pensively over the example that it sets before us.

> *Have this mind in you, which was also in Christ Jesus: who, existing in the form of God, counted not the being on an equality with God a thing to be grasped, but emptied himself, taking the form of a servant, being made in the likeness of men; and being found in fashion as a man. He humbled himself, becoming obedient even unto death, yea, the death of the cross.*

We have earlier observed the four levels here: (1) God, (2) man, (3) bondslave, (4) felon. Whenever we reflect on that sheer mystery of divine grace are we not "lost in wonder, love, and praise"? But the gracious marvel of it is matched by its moral challenge, for he who was in the form of God yet became in the likeness of men is portrayed as being thereby the supreme example that we are to follow: "Let this mind be in you" says the text! Reflect on it again in that light.

"Who being in the form of God thought it not robbery to be equal with God." As we read those words we are atmosphered in infinite mystery. "In the form of God": that word "form" here cannot mean shape, for shape belongs to material things, whereas God is purely spirit. It must mean that in the closest possible way he was like God, and he could be so only by being of identical nature, just as a man can only be truly like a man by actually being a man. The reason why two human beings are fundamentally alike is that they have the same human nature. That our preexistent Lord was in the very form and likeness of God involves his own deity, which indeed is endorsed by the added word that he "thought it not robbery [i.e., something to be graspingly retained] to be equal with God."

Besides, if our Lord were not truly the Father's coequal, the very idea of his being an example would border on the bathetic and blasphemous, for where would there be any moral example in a mere creature Christ thinking it not robbery to be "equal with God"? What could there be to emulate in a creature's not grasping after that! On the contrary, a mere creature Christ's grasping after that would have made him a second Lucifer!

The soul-subduing mystery is that this glorious One who is in the form of God and equal with God, and therefore absolutely divine, takes out a blood relationship with me through human birth and actually becomes human in order to redeem me! As the text says, he became "in the likeness of men." Out of his infinity and invisibility the Architect of the universe walks to me in human form! He looks on me through human eyes, beckons to me with human hands, feels for me with human emotions! Oh, sacred marvel of Bethlehem, Nazareth, and Calvary!

Before I see God in Jesus, he is unknowably distant in his superstellar transcendence. He is incomprehensible in his unimaginable immensity. But in Jesus I see him, recognize him, understand him, and although his sin-exposing holiness still awes and shames me, I am drawn to him. Yes, as I see God in the holy but meek and lowly Jesus, I reverently like him, I want him, I trust him and love him and possess him!

"In the likeness of men"—not just the likeness of a man but of all people. He is the "Son of Man," not just of a man. He is not merely a Jew, a Roman, a Greek, or an Englishman, American, European, Asiatic. As the "Son of Man" he is the universal Human. The blood of the whole human race courses in his veins. He is the only One who ever walked this earth who is big enough to hold all the millions of us in his heart and to represent all the millions of us in his substitutionary sin-bearing.

Yet his universality does not in the least blur or diminish his human individuality, for not only is he made "in the likeness of men"; the text adds that he is found "in fashion as a man." He has his individual likes and dislikes. He has his special friends. He has the concern of a loving human son for his mother. He hungers and thirsts. He sighs, he thrills, he weeps, he sympathizes, he knows weariness and sits by the well and politely asks for a drink of water. All this brings him closer still to me, for I discern that before he ever bore my iniquities on Calvary he "took my infirmities" into his compassionate humanity (Matt. 8:17).

But further: he who was "in the form of God" and came "in the likeness of men" and was found "in fashion as a man," compresses his manhood into the narrower limits of a "bond-servant," for the text says, "He took upon himself the form of a bondman"! He who is "over all, blessed for evermore" (Rom. 9:5) places himself beneath all, that he may serve all! The richest becomes the poorest; the highest becomes the low-liest; the strongest becomes the meekest, so that he may reach down to the poorest, the lowest, the weakest, the oldest, the youngest, the needi-est, and the most sinful.

Yet even that is not the terminus. There is the final, deepest plunge: "He humbled himself, becoming obedient even unto death, yea, the death of the cross"! Can we ever cease to be astounded? He not only submits to servanthood or, rather, to the lower level of a bondsman, but he takes the place of the criminal before the bar of divine law! As a mere bondsman he has no counselor to speak on his behalf. Nor does he open his mouth to utter one plea of innocence or one protest against the merciless severity of the law. The One who hung on that Cross in public execution was hang-ing tortured there not only as bondsman but as felon! Besides the un-speakable agony there was the depthless shame: "even the death of the cross"!

It had to be so if we were to be saved. Law is the opposite of mercy. Justice is the opposite of clemency. It has been truly said: "The moment a judge becomes merciful, he ceases to be strictly just, for as long as he remains strictly just he cannot be merciful." Sin is moral and spiritual criminality against God, against light, against absolutely necessary moral law. Sin must be punished. Take away holiness, righteousness, justice from the being of God, and you undeify him; the very throne that secures the universe totters.

The Cross has to be, or mankind must perish under eternal sentence. Gathered up into that infinite God-Man who hangs on that Cross is all the guilt of the whole human race. The divine Law sees him as the aggre-gate criminal. As the race's Guilt-Bearer he must experience that awful death, the depthless darkness of which wrung from him the cry, "My God, my God, why hast thou forsaken me?" Infinity and eternity and the starkest agony ever known were concentrated in that desolate wail from Calvary.

But how can all that, with its immeasurable proportions and mysterious meanings, ever be an example to you and me in our finite littleness and human sinfulness? What parallel can there possibly be between that only-begotten Son of God and ourselves, infinitely distanced from us as he is in his absolute deity? There is only the one Incarnation, only the one Calvary, only the one Atonement. What exemplary parallel can they have with any behavior of ours?

Well, in its divine dimensions and redemptive uniqueness our Lord's saving work cannot be an example for us: it is beyond all parallel. Yet, paradoxically, it is in the very contrasts between him and us that the similarities most vividly appear and make him our example par excellence. Because of who he was and is, he gave up so much more than we can ever be called upon to give up. In his sensitive sinlessness and infinite capacity to feel, he suffered so much more for others than we can ever be called upon to suffer. His substitutionary self-offering in Gethsemane and on Golgotha was so much more costly in every way than anything we could ever be called upon to undergo. Those very differences between him and us emphasize the example, for if he, so incomparably different from us, voluntarily chose, without obligation, to forego so much and endure so much for sinners, rebels, enemies, perishing souls, is he not thereby the supreme Pattern for his people?

Thus, although in the solitary splendor of his deity and saviorhood he is beyond all parallel, in his motive and response, that is, in his purpose and love and self-sacrifice, he becomes the highest, loveliest, sublimest Example ever seen by humans or angels in time or eternity. Paul says, "Let *this mind* be in you which was also in Christ Jesus." That is the vital point of parallel.

The true zenith of Christian idealism is Christ-mindedness. The peak concept of Christian character is Christlikeness. Although we can never have it in the same perfection or degree, we are meant to have the same kind of disposition or mindedness, the same kind of motive, response, love, and willingness to sacrifice. What an ideal! What an example! And what a possibility! The resurrected Exemplar himself now lives to indwell us by his own Spirit, to make the ideal an experiential reality, if we will but let him!

The apostle Peter brings this Pauline passage nearer to our hearts in a paragraph that he pens in his first epistle. With his eyes fixed on that exemplary manhood and saviorhood, he writes:

> For even hereunto were ye called: because Christ also suffered for us, leaving us an example, that ye should follow his steps: who did no sin,

neither was guile found in his mouth: who, when he was reviled, reviled
not again; when he suffered, he threatened not; but committed himself to
him that judgeth righteously: who his own self bare our sins in his own
body on the tree, that we, being dead to sins, should live unto righteous-
ness: by whose stripes ye were healed. For ye were as sheep going astray; but
are now returned unto the Shepherd and Bishop of your souls. (1 Peter
2:21–25)

This passage plainly declares that our Lord's life and death on earth are
an intended example for us: "Hereunto were ye called: because Christ
also suffered for us, leaving us an example. . . ." We are to follow that
example in no merely perfunctory way, but with constancy and particular-
ity, for the text says, "Leaving us an example, that ye should follow his
steps." We are to be his close followers, step by step treading in his sandal
prints, testing each motive, ambition, habit, and our whole behavior by
that perfect File leader! Observe, then, the four salient features here:

1. a stainless walk—"who did no sin"
2. a guileless mouth—"neither was guile found in his mouth"
3. a yielded will—"he committed himself to him who judgeth
   righteously"
4. a quenchless love—"who his own self bare our sins in his body on
   the tree"

Yes, again, what an example, and most of all in that Cross, its culmination point! Translated into English, this is what a learned Brahman said to
a Christian missionary: "The Jesus of your theology is not easy to me, but
in the book you gave me, the Jesus who died such a death after such a life
is the most heart-drawing character ever shown to me."

How many (or how few) of us, I wonder, truly and deeply accept that
Cross as our standard of behavior? How many (or how few) of us have
really driven the nails through the self-life: through unforgivingness,
retaliativeness, grumbling, grudge-nursing, conceit, envy, rivalry, resent-
ment, touchiness, self-praise, self-pity? In the light of that example, how
many (or how few) of us are truly Christlike?

In a devotional study like this, ought we not stand again before that
Cross now, contemplating its melting yet challenging example? Hear again
that first of our Savior's seven utterances from the Cross: "Father, forgive
them, for they know not what they do." Even the hardened soldiers must
have been taken aback, for that gracious plea was spoken just at the point
when most crucified criminals shrieked curses at the executioners and
spectators. Presumably our Lord would have been nailed to the cross
while it was still lying on the ground. Then strong hands would have

raised the impaled Victim and dropped the perpendicular stake, with him already fastened to it, into a deep hole already prepared. As the prisoner was thus hoisted upright, the whole weight of his body became suspended entirely by the nails, and that first excruciating jolt into the ground would send shuddering spasms of pain through his frame, turning every nerve into a strand of fire and every vein into a river of anguish.

What shrieks of frantic blasphemy and impotent rage those soldiers had heard from crucified criminals at that moment of convulsive torture! But now for the first time they hear, "Father, forgive them"! They had taken away everything he had, yet even crucifixion could not take away his love! This was the love that fiercest flames could not quench and many waters could not drown.

"Father, forgive them." Mark the selflessness of it. Acute suffering often so contracts the mind that the sufferer can think only of himself and what he is enduring, but the sublime otherism of Jesus came out even more in his crucifixion torture than ever before!

"Father, forgive them." What concern his plea expressed! He himself needed no forgiveness, but they did. Now more than ever they would need forgiveness, and he knew that through his own atoning suffering they could have forgiveness.

> Seven times He speaks, suspended there,
>   As Satan's henchmen do their worst;
> Seven calls of gracious love and care,
>   "Father, forgive them," is the first:
> The very Cross where thus He pleads
>   Becomes the answer to His call,
> For as He there redeeming bleeds,
>   He makes forgiveness free to all.

Do we call ourselves disciples of Jesus? Do we then have the same forgiving love? Being able to pass a test in theology or being zealously sound in doctrine or being able to speak in tongues or being able to work miracles of healing—all these are poor compensation for lack of this forgiving love. How we need to keep coming back, in mind, to linger at that Cross and in its searching light to ask ourselves, Do I have that forgiving love?

"Father, forgive them." Those words are echoed by Peter in Acts 3:17, "And now, brethren, I know that through ignorance ye did it." There is a further echo by dying Stephen in Acts 7:60, "Lord, lay not this sin to their charge." Even so, there ought to be a continuing echo of it in every Christian heart: "Father, forgive them." Alas, how unlike Jesus many of us are! How unforgiving, how self-justifying, how resentful, how hard! How prone we are to reprisal, to drastic verdicts, and to caustic retorts!

How big we seem in our self-imagined right to hold a grudge! How petty, how ugly, how pigmy-little we really are in our unforgiving snobbery! Lord Jesus, melt our hearts by your own example. Shame us by that Calvary prayer for your traducers and slayers. If we cannot cure our own wretched unlikeness to you, help us so to surrender ourselves to the inflow of your own noble love that our inborn pride and hate may be completely supplanted by it.

> "Father, forgive them," help me pray it,
>   Tho' they hate me without cause;
> "Father, forgive them," help me say it,
>   Tho' they tear with fang and claws;
> "Father, forgive them," Jesus, save them,
>   For they "know not what they do";
> Help them learn through my forgiveness
> Of Thine own forgiveness too.

"Father, forgive them." Yes, even them—those gloating hypocrites, those chief priests and scribes, their nation's religious leaders and doctors of divinity! Listen to their mocking taunt, "He saved others; himself he cannot save." However raw their jealousy of the pure-souled Nazarene, they ought at least to have been subdued now that he was hanging helpless on that torturing cross. He had committed no crime. His character was unimpeached. The very fact that he was willing to die in such agony for his claim to be their Messiah should have sobered them. Even their knowledge that the people looked up to them as religious examples should have begotten restraint in them. But no, not only did they fling away all reserve and dignity, they led the chorus of ribald mockery: "He saved others; himself he cannot save!"

"He saved others; himself he cannot save." The taunt expressed intensest hatred. Had it been the disciples who were the speakers, it would have vented their bewildering disappointment and brokenhearted sympathy, but from those Satan-perverted priests and scribes the words were flung at the pinioned Sufferer as a malicious jibe. It is strange, but there seems to be scarcely any hatred worse than religious hatred. There can be a fanatical fierceness in it. There certainly was at Calvary.

It is awful to have to say it, but there are those who in the name of religion can laugh fiendishly over the fall and shame of others. Oh, how we need beware of any such hatred in ourselves toward those who are holier than we ourselves are or who have gifts that we do not possess or whose views differ from ours in religious matters! However much we may hate heresies, let us love the heretics! God loves them. Christ died for them. And when we ourselves are persecuted for righteousness' sake, let us pray for grace always to be able to say with that pain-racked, humiliated, sublime Sufferer on Calvary, "Father, forgive them."

"He saved others; himself he cannot save." The words unmasked despicable hypocrisy. Hitherto those chief priests and scribes had charged that our Lord's miracles were fakes, that he had a demon, and that his supernatural cures were activities of Beelzebub. Yet as soon as they had him fastened up there in ignominious execution they confessed what they had known deep down in their hearts all the time: "He saved others." How we ourselves need to guard against such hypocrisy—for we are human! I have seen otherwise venerable lives disfigured by hypocritical jealousy of prestige and position. It can exist among workers in a small mission hall as well as among dignitaries in a cathedral or in the high places of society. God save us from it, for it is the venom of the viper!

"He saved others; himself he cannot save." Perhaps the most striking feature in those words is their challenge to all of us who are disciples of our Lord. Unwittingly the taunt crowns the Victim as the supreme example of moral sublimity. When those chief priests and scribes thus jeered, had they only known it, they were enunciating the binding law of all true service: you cannot save others if you save yourself. As our Lord says elsewhere, "Whosoever will save his life shall lose it, and whosoever will lose his life for my sake shall find it" (Matt. 16:25).

That which counts is always that which costs. We must bleed if we would bless. We must lose ourselves if we would save others. Jesus did, and so must we, in our lesser way. What we selfishly retain we lose. What we sacrificially give up we gain. We conquer by yielding. We gain by giving. We win by losing. We live by dying. We save others only when self-absorption gives place to compassionate otherism. A contemporary novel describes a certain female thus: "Edith was a little country bounded on the north, south, east, and west, by Edith." To this we may add, "And, behold, the country of Edith was desert."

See our Lord, again, on that cross, then recall his words, "Except a seed of wheat fall into the ground and die, it abideth alone, but if it die, it bringeth forth much fruit." If our Lord had saved himself, he could not have saved us. To save us, himself he could not save. How like or unlike him are you and I, who call ourselves his followers? All around us are Christless souls. What are we doing to win them? Is it inconvenient? Does it bring rebuff? Does it hurt? Does it cost? Is it tiring? Well, listen again to those priests and scribes: "He saved others; himself he cannot save"!

> As our dear Lord hung crucified,
>   Wicked men mocked Him as He died;
> "He saved others," loud they cried,
>   "Himself He cannot save."

How strangely true, as then so now!
    Would we save others? This is how—
In our own hearts the iron must plow;
    Ourselves we cannot save.

Ere roses grow the stem oft bleeds,
    All harvests come from buried seeds,
And truth survives by martyr deeds;
    Themselves they did not save.

When blessing flows in copious tide,
    Pleaders for souls have wept and cried,
And saints to selfish ease have died;
    Themselves they would not save.

Lord, in my soul this truth impress:
    If others I would save and bless,
And Thine own saving love express,
    Myself I cannot save.

"He saved others; himself he cannot save." In that spiteful sneer—so strangely wicked yet so strangely true—see finally the supreme meaning of our Lord's life and death. It was his crucifiers themselves who confessed it: "He saved others," or, to translate it more exactly, "He has saved others." Yes, he has, in their millions. It was in order to save that he came and lived and died and rose again. Had Israel's priests and scribes only realized it, even as they were sarcastically admitting that he had saved others, his very dying was to save them. But those hardhearted leaders, by their own use of that word "others" placed themselves outside his saving reach.

What they were unthinkingly indicating was, "He saved others, but he has not saved us." By that word "others" they excluded themselves. And it is still true that the only ones excluded are the self-excluded. "He saved others." He still saves others. If he has saved you and me, let us be out to tell them!

    Out to tell them! Out to tell them!
        Tell them of the Crucified!
    Urge, allure, persuade, impel them,
        Souls for whom the Savior died.
    Is it costly! Does it hurt us?
        Easier far be dumb than brave?
    Then remember, "He saved others,
        But Himself He would not save"!

Appendix
Isaiah 53:3-15

UNDOUBTEDLY, SINCE THE ADVENT of scientific higher criticism, Old Testament prophecy has become much more intelligently appreciated. Gone forever is the mistaken idea that all the Old Testament prophecies were direct and exclusive predictions of events in the distant future without any reference to the times and circumstances when they were uttered. It is now realized that for the most part they grew out of, and had their primary application to, the times and peoples amid which the prophet himself lived.

This does not detract from their supernaturalness, but it greatly clarifies their coherence and original pertinence. The mistake comes when philological critics so desupernaturalize Old Testament prophecies that they supposedly have little or nothing but their first and local reference.

With a certain class of Bible scholars and expositors, the attitude to Isaiah 53, as also to various other passages in the Old Testament prophets, is: "If you study the original, with a mind freed from traditional presuppositions, and apply to it the historical method of examining ancient documents, you will soon be convinced that it refers solely to the prophet's own times and not to the Jesus of the future New Testament."

Is Isaiah 53 Postexilic?

They base their argument mainly on two grounds: (1) that the whole of Isaiah 40-66, whether it is the work of one writer or a composite, is a post-Exile product and (2) that right through it the "Servant of Jehovah" (its recurrent central figure) is the nation Israel. The underlying reason for this late dating of the poem-prophecy is to make the sufferings of Jehovah's Servant in Isaiah 53 mean more clearly the sufferings of the deported nation Israel in its Babylonian exile. With some, though not all, a further reason for their thus delimiting the Servant of Jehovah to mean only Israel, then and there, is to empty the prophecy of the supernatural, that is, of divine prediction.

My own belief is that both the above assumptions are demonstrably wrong. The Babylonian exile, although often spoken of as "the seventy-years exile," lasted only fifty-one years, that is, from 587 to 536 B.C., at which latter date Cyrus the Persian issued his edict freeing the Jews. One of the things that deeply affected Emperor Cyrus was that he had been foredesignated by his very name in the Hebrew prophet Isaiah as Jehovah's appointed servant for that time. It certainly was not a doubtfully late "prophecy" of the Exile period that so astonished Cyrus; it was the surprise that even before he was born he had been thus divinely anticipated by name.

That, however, is not the only evidence for the pre-Exile date of Isaiah 40–66. There is the testimony of the Septuagint, the standard version of the Hebrew Scriptures into Greek (third century B.C.), also of the book Ecclesiasticus (third century B.C.), also of Josephus (first century A.D.) who actually reports Cyrus's reading "the book which Isaiah left behind him." But for a discussion of these and other evidences, I refer the interested reader to volume 3 in my series *Explore the Book.*

The only other evidence that need be submitted here is one which, to any unprejudiced mind, must surely be conclusive, namely: there are quotations from that second part of Isaiah (chapters 40–66) in other Old Testament prophets who, by general consent, are pre-Exile. But here again, see volume 3 of *Explore the Book.*

Suppose, however, we were momentarily to concede, for argument's sake, that Isaiah 40–66 was of post-Exile origin; even then, could we honestly believe that the sufferings of Jehovah's Servant in chapter 53 depict the sufferings of the exiled Jews? No, the suffering of those intransigent idolaters was inflicted for their own persistent infidelity and immorality, whereas the sufferings in Isaiah 53 are those of a guileless, inoffensive, nobly submissive Victim who, although he suffers under the hand of Jehovah, is nevertheless pleasing to Jehovah.

Even more decisive is the fact that while the sufferings of the guilty deportees in Babylon were a penalty on their own misdeeds, the sufferings of Jehovah's Servant in Isaiah 53 are on behalf of others—which is indeed their most dominant peculiarity. Furthermore, the Sufferer in Isaiah 53 is distinguished from the people of Israel by the very fact that he is substitutionarily smitten for them.

Added to all this is the feature that the Sufferer in Isaiah 53 is so personalized as to make the passage inapplicable either to the disobedient nation as a whole or to any elect group within it. Some of those who have tried to make it refer, more or less, to the Israelite nation admit that in other parts of the poem-prophecy (42:1–7; 49:5–6; 50:4–10) the "Servant of Jehovah" is so personal as to make those parts exclusively messianic. They are so strongly individualized, in fact, that no open-minded reading can take them as mere poetic personifications of the nation.

If that is true of those other parts, it is equally so in chapter 53. Especially in those verses that detail the death and burial of Jehovah's Servant, the offering of his soul for sin, and his making intercession for the transgressors, the individuality is so marked as to pass beyond any mere personification of the nation.

About the Interpretation of Prophecy

Nevertheless, let me make two things clear. First, I agree that prophecy in general (as distinct from direct prediction) has a first meaning for the times and people and circumstances in which it was first uttered or written. Second, I agree that in Isaiah 40–66 there is much reference to the nation Israel both directly and pictorially. I believe that the historical approach to Old Testament prophecy is sound and necessary, but it is not the only true approach. I am quite prepared to accept tentatively, for instance, that Psalm 2 was originally a battle song, that Psalm 45 was an epithalamium for Solomon or maybe for Jehoram, that Psalm 110 may have had contemporary connection with a Davidic war, and even that Psalm 22 may have had some strange, prior reference subsidiary to its profound fulfillment on Golgotha.

Where such contemporary connection exists as well as the culminating fulfillment in Christ, that only makes Old Testament prophecy the more wonderful, just as the Mosaic rituals and sacrifices become the more wonderful because in them there was both a symbolic meaning for Israel then and a typical meaning that looked ahead through coming centuries to their grand fulfillment in Christ.

That many Old Testament prophecies do have a larger, ultimate fulfillment in our Lord Jesus, beyond their merely local and temporary connection, even a nonconservative critic like the late Dr. Cheyne conceded in his exposition of the book of Jeremiah. I quote:

> As a rule, the details of a prophetic description cannot be pressed; they are mainly imaginative elaborations of a great central truth or fact. Occasionally, however, regarding the prophecies in the light of Gospel times, it is almost impossible not to observe that the Spirit of Christ which was in the prophets has overruled their expressions, so that they correspond more closely to facts than could have been reasonably anticipated. Such superabundant favours to believers in inspiration occur repeatedly in the prophecies respecting Christ.

To my own mind, of course, that is a pathetically poor view of Old Testament inspiration. The Holy Spirit did much more than "overrule" expressions used by the prophets. He inspired both thoughts and words in a direct and unique way. He guided their expressions, and in that way he certainly did superintend them to describe evangelical realities that were to be revealed centuries later. Moreover, that phenomenon is found in the prophetic oracles not just "occasionally" (to use Dr. Cheyne's word) but again and again, all through the prophetic books. If scholars of the purely historical approach have to concede that this far-reaching messianic element is found in some prophecies, then whether it occurs in any given passage must be determined solely on evidence.

What, then, is the principal mark of this bigger, messianic content in any passage where it occurs? It is that the language, ideas, and statements of the passage unmistakably transcend a limiting of them to lesser subjects or events around the prophet's own day. This bigger and further reach does not necessarily exclude a smaller, temporary reference at the time when the man of God wrote, but it is unmistakably too big for confinement to then. Of course, we know for certain that many such Old Testament prophecies do have this latent onreach by the very fact that they have had actual fulfillment in our Lord and are authoritatively endorsed by the New Testament as being intendedly fulfilled in him.

Various Views of Isaiah 53

So far as Isaiah 53 is concerned, several supposed interpretations of it have been advanced by those who would deny or greatly modify its application to our Lord. Back in the third century A.D., when Origen used that chapter in debate with the Jews, they explained it to mean their own nation and its sufferings. That idea has been revived and popularized in our own time not by Jewish rabbis but by Christian teachers of the "historical approach" school.

Grotius (1583–1645) was the first Christian scholar to interpret the passage of any other than our Lord. To him it photographed the prophet Jeremiah. Others have seen in it a picture of the "godly remnant"—the true Israel within the apostate Israel. Others have seen in it good King Josiah. To still others it describes the ill-treated Hebrew prophets as a collective body. Evangelical expositors have almost uniformly interpreted it as messianic, and therefore forepicturing our Lord Jesus.

One of the most cogent arguments that the passage fore-pictures our Lord is that all attempts to interpret it as picturing others have failed. Why have they failed? It is because, although some clear correspondences with others than our Lord may be found in the chapter, they are heavily outweighed by wording and statements in it that simply cannot be made to fit without exegetical torture. On the contrary, all the wording and statements, right to the last detail, do fit our Lord.

Along with that, as already remarked, is the witness of the New Testament. Wherever the Gospel or the Epistles quote or allude to Isaiah 53 they apply it clearly and solely to him. That will be sufficiently conclusive to all who accept the New Testament as having divine authority.

Somehow, from earliest times, nearly all thoughtful readers and students of Isaiah 53 have sensed that it had the mark of that bigger, messianic reference in it. The ancient rabbis of Israel, puzzled though they were how to combine such a sorrowful strain as Isaiah 53 with their jubilant messianic hope and in spite of their strong desire to rip away the witness of Old Testament prophecy from Jesus of Nazareth, found themselves compelled to acknowledge a mysterious connection between this suffering "Servant of Jehovah" and the King-Messiah who in the latter days should gather the outcasts of Israel.

Is the Sufferer the Israel Nation?

We might comfortably dismiss the matter there were it not for the wide impression abroad nowadays that modern Old Testament scholarship has finally settled it that Isaiah 53 belongs mainly, if not wholly, to the nation Israel. It may be worthwhile to take a brief but thoughtful look again at that idea. To my own mind, it is surprising how many evangelical writers apparently feel obliged to doff their caps at that fashionable idea and apply the chapter largely—sometimes mainly—to the suffering Jews in their Babylonian exile.

That fifty-third chapter is a part of the "Book of Consolations," as the rabbis call Isaiah 4–66 (from its opening words, "Comfort ye, comfort ye my people"). Its standpoint is supposed to be that of someone who is among, or about contemporary with, the exiled Jews in Babylonia. He sees around him the shattered wreck of his nation, a people now in the crushing grip of a Gentile despot. The corporate and political character of the elect nation seems mutilated beyond recovery. Born of this agony is the suffering prophet's message of comfort that Israel is still Jehovah's servant and shall eventually be delivered. "Thou, Israel, art my servant; Jacob whom I have chosen; the seed of Abraham my friend. I, Jehovah, will hold thy right hand, saying unto thee: Fear not, I will help thee. This people have I formed for myself: they shall show forth my praise."

This prophet of the Exile is supposedly given to see more deeply than others into the mystery of Israel's sufferings.

Here is the elect nation, charged with a messianic function, and still bearing in its mangled bosom the mystery of redemption: here it is, passing, by God's appointment, through the deep waters of affliction. How can this baptism of suffering be other than a part of the process through which it moves onward to the fulfillment of its divine calling? What is more natural than that the wasting and agony before the prophet's eyes should shape itself, in his mind, into a sort of redemptive passion endured by Israel as Jehovah's chosen servant in pursuance of its divine destiny to be his channel of blessing to the world?

Others might cast a contemptuous glance on its misery, and be satisfied with saying that God had smitten it as its sins deserved. But to the prophet's mind, illuminated by the revealing Spirit, the suffering would assume a vicarious aspect, and be viewed as instrumental to the advancement of God's saving purpose. The holy nation, bowed down to the dust and trampled upon by the heathen oppressor, would appear as if agonizing in sore travail, and bringing forth in labor-pangs the universal kingdom of God.

Well, all that is vividly imaginative, but to say that the revealing Spirit put such an idea into the prophet's mind is, to me, a daring presumption. How can there be any genuine identifying of such a people, punished and exiled for idolatry, infidelity, and gross immorality, with the innocent, sinless, sublime Sufferer in Isaiah 53? To refer that chapter in any way to such an insensately wicked people, dragged into penal captivity as the inveterate betrayers of Jehovah, certainly does need imagination! Is it not strangely naive? Surely it is far more in keeping with the facts to believe that Isaiah 53 was written before the Exile (as was the prenaming of Cyrus) in order to be ready for the Exile, so that the people, suffering for their own impenitent apostasy, should be led to repent and look away to the great Sin-Bearer in whom should be their ultimate salvation both as individuals and as a nation. Amid their exile, this was the one true "comfort," if only they would believe it and respond to it and return in heart to Jehovah.

It is equally wrong to say that exiled Israel's "baptism of suffering" was a "part of the process" in fulfillment of the nation's divine calling. No, that would make the depraving idolatry that caused the Exile part of the process!

It is even worse to say that the Holy Spirit "illuminated" the prophet to see in disobedient Israel's sufferings a "vicarious aspect." That is an aspect that those sufferings could not have had, for again and again God told the recalcitrant generation that they were being judged and punished for their own sins.

As for that further idea that is supposed to have developed in the prophet's mind, namely, that Israel in the Exile was, so to speak, "agonizing in sore travail, and bringing forth in labor-pangs the universal kingdom of God," that is indeed a big feat of imagination when one considers what the Exile actually did bring forth. It certainly did not "bring forth" the "kingdom of God" to fill the earth, nor by any delayed action has it done so yet, twenty-five hundred years later.

Only too willingly can I concede that the whole story of Israel, the nation of divine election, including and culminating in the Messiah, has an "ideal unity" and embodies the conception that "Israel itself in its corporate and collective capacity has a messianic character." Yet that does not give any warrant whatever for assuming that it is the nation that is the subject in Isaiah 53, any more than in various other passages where the language can be applied only to the personal Messiah himself. It is never sound exegesis to make any passage of Scripture fit to ideas imported from other passages. The interpretation of each must be decided by its own wording and other internal evidence. On the grounds of strict exegesis Isaiah 53 does not fit the Israel nation.

Inconsistent Suppositions

We must therefore disagree with the following:

> Let it be remembered that in their higher and ideal character the main lines of Israel's story are typical, and it must be admitted that this holds good above all else in such a catastrophic event as the crushing of the nation beneath the heel of Babylon, with its subsequent exile and misery, followed by its marvelous restoration. If a type of the Messiah at all, Israel must have been a type of him here.

Thus Isaiah 53, with its substitutionary sufferings and final triumph, is supposed to have its fulfillment, or at least its primary fulfillment, in Judah's Babylonian exile and the "marvelous restoration" that followed it.

We have already shown how impossible it is to see any real likeness between the vicarious sufferings of the innocent Substitute in Isaiah 53 and the retributive scourging that the Babylonian exile inflicted on guilty Judah. As for the "marvelous restoration" that followed it (according to the above quotation), it was anything but that! When Cyrus issued his famous edict in 536 B.C., allowing all the Jews to leave for their own land, the great majority of them did not go—did not even want to go! A mere "remnant" of some forty-six to fifty thousand struggled back under Zerubbabel's leadership. Nor is the checkered story of that remnant any too happy, either morally or politically, during the five hundred years between then and the time of our Lord's birth in Bethlehem.

The exile in Babylon certainly cured the Jews of idolatry and made them the most rigid monotheists in history, but instead of their being changed by the "marvelous restoration" into evangelists of the kingdom of God, they developed such bitter, relentless anti-Gentile hatred and such isolationism that they blinded their own minds even beyond recognizing the kingdom when Jesus came and offered it to them!

In that blinding hatred they even crucified their divine King, mocked and murdered his followers, and brought on themselves the fearful destruction of Jerusalem in A.D. 70.

Therefore, to see in that long-ago return of the Jewish remnant a fulfillment, or even a faint picture, of the Messiah's final triumph as worded in Isaiah 53 is even more pathetic than to see in exiled Judah a "primary sketch or prelusive outline" (as one writer calls it) of our Lord's Calvary sufferings.

Defective Views of Inspiration

Of course, it needs to be realized that most of those who insist on interpreting Isaiah 53 of the Israelite nation have a different view of inspiration from mine. With some of them, the recurring concept of "Jehovah's Servant" in Isaiah 40-66 seems scarcely more than a remarkable product of perceptive evolution in the prophet's own thinking or in the conglomerate thinking of a plurality of contributors.

Those who hold that all those chapters (40-66) are from one writer—an anonymity whom they please to call "Deutero-Isaiah"—tell us we must bear in mind that the prophet was not writing with didactic calmness but in a "white heat of emotion and desire, of faith and hope" (a strangely different attitude from the overwhelming bulk of his earthly-minded people, who no more saw themselves or Israel as a type of some promised suffering Messiah than they saw the need of returning to their homeland when the opportunity came).

Basic to everything, modernistic scholars tell us, was the prophet's conviction that Israel was an elect and "anointed" nation, that is, a "messianic nation," Jehovah's servant to fulfill a divine purpose toward all mankind. But amid the humiliation and wreckage of his nation in Babylonia the prophet came to see through his tears (so they say) beyond the actual Israel to an ideal Israel, a true "Servant of Jehovah," in which the purpose should be realized. "Yes, an ideal Israel of the future!"

Then, while he muses as to how such an ideal Israel should emerge, he rises to a yet higher, personalized concept. I quote:

> What if the nation were to produce and culminate in one perfect "Servant of Jehovah" through whom its vocation were to be accomplished! Other prophets had looked forward to a Davidic King reigning in righteousness and bringing peace and salvation to Israel. Why should not the same hope now take form in an individual Servant, raised up of God out of the bosom of the nation, through whose travail the kingdom of God should at last be born into the world?

My own persuasion is that any such accounting for the Servant of Jehovah as the excogitation of a fertile religious imagination, which the Holy Spirit, so to speak, adopted and adapted, is scarcely worth calling inspiration. In fact, it is not inspiration in the true and vital scriptural sense. I believe, on ample scriptural grounds, that the Holy Spirit directly revealed what he wanted those Old Testament prophets to see and to say. There was no swamping of their individuality, but there was direct, supernatural, and inerrant inspiration. What Isaiah saw and then wrote about the Servant of Jehovah was directly revealed to him. As I read through Isaiah's "Book of Consolations" (40-66) I am prepared to see as the Servant of Jehovah: (1) the nation Israel in some passages, (2) an ideal Israel of the future in others, (3) the personal Messiah, our Lord Jesus Christ, in others. In each case, evidence in the passage itself must decide. All three do not coincide in any one passage. In Isaiah 53 it is neither the actual nor the ideal Israel nation that is in view. All the evidence is that it refers to our Lord Jesus, and to him alone.

The Popular Presentation

I do not wish to lengthen this appendix disproportionately, but let me add one further culling—from a book that was published some years ago and that presents in specious form for the general reader this newly popularized idea that the Suffering Servant of Isaiah 53 is the nation Israel. Its able penman is very "modern" in his approach to the four Songs of the Suffering Servant in Isaiah (42:1-4; 49:1-6; 50:4-9; 52:13-53:12). While apparently accepting the "bulk" of chapters 40-55 as written by the so-called Deutero Isaiah, he tells us approvingly that some scholars believe the four songs to be insertions from another hand.

Some of us wonder with solemn awe at the confidence with which those scholars can detect changes of authorship in this and that and the other paragraph and dissect the book of Isaiah into the many fragments that together, supposedly, form the total mosaic called "Isaiah." Often a detailed comparison of the segments shows that the asserted differences of vocabulary, style, background, etcetera, which are supposed to indicate different authors, are fanciful rather than factual. Over against the doubtful dissimilarities are the far more patent similarities that betoken the unity of the whole book from the one well-known prophet Isaiah of Hezekiah's time.

The modern author of the publication that we now quote represents many preachers in our main Protestant denominations. He writes as follows:

Israel is to be restored with this larger purpose in view, to bring all men to the truth of God. . . . In the third Song the insults and cruelties which the Servant has had to endure are mentioned. In spite of everything he maintains his confidence in Jehovah his Instructor and is certain that the time of his vindication is at hand. The fourth Song (Isaiah 53) describes this vindication: just as many had been astonished at his sufferings, so shall they be startled by the glory that shall be given him. Even kings shall be hushed to silence at so great a transformation: the nations will exclaim, "Who would have believed it? For Israel was a thing of no account; men even turned away in revulsion from so despised a nation. We thought that the Servant's sufferings were God's punishment for his sins, but now we recognize that it was our sins that caused his pain. It was to win peace for us that he suffered chastisement. For we (i.e., Gentiles) like sheep had gone astray, and needed to be rescued. And in all that he endured he made no complaint, even when he, although innocent, was stricken to death [a supposed reference to Israel's loss of national existence in the "death" of the Exile!]. And then Jehovah delivered him, and gave him a position of great exaltation. . . ." The literature of the Exile is full of this hope of better days to be; days of national restoration and of spiritual and moral transformation.

The contradictions in such an interpretation of Isaiah 53 are so glaring as scarcely to need pointing out. To say of that stiff-necked generation of obdurate offenders, ejected from Canaan into humiliating retribution, that "in spite of everything he maintains his confidence in Jehovah his Instructor, and is certain that the time of his vindication is at hand," makes a travesty either of Bible prophecy or of some modern scholarship.

It is egregiously worse to make out that the nation's sufferings were not for its own sins but the sins of other nations, so that at last the Gentile nations say, "We thought that the Servant's sufferings were God's punishment for his sins, but now we recognize that it was our sins that caused his pain; it was to win peace for us that he suffered chastisement. For we like sheep had gone astray and needed to be rescued"!

What God actually says through Isaiah is that it was Israel that had gone astray (the "all we" in verse 6 is Isaiah the Jew speaking as being one with his own Jewish people, as is confirmed by verse 8, "For the transgression of my people . . ." that is, the covenant people).

As for the return from the Exile being the "vindication" and "transformation" of the Servant, we have shown already how absurd that idea is. Not only did a mere handful return, comparatively speaking, but they came back to wrecked cities and silted debris as a vassal people with no longer any king or throne or independent government of their own. Their fortunes were henceforth tossed about by successive ruling powers. Only once was there a short interval of tenuous independence (part of the Maccabean period: 163-67 B.C.).

Then came subjection to imperial Rome, followed in A.D. 70 by the fearful climax of that post-Exile period, the still deadlier destruction of Jerusalem, and a worldwide further scattering of Jews that has lasted until present times. Yet we are asked to believe that this was the foreseen "vindication" and "transformation"! It would seem as though some people will swallow anything rather than accept the traditional and supernaturalist view of the Bible.

Israel: The Actual Versus the Ideal

However, the author of the above-quoted book must have had some secret discomfort about his interpretation of the Servant in Isaiah 53, for he goes on to bring him into focus as being the "ideal" Israel (though no such phantom has ever yet suffered and fulfilled Isaiah 53!). He tells us that the "Second Isaiah" now sees "with truly amazing spiritual insight . . . that the very sufferings of the nation have their place in this great redemptive purpose. If only the actual Israel will act as the ideal Israel whom he [Deutero-Isaiah] portrays in the Songs of the Suffering Servant; if only the real Israel in exile will accept suffering without complaint or bitterness, then the very sorrows themselves will lead to the exaltation of the nation as the faithful steward of the salvation of God for all mankind."

That, pathetically enough, reduces Isaiah 53 to a wishful "if only" appeal to the obdurate nation, instead of direct divine prediction of something predetermined.

Even then the author is obliged to add, "Alas, the nation failed to rise to the challenge and call of this noble teaching. In all history only One has done so." Why then does not our modern author come right out and agree that Isaiah 53 is a direct prediction pointing on through the centuries to that "only One" in all history who fulfills it? Apparently it is just because he is a bit too modern. He says, "The prophet discerned a spiritual truth which only Jesus has fulfilled. That is why for centuries, some have taken this part of his prophecy as a direct foretelling of the coming of our Lord Jesus Christ."

To my own mind, that author has a pretty poor concept of biblical inspiration (that is nearly always the trouble) when he says that Isaiah 53 was merely something that "the prophet discerned." My own view is that it was something that God directly revealed, for in verses 11–12 it is God himself speaking: "By his knowledge shall my righteous servant justify many." It cannot be merely that the prophet "discerned a spiritual truth," for he describes centuries in advance and in remarkable detail the submission, sufferings, death, and ultimate postmortem triumph of the most wonderful Being who ever came into human history.

So decidedly do the description and details fit him and him exclusively that for Christian expositors to insist on bending them into any other direction not only impoverishes the prophecy, but seems almost an irreverent impertinence to clearly worded divine revelation.

Why It Cannot Mean the Nation

To sum up, we submit six reasons in brief why the Suffering Servant of Isaiah 53 cannot be the nation Israel.

1. The singular personal pronouns "he," "him," "his" in this chapter separate the Sufferer from the Israel nation, for the nation speaks in the plurals, "we" and "our" and "us" in verses 4-6. Furthermore, those plurals cannot be the Gentile nations addressing the Israel nation because they are ascribed to Israel, "my people," verse 8.

2. The sufferings of Jehovah's Servant in Isaiah 53 are vicarious, as is corroborated again and again in other parts of Scripture, whereas the Israel nation's sufferings were penal and corrective, as is stated repeatedly in Scripture, without the faintest suggestion anywhere that they were otherwise.

3. The Sufferer in Isaiah 53 suffers vicariously for the nation, so he cannot very well be the nation on behalf of which he substitutionarily suffers.

4. He suffers both voluntarily and submissively without complaint or resistance. That is far from true of the Israel nation, as everyone knows. For centuries after the Exile the Jews broke out in fierce, desperate insurrections, nor did these cease even with the butchery and scattering of them from Judea in A.D. 70. Their hatred not only of the Romans but of all the Gentiles was proverbial. Right up to the seventh century of our Christian era these revolts periodically occurred.

5. The sufferings of the innocent Victim in Isaiah 53 ended in death and burial. That is the very opposite of what is foretold again and again of Israel's sufferings as a nation. No earthly power shall stamp out the Jews. No scattering, however prolonged, shall extinguish them. At the same time as they are punished they shall be preserved, and most certainly in the end they shall be regathered. See passages such as Jeremiah 30:11; 31:35-38; 33:20-21; Isaiah 11-12; Ezekiel 11:16-20; Psalm 89:28-37; Romans 11:1-2, 25-29.

6. The sufferings in Isaiah 53 were personally undeserved and were borne by One whom Jehovah himself calls "My righteous Servant" (v. 11), which at once separates the Sufferer from the nation against which Jehovah alleges the very opposite of righteousness over and over again.

Why It Cannot Mean the "Godly Remnant"

But if the Suffering Servant is not the nation Israel, is he the "godly remnant" personified—the faithful few among the impenitent many? That is an alternate view held fairly widely. Here are six reasons that to me seem valid and cogent why Isaiah 53 cannot refer to the "godly remnant."

1. The sufferings in Isaiah 53 are inflicted by Jehovah himself (vv. 6, 10). One of the sad ironies of history is that through social complexity the innocent all too often suffer with the guilty in some general calamity brought on by the wicked. But it is simply unthinkable that God himself would directly inflict punishment and death on an innocent minority instead of on the guilty. Yet that is what Isaiah 53 would teach if the Sufferer were the godly remnant in Israel.

2. If the Sufferer in Isaiah 53 is the godly remnant in Israel, then godly Isaiah is made to place himself not with them but with the ungodly who went "astray" and "turned everyone to his own way," for he includes himself in the "our" and "we" and "us" of verses 4–6. Isaiah thus separates himself from the godly remnant and becomes one of the "despisers" (v. 3), if the Sufferer is the godly remnant!

3. Some of the wording simply will not fit any such godly remnant— for example, being buried "with the rich" (v. 9); the pleasure of Jehovah prospering in their hand (v. 10) when the very opposite has been the case; the being regarded as "afflicted of God" (v. 4)— for the ungodly in Israel never so regarded the godly: they knew well enough that it was they themselves (not God) who afflicted the godly.

4. The most startling peculiarity of the Servant's sufferings is that they were vicariously atoning. Will any of us dare to say that the persecutions of the godly by the ungodly in Israel were either vicarious or atoning? Sin, basically, is rebellious disobedience and transgression against an infinite God and requires infinite reparation. One has only to reflect on this to realize that substitutionary atonement such as is indicated in verses 5–6, and 10 is utterly beyond any merely human group. Moreover, even the godliest humans are still sinners themselves. No human being can make atonement even for his or her own sin, let alone for the vast guilt-aggregate of the many!

5. The sufferings of Jehovah's righteous Servant in Isaiah 53 terminated in death and burial. In the words of verse 8, he was "cut off out of the land of the living." That is not true of the godly remnant. As a group they are to persist right on to the future consummation. They will never be "cut off"; Jehovah will always have his loyal inner circle within Israel. See, for instance, the "seven thousand" in 1 Kings 19:18 who had not "bowed the knee to Baal,"

with Paul's comment in Romans 11:5; also Malachi 3:16–17, Ezekiel 9:4, and the 144,000 of Revelation 7 and 14. The One who was "cut off" out of the land of the living, as in Isaiah 53, was Israel's Messiah, of whom we read in Daniel 9:26, "And after threescore and two weeks shall Messiah be cut off."

6. Isaiah 53:11 says, "By his knowledge shall my righteous Servant justify many, for he shall bear their iniquities." More recent translations are helpful in bringing out the full meaning: "Through the knowledge of himself (by others) my righteous Servant shall obtain righteousness for the many." So there, away back in the Old Testament, as clear as can be, is the doctrine of justification through the imputed righteousness of a substitutionary Sin-Bearer.

Let it be said with categorical decisiveness: no godly remnant ever did, ever could, or ever will bear sin and provide justification for others in that way. That the perverted majority in old-time Israel or the majority at any other time, present or future, should be exonerated, excused, or in any way justified by the suffering of the godly remnant is an idea that cannot be entertained for one moment.

The One True Fulfillment

Finally, here are twelve fulfillments of Isaiah 53 in our Lord Jesus that confirm that he is the one and only figure in all history who obviously and completely answers to all the requirements of the prophecy.

1. He came of the lowliest human stock, answering to verse 2: a "root out of a dry ground."
2. He was despised as the Nazarene of mean birth, in line with verse 3: "despised and rejected of men."
3. He suffered for sins in the place of others, as he himself taught (Matt. 20; 28, etc.), thus fulfilling verses 4–6: "wounded for our transgressions," etcetera.
4. He was actually "delivered up" (Rom. 8:32) by God the Father (Acts 2:23), thus strikingly answering to the words of Isaiah 53:10, "It pleased Jehovah to bruise him."
5. He submitted with uncomplaining, utter resignation, thus sublimely implementing verse 7: "He was oppressed, and he was afflicted, yet he opened not his mouth."
6. He was executed as a felon between two outlaws, thus bringing to pass verse 8, "taken from prison and judgment," and verse 9, "made his grave with the wicked."
7. He was cut off prematurely, in his early thirties and in sudden abortion of his impact on the people, thereby fitting the wording

of verse 8, "cut off out of the land of the living."

8. He was personally guiltless and guileless, so much so that his accusers contradicted and confounded themselves and could only charge falsely the utterance of blasphemy, which was exactly as foretold in verse 9, "He had done no violence, neither was any deceit in his mouth."

9. He was to live on (strange as the prophecy seemed) even after his sufferings and death, according to verse 10, "He shall see his seed [or followers]; he shall prolong his days." This seeming enigma suddenly began to be unlocked when Jesus rose from the grave in resurrection life.

10. He thus began to unloose the meaning of those further words in verse 10, "The pleasure of Jehovah shall prosper in his hand."

11. As the risen Victor he declared, "All authority is given unto me in heaven and on earth," and the whole New Testament rings with his victory and exaltation and with the hope of his second advent in glory and global empire. What abundant and unique fulfillment of verse 12: "Therefore will I divide him his portion with the great, and he shall divide the spoil with the strong"!

12. By all this and by "justifying many" and saving a "multitude which no man can number" he gives everlasting fulfillment to the words of verse 11, "He shall see of the travail of his soul, and shall be satisfied."

As trait after trait swings into focus and fulfillment, can we write any other name under Isaiah's amazing portrait of the sublime Sufferer in chapter 53 than Jesus of Nazareth? And can we fail to marvel at the miracle of inspiration in this prophetic anticipation of the lovely "Man of Sorrows" when we reflect that it was written some seven hundred years B.C.?

Notes

Chapter 1: The Revelation of the Lamb
1. To my own mind, it is a minor tragedy that verse 37 is omitted, except by marginal acknowledgment, in ERV, ASV, and RSV, as well as in such modern-language versions as NIV. Our earliest New Testament manuscripts go back only as far as the fifth century, whereas Irenaeus, in his third book, *Against Heresies,* written as early as A.D. 180-188, distinctly quotes that part of verse 37 which says, "I believe Jesus Christ to be the Son of God." And Cyprian (A.D. 200-258), in his third book of *Testimonies,* quotes the other part of the verse. So, long before the oldest existing manuscripts, verse 37 *must* have been in the codices of both the Greek and Latin churches.
2. Let it be noted that in this one instance, and for a very meaningful reason, the two goats represent the one Lamb. Why were not two *lambs* chosen? The reason seems clear. Not in any detail must the typical ceremonies and offerings of the Mosaic ritual suggest that there is more than the one "Lamb of God which beareth away the sin of the world."
3. On meaning of "sprinkling" here see Ellicott Commentary *in loco.*

Chapter 3: The Sovereignty of the Lamb: (1) Preincarnate
1. In the *Cambridge Bible for Schools and Colleges* Professor Skinner wrote: "The book which bears the name of Isaiah is in reality a collection of prophetic oracles showing manifest traces of composite authorship, and having a complicated literary history behind it. Not much less than two-thirds of its bulk consists of anonymous prophecies . . . to this class belongs first of all the whole of the latter part of the book . . . but even when we confine our attention to chapters 1 to 39 we still find abundant evidence of great diversity of authorship." So there we are!—our "book of Isaiah" is a sheer patchwork from a combination of anonymous authors whose number no one knows!

Chapter 4: The Sovereignty of the Lamb: (2) Postresurrection
1. It is unfortunate that the AV, ERV, ASV, and RSV, as well as the NIV and the NASB, all render the Greek aorist in this verse as a present perfect: "hath," or "has," "overcome," which suggests that the overcoming was somehow at the time of the vision. The true translation of the aorist here is "over-*came,*" and of course it repeats our Lord's own word in chapter 3:21,

"Even as I also *overcame*" (emphasis mine), referring to what happened when he was on earth as the Second Adam, our new champion.

Chapter 6: The Finalities of the Lamb: (1) Lord and Savior
1. Further comment on this is in volume 1 of *Explore the Book*.

Chapter 8: The Cross as a Superlative Wonder
1. The difference between the essence of the attributes of the divine Being is decided by whether we can use a noun or only an adjective after the words, "God is." Thus, "God is love"—noun—so in his very essence that is what God is. But, "God is triune"—adjective, and "God is eternal"—adjective, and "God is omnipotent"—adjective, all indicate attributes, not essence, because we cannot change the adjectives *triune, eternal,* and *omnipotent* into nouns and say "God is triunity," or "God is eternality," or "God is omnipotence"—the essence of what God is. The attributes are what God has, i.e., the qualities that belong to the essence.

Chapter 11: The Cross as the Ensign of Creation
1. Let me here make clear that by the "cosmos" (Greek, *kosmos*), I mean, unless otherwise indicated, our earth and the "world system" or order of things in operation upon it and around it. I know, of course, that there are those who often use the word to mean the whole universe, because the Greek *kosmos* means order, system, harmony, and the whole universe in that sense is the vast cosmos. However, in classic Greek philosophy it seems to mean at most only our own solar system, and in the New Testament it is used solely of our own world.
2. That as late as the fifteenth century educated Europe should still be thinking of the earth as flat is the more remarkable because Aristotle, away back in the fourth century B.C., had demonstrated convincingly (philosophically) that the earth was not a disc, a cube, or a cylinder but a globe. In Europe, about the fourteenth century A.D., the usual idea was that the earth was a disc that supported the big dome of the starry sky!
3. It is pitiful to see how some modern Unitarian cults try to minimize the force of John's wording. It is argued that the clause, "and the word was God," should be translated, "and God was the Word," because that is the order of the wording in the Greek. But the best Greek scholarship concurs that according to idiomatic Greek construction the true subject of the sentence is "the Logos." Furthermore, if we read it, "and God was the Word," thus making God and the Word identical, we thereby at once destroy the distinction that John has just made between them, i.e., "The Word was *with* God" (emphasis mine).
4. See Liddell & Scott, *Greek-English Lexicon*.
5. I have quoted Revelation 13:8 from the KJV and the ERV. Several other versions transpose clauses to make the text read, "Whose names have not been written from the foundation of the world in the book of life of the Lamb." This makes it mean that it was the Lamb's book that was "from

the foundation of the world" rather than the Lamb's being slain then. I think, however, that the learned Alford's comment on the Greek here is decisive in favor of the AV and ERV, and I am glad to find that most translations, including the NIV, agree with him. But whether we read it that it was Lamb's book or the Lamb slain from the foundation of the world, the import is the same, that the Lamb was already there, which means that the Cross was there before human history began.

Chapter 12: The Cross as the Rainbow of Government

1. We are plainly told in John 8:41 that in Isaiah 6 it was Christ preincarnate whom Isaiah saw on that heavenly throne.
2. On this see later pages.
3. According to Josephus and Jewish tradition, Isaac at that time was twenty-two years old.
4. Some exegetes take the phrase "the eternal Spirit" in Hebrews 9:14 as meaning not the Holy Spirit himself but the Spirit of *God* who is alone the "eternal Spirit." My own persuasion is that the reference is to the Holy Spirit himself, but in either case the force is the same so far as our use of the above quotation is concerned.

Chapter 13: The Cross as the Victory of God

1. Expositors might with even more reason limit the less abnormal phraseology of the Isaian prophecies on *Babylon* and insist that the reference is *only* to ancient Babylon. Yet it turns out that there is a further, distant reference to the "Mystery Babylon" of Revelation 17–18. Practically identical clauses reappear in Revelation, e.g., "I shall sit as mistress [queen] forever" (Isa. 47:7; Rev. 18:7). "I shall not sit as a widow" (Isa. 47:8; Rev. 18:7). "Babylon is fallen, is fallen" (Isa. 21:9; Rev. 18:2), etc.
2. Literally, "prevailed," and therefore "was not needed" there any longer: see ASV mg.
3. That the word "prince" here means an evil angel or evil spirit power is made clear by verses 13, 21, where the archangel Michael is called a "prince" and "one of the chief princes."
4. Perhaps those two passages in Isaiah 14 and Ezekiel 28, like some other Old Testament prophecies, have a double reference, i.e., not only Lucifer's deposition from his original status and authority, but his yet further and final expulsion and doom.
5. I believe that the genealogical tables in 1 Chronicles, from Adam downward, and in Matthew, from Abraham backward, and especially from Noah back to Adam, they become indefinite geological periods, as some try to argue in order to push much further back the appearance of humans on the earth and thus make the Bible tally more apparently with geological findings. It is geology that must and will yet fall in line with Scripture, not vice versa. If, then, we keep to those Bible genealogies, they confirm each other, and us, that Adam was on earth approximately some six thousand years ago.

6. If the wonderfully exact measurement of age now ascertainable by the isotope or 14 C method is to guide us (the means first discovered in 1947 by the now famous Professor Willard P. Libby), it may well be that the interval during which our earth became "without form and void" was not more than some three thousand years, for there are evidences of organized, intelligent beings on earth nine or ten thousand years ago. That, however, is a far too dusky matter for consideration here!

7. Nor must those angels that "kept not their first estate" ever be thought of as those "sons of God" in Genesis 6 who coveted the "daughters of men" because they "were fair." Such an idea is utterly unallowable on both exegetical and physiological grounds. For a full treatment of this, perhaps we may usefully recommend a perusal of "Who Were Those Sons of God?" in Studies in Problem Texts, by J. Sidlow Baxter.

8. Presumably having acquired thereby long experience in judging!

9. Yes, after considering all the amillennial arguments, with as little prejudice as possible, I believe they are not true to many clear statements of Scripture or to the full data of the evidence in favor of a coming millennial age.

Also by J. Sidlow Baxter

His Deeper Work in Us

Baxter explores the topic of holiness, answering questions such as, Does the Bible teach a deeper, further work of the Holy Spirit in the believer? and Is there a complete freedom from sin?
2172-1   256 pp.

Our High Calling

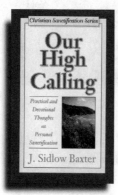

This volume offers devotional and practical studies to affirm the need for personal sanctification, pointing to the New Testament's emphasis on the call to sanctification as "one of the most ringing of its imperatives."
2171-3   208 pp.

A New Call to Holiness

This volume examines the right approach to Scripture while guarding against the errors that have beguiled others in discussing the question, What is holiness?
2170-5   256 pp.

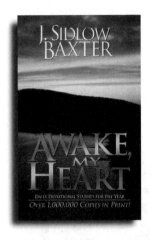
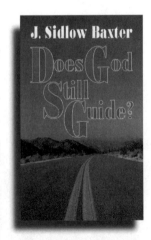

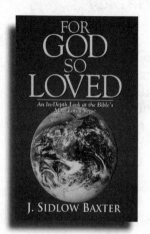
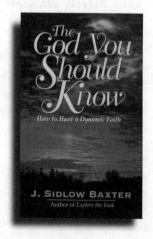

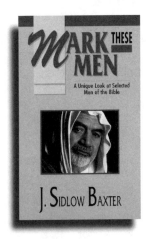

Mark These Men

A treasure-house of Bible biographies including Elisha, Elijah, King Saul, Daniel, Gideon, Balaam, and Nehemiah. Also New Testament characters such as the apostle Paul, Lazarus, the rich young ruler, Ananias, and Simon of Cyrene.

2197-7   192 pp.

The Strategic Grasp of the Bible

An extensive look into the origin, structure, and message of the Word of God. A condensed version of the author's well-known work, *Explore the Book.*

2198-5   406 pp.

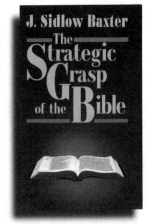